"Soldiers Sportsmen All"

The Great War Story Of The 24ᵗʰ Battalion, The Royal Fusiliers

By Dr Robert Wynn Jones

www.publishnation.co.uk

The Sportsmen

Sportsmen of every kind,
God! We have paid the score
Who left green English fields behind
For the sweat and stink of war!
New to the soldier's trade,
Into the scrum we came,
But we didn't care much what game we played,
So long as we played the game.

We learned so much in a hell-fire school
Ere many a month was gone,
But we knew before hand the golden rule,
"Stick It, and Carry On!"
And we were a cheery crew,
Wherever you find the rest,
Who did an Englishman can do,
And did it as well as the best.

Aye, and the game was good,
A game for a man to play,
Though there's many that lie in Delville Wood
Waiting the Judgement Day.
But living and dead are made
One till the final call,
When we meet once more on the Last Parade,
Soldiers and Sportsmen all!

"Touchstone" (Claude Edward Cole-Hamilton Burton), "*Daily
Mail*"

DEDICATION

I dedicate this book to my mother, Peggy Anne Jones, *nee* Clements, and to the memory of her father, and my grandfather, Private Charles Reuben Clements of the 24th (2nd Sportsmen's) Battalion, the Royal Fusiliers.

CONTENTS

PREFACE

Contained within is the Great War story of the 24th (2nd Sportsmen's) Battalion, The Royal Fusiliers (The City of London Regiment). The Battalion served on the Western Front for over three years, fighting in the Battles of the Somme in 1916, in the Battles of Arras and Cambrai in 1917, and finally in the First and Second Battles of the Somme, 1918, the Battles of the Hindenburg Line, and the Final Advance in Picardy, in 1918. It sustained just over eighteen hundred casualties over the course of the war, including just under six hundred fatalities. Even those who survived the war are also now long-dead; the war itself, no longer living memory but history.

The story is one of ordinary men, of diverse origins, living and dying in the midst of an extraordinary time in history. It is told from the – contextualised - viewpoint of an ordinary, cold, hungry soldier in a dismal, miry trench somewhere in France, peering through a periscope at another soldier in another trench, on the other side of No Man's Land, peering back. It features photographic images and/or at least brief biographical sketches of a sample of 288 such men from the 24th Battalion. Out of a further sample of 211 men, seventy-eight (37%) were originally from London or the contiguous Home Counties, thirty-six (17%) from the West of England, where there had been a targeted recruitment drive, thirty-six (17%) also from the North, seventeen (8%) from the Midlands, eleven (5%) from the East, and seven (3%) from the South. Seven (3%) were from Scotland, five (2%) from Wales, and four (2%) from Ireland. And ten (5%) had been born overseas: two (1%) of them in New Zealand, and one (<1%) in Australia, which at the time of the Great War were Dominions of the British Empire; two (1%) in Trinidad, one (<1%) in Ceylon (now Sri Lanka), one (<1%) in India, and one (<1%) in Jamaica, which were Crown Colonies; one (<1%) in the Netherlands; and one (<1%) in the United States of America. At least two (1%) had Germanic ancestry on either their father's or their mother's side. Many men had joined the Army straight from school or university at the outbreak of the war. More than a few had been under-age; and a few, over-age. Eleven had previously worked in the banking profession or allied financial services, one part-time in insurance and part-time as an actor, and one full-time as an actor; five as schoolmasters or teachers; three each as legal clerks and newspaper reporters; two each as writers, architects, and artists; and one each as the managing director of a firm of antique dealers, an engineer, an aeronautical engineer, a civil engineer, an electrical engineer, a mining engineer in Australia and West Africa, a trainee locomotive engineer, an estate agent, a law agent, an ordained minister, a pharmacist, and a political agent. One had been a sitting Member of Parliament, and one a lawyer and former M.P. Two had worked in the licensed trade, two as shop assistants, and two as travelling salesmen; one in the motor manufacturing industry, one in a tin-plate factory, one as a watch-maker, and one a joiner's apprentice; one as a rubber planter in the Malay States (now Malaysia), one a farmer in Argentina, one a farmer in Southern Rhodesia (now Zimbabwe), and one a farm-hand in Canada; one as a farmer in Buckinghamshire, one a duck-breeder's help and farm-hand in Bedfordshire, one a gardener in Cornwall, and one a market gardener; one as a carter's boy and later a market gardener, one a baker's boy and later a baker, and one an errand-boy; and one each as a barber, a clerk in a shirt collar factory, a draughtsman in a lace embroidery, a labourer, a bricklayer's labourer, a colliery labourer, a garden labourer, a porter in a paper warehouse, a printer, a wholesale merchant, and a merchant seaman. Three had been professional footballers, and one a semi-professional player; one a county and international cricketer who also played occasional club football, and one a minor counties cricketer; one a former club and international rugby player; one a professional golfer, and one a golfer and club-maker; one probably the best rock climber in England; and one a renowned hunter of big game in Africa. Every one was a loved one.

One of the men who served in the 24th Battalion in the Great War was Private Charles Reuben Clements from Hammersmith in what was then Middlesex and is now London, a former shop assistant - and the author's maternal grandfather. Private Clements was seriously wounded in the Battle of Havrincourt, the first of the Battles of the Hindenburg Line, on September 12th, 1918. He was then treated at a Casualty Clearing Station and at a General Hospital in France before being repatriated to the U.K. on September 15th. He spent the remaining two months of the war in hospitals in the U.K.

ACKNOWLEDGMENTS

I would like to acknowledge the following institutions and individuals for their assistance with one or other of my soldierly and sporting lines of research: the Commonwealth War Graves Commission, in particular Records Data Manager Roy Hemington; the Imperial War Museum, in particular Research Support Librarian Elizabeth Smith and Media Sales & Licensing Executive Sophie Fisher; the National Archives, in particular Remote Enquiries Duty Officer Katherine Howells; the National Library of Scotland; the church of St Sepulchre-without-Newgate (Holy Sepulchre London), in particular Chairman of the Royal Fusiliers Memorial Chapel Committee, Colonel Mike Dudding; the Thiepval Memorial Project, in particular Pam and Ken Linge; Fulham Football Club, in particular Historian Alex White; and the Football Historians Research Group, in particular David Bauckham. I would also like to acknowledge Mme. Diane Deleporte of Arras for the hospitality she extended to me during my visit to Arras, Vimy, Cambrai, Havrincourt and Bac du Sud at the time of the Great War centenary commemorations.

Finally, I would like to thank my lovely and long-suffering wife, Heather Suzanne Jones, and all at PublishNation, for helping to see the project through to publication.

THE 24th BATTALION, THE ROYAL FUSILIERS

The Royal Fusiliers - the City of London Regiment - was founded as long ago as 1685, in the aftermath of the failed Monmouth Rebellion, from two companies of guards from the Tower of London (31; *Figure 1*). It went on to see service in, among others, the American War of Independence, the Napoleonic Wars, the War of 1812, the Crimean War, the "Indian Mutiny", the Second Afghan War, the Boer War, the Great War, the Second World War, and the Korean War, before being incorporated into the Royal Regiment of Fusiliers in 1968 (31; 62). There is a fine Fusilier Museum in the Regimental Headquarters in the Tower of London, which houses an extensive archive together with a range of artefacts, including the colours of the 24th Battalion. There is also a regimental war memorial, dedicated "to the glorious memory of the 22 000 Royal Fusiliers who fell in the Great War" at Holborn Bars at the western entrance to the City of London (21; 28; *Figure 2*). The memorial, designed by Alfred Toft, features the figure of a fusilier on a parapet, "encircled by the vast radius of air that extends from head to bayonet tip to trailing foot", with "this framing circle ... [rendering] ... the sculpture ... both more powerful and more vulnerable, ... fixing our attention, as if through a sniper's sights, on the soldier at its dead centre" (28). And, in the city church of St Sepulchre-without-Newgate (Holy Sepulchre London), on Newgate Street, a few minutes walk east of the war memorial, there is a Royal Fusiliers Memorial Chapel, and a Garden of Remembrance, dedicated in 1950 (*Figures 3-6*).

The 24th (2nd Sportsman's or Sportsmen's) Battalion, in contrast, was only raised in 1914, in the Hotel Cecil on the Strand in London, part of which served for a while as a Drill Hall (62). The Battalion was raised by a remarkable woman named Emma Pauline Cunliffe-Owen (*Figure 7*). Emma was born in 1863, to an English father, Sir Francis Philip Cunliffe-

1

Owen, the Director of the South Kensington Museum (now the Victoria and Albert), and a German mother, Jenny von Reitzenstein, whose father, a Baron, had been an *aide-de-camp* to Frederick Wilhelm of Prussia. She married her cousin, Edward Cunliffe-Owen, a barrister, in 1882, and the couple settled in London, and had four children together, before becoming estranged. After Edward died in 1918, Emma married Robert Basil Stamford, a surgeon, in 1919. She eventually died, aged eighty-seven, in 1950. The story goes that in 1914, on the outbreak of war, Mrs Cunliffe-Owen chanced to meet two big-game hunters of her acquaintance while walking down Bond Street, and, half-jokingly, asked them why they had not yet enlisted in the Army. They in turn, and in similar vein, asked her why she had not yet raised her own battalion. And so she did. She and her husband, with the sought approval of the Secretary-of-State for War, Lord Kitchener, advertised in *The Times* for "Sportsmen, aged 19 to 45, upper and middle class only", to sign up at the Hotel Cecil "at once", to constitute a Sportsmen's Battalion around fifteen hundred strong. In the event, the response was such that two Sportsmen's Battalions were constituted, the 23rd (1st Sportsmen's) Battalion, the Royal Fusiliers, on September 25th, 1914, and the 24th (2nd Sportsmen's) Battalion, on November 20th (30; 98). Essentially an entire Company of the 24th Battalion was raised in a recruitment drive in the West Country in December, 1914-January, 1915, organised by Captain Albert Edward Dunn (*Plate 1*; see also Appendix 1). One of these men, Private Thomas Ladas Powers, aged twenty, died at his temporary billet in Exeter on February 26th, 1915, and was buried in Exeter Higher Cemetery (see also Appendix 1). As might be expected, many of the 24th (2nd Sportsmen's) Battalion's recruits came from sporting backgrounds, or could at least shoot or ride. And, although equally many were working-class, proportionately more were middle- or upper-class, as intimated in the "Preface" above. This was perhaps in part because "working-class men in London were in general less well fed and less fit than middle-class Londoners" and "many failed to reach the exacting standards then enforced"; and in part because "some ... were less dispensable to the war

2

effort", because they were in "reserved occupations" (100). A Special Variety Concert in aid of the 24th Battalion, organised by Mrs Cunliffe-Owen and Corporal Gaetano Musitano, "the tenor of the battalion", took place at the Hotel Cecil on February 5th, 1915. What was described as "a very pleasant and enjoyable evening" was brought to a close by the singing of the National Anthem, "in which the whole audience joined with fervour". On March 17th, 1915, the 24th Battalion was inspected, in the presence of Mrs Cunliffe-Owen, at Horse Guards' Parade in Whitehall, before being marched up the Strand, Fleet Street, Cheapside and Threadneedle Street to Liverpool Street Station, to board a train to Hare Hall Camp in Gidea Park in Romford, there to begin their basic training (*Figure 8*). Before they were deployed to the Western Front, all ranks were presented with a silver medallion by Mrs. Cunliffe-Owen, bearing her signature and the words "God guard you". It is believed that only six men from the 1914 cohort served with the 24th Battalion throughout the Great War. One of them was Warrant-Officer Second-Class Joseph Henry – "Joe" – Hughes, M.M. (see also Appendix 1).

The 24th was a so-called "Pals Battalion", a part of Lord Kitchener's "New Army" (as distinct from the established professional "Regular Army", also known as the "Old Contemptibles", and the semi-professional, part-time "Territorial Force"). The "New Army" began its life in 1914 as a volunteer force, characterised, as Rudyard Kipling put it, by "pride of city, calling, class and creed", and "standards and obligations which hold men above themselves at a pinch, and steady them through long strain" (46). Contingents from it were first deployed on active service on the Western Front, in the Battle of Loos, in the early autumn of 1915. Conscription was only introduced - following the passing of the Military Service Act - in January, 1916.

One of the men who served in the 24th Battalion in the Great War was Private Charles Reuben Clements, who was my maternal grandfather (see Appendices 1 & 2).

3

Training for the Great War

The 24th Battalion began basic training at the newly-built Hare Hall Camp on March 17th, 1915 (30; 101). Incidentally, the eighteenth-century Hare Hall that gave the former camp its name, and provided its officers with their quarters, still stands, although it is now part of the Royal Liberty School. And at the site of the former entrance to the camp, on Main Road, is a 2019 memorial to the "Artists' Rifles" Officers' Training Corps, which was based there from 1915-1919 (*Figure 9*). However, no trace remains of the camp itself, which was the size of a small town, and remarkably well appointed, with fifty wooden barrack-huts, each built to house thirty men, a tailor's hut, a boot-maker's hut, a barber's hut, a guard-room, a serjeants' mess, a stores, a cook-house and canteen, an ablutions shed, a laundry, and even its own twenty-four bed hospital staffed by the Royal Army Medical Corps, not to mention its own electricity generator and its own post office (101). The majority of the 24th Battalion relocated from Hare Hall Camp to Clipstone Camp near Mansfield in Nottinghamshire sometime in July, 1915, to continue their training (the remaining minority later coming to form part of the 30th (Reserve) Battalion). The Battalion transferred again to "Candahar Barracks" in Tidworth Camp on Salisbury Plain, on the Hampshire/Wiltshire border, in or around September, 1915, to complete their training.

As already intimated above, among the 24th (2nd Sportsmen's) Battalion's trainee recruits at one time or another there were, unsurprisingly, a number of sportsmen (30; 62). These included three professional footballers, Serjeant Adams (*Plate 2*), who played for Southend United and Fulham; Serjeant Arthur Nicholas Evans (*Plate 3*), who played for Manchester City, Blackpool and Exeter City; and Private Henry George Purver (*Plate 4*), who played for Brentford (see also Appendix 1). (Sadly, Evans and Purver went on to killed in the Battle of Delville Wood on July 31st, 1916). And Charles Percy – "Charlie" – McGahey, who played first–class cricket for Essex and the M.C.C., and was voted one of Wisden's "Cricketers of the Year" in 1901, and who also played at least occasional top-tier football for Millwall, Woolwich Arsenal and Tottenham Hotspur, once breaking an opposing goalkeeper's collar-bone with a particularly hard shot (*Plate 5*; see also Appendix 1). Also Harry Packer, who had played first-class rugby for Newport, and internationally for Wales (see also Appendix 1). Not to mention the big-game hunter and explorer Frederick Courteney Selous, the inspiration for the Allan Quatermain character in H. Rider Haggard's stories, who would go on to transfer to the 25th (Frontiersmen's) Battalion (*Plate 6*; see also Appendix 1). And the similarly adventurous and dare-devil Reginald Alexander John - "Reckless Rex" – Warneford, who had joined the Merchant Navy aged only thirteen, and who would go on to join to the Royal Naval Air Service, and then to win lasting fame – not to mention a Victoria Cross - as the first airman to bring down a Zeppelin (*Plate 7*; see also Appendix 1). Warneford described the 24th Battalion's training camp as "a sort of Boy Scouts' Jamboree for old gentlemen" (32). Perhaps more surprisingly, also among the Battalion's recruits were two artists who had exhibited at the Royal Academy, Frank Gascoigne Heath, who went on to transfer to the 30th Battalion, and Frank Edward Southgate, who went on to die on active service with the 24th Battalion in February, 1916 (see also Appendix 1). As were the Reverend Frank Edwards (*Plate 8*), an ordained minister from Hull; Frederic Thomas Horne, the Liberal Agent for West Gloucestershire, who went on to be killed on the Somme in September, 1916, and Herbert Henry Raphael (*Plate 9*), the millionaire Member of Parliament for South Derbyshire (see also Appendix 1). And various others of the upper classes who had joined as officers, despite having no military experience outside the Officers' Training Corps in their public schools. Most "Other Ranks" appear to have been more or less content to defer to, and obey orders from, higher-class officers. It was a more deferential time.

At least for the "Other Ranks", basic training seems to have consisted for the most part of drilling, marching, digging trenches, and practice in the use of weapons, with little instruction on battlefield tactics, and less, if any, on strategy (30; 98; *Figures 10-11*). It was evidently not without its

5

dangers, though - one man, Private James Lambert Jenkin, aged twenty-five, died suddenly during training on July 15th, 1915, and was buried with full military honours in Romford Cemetery (30; see also Appendix 1). On a typical training day in Romford, the men might march to the railway station to catch a train to Wickford, then march for an hour to their allotted place of work to dig the trenches that would form part of the defences for North London. They would get a half-hour break for a lunch of bread and cheese in a local pub. The fortunate few who knew the aforementioned Herbert Henry Raphael might also be treated to beer and cigarettes. As regards weapons, the standard issue was the bolt-action .303" Calibre Short Magazine Lee-Enfield or S.M.L.E. ("Smelly") Mk. III rifle, which came with a Pattern 1907 Mk. I sword bayonet attachment (63). At 44.6" long, the Lee-Enfield rifle was significantly shorter than the German equivalent, the Mauser Gewehr-98 or G-98, and, in order to compensate, the bayonet was significantly longer, at 17" long. It was capable of a rate of fire of at least fifteen aimed rounds per minute, twice that of the Mauser, and it had an effective range of around 550 yards. In skilled hands, it was capable of thirty or more r.p.m. In 1914, one Serjeant-Instructor Snoxall used a Lee-Enfield to squeeze off no fewer than thirty-eight shots in sixty seconds, and hit a one-foot diameter target three hundred yards away with every one.

There was, though, at least a certain amount of free time (*Figures 12-14*). There was even time for a football match between the 24th (2nd Sportsmen's) and 23rd (1st Sportsmen's) Battalions at Romford Town's football ground, which the 23rd won, 2-1. And on Sundays, there was religious instruction. Private W.S. Ferrie of the 24th Battalion, who had been a Minister before enlisting, was an enthusiastic member of the congregation in the Congregational Church in Romford (30; see also Appendix 1). Charles Edward Montague, M.B.E. (*Plate 10*), on the other hand, wrote in his book *Disenchantment*, "like the infinite cleaning of brass-work, the hearing of many well-meaning divines in the Tidworth garrison church had been one of the tribulations through which the defender of Britain must work out his passage to France" (60;

see also Appendix 1). On reflection, Montague also wrote, "The old time seems like one's youth. It was merry and friendly and full of the vague thrill of greater experiences lying ahead. Most of us privates had gone back, as by a miracle, to the irresponsibility of childhood. ... [A]nd when the day's work was done, it was all rest and play. I remember, in May and June 1915, the half-hour before lights-out was blown on the bugle, the thirty men going to bed laughing .... and singing together and telling stories and there were nightingales singing in the trees outside. It's all gone as childhood does".

An annotated photograph of the 24th Battalion's officers - "Fighters for the Freedom of Europe" - taken at Hare Hall Camp in Romford, and published in *The Illustrated War News* on August 8th, 1915, included a Colonel A.de B.V. Paget, Major and Adjutant H.H. Enderby, Major P. Elwell, Captains G.W. Bagot, C.E. Browne, G.A. Franks and P.J. McRedmond, Lieutenants A.R. Cunliffe-Owen, A.A. Enderby, W.C. Green, J.S.G. Kay, W.G. Perkins, R.H. Shaw and F.J. Templeman, and Second Lieutenants H. Blaauw, R.A. Durand, G.T. Edwards, W.T.H. Montgomery and S. Smith (*Figure 15*). Temporary Quarter-Master and Honorary Lieutenant Bertram Edward Crosse joined the ranks in February, 1918 (see also Appendix 1). Colonel A. de B.V. Paget had at the outbreak of the Great War returned from a decade-long retirement to help train the 24th Battalion (see Appendix 1). He was characterised by Montague, again in *Disenchantment*, as "the old, cold, colonel, upright, dutiful, unintelligent, waxen, drawn away by a genuine patriotism from his roses and croquet to help joylessly in the queer labour of trying to teach this uncouth New Army a few of the higher qualities of the old". Paget, Montague added, "too honest a man to pretend that he was not taking all that he said in his lecture out of the Army's official manual, *Infantry Training, 1914, ...* held the little red book in his hand, read out frankly from that terse and luminous masterpiece of instruction, and then ... tried to "explain" it while the men gaped at the strange contrast between the thing clearly said in the book and the same thing plunged into obscurity by ... woolly and faltering verbiage. ... [H]ere was the colonel bringing his laboured jets of darkness to show the

7

way through sunlight; elucidating plainness itself with the tangled clues of his own mind's confusion". Lieutenant Alexander Robert Cunliffe-Owen was the Battalion's founder Mrs Emma Cunliffe-Owen's younger son (her elder son had died before the war) – promoted, perhaps, beyond his youthful experience (see also *Figure 7* and Appendix 1). Lieutenant Arthur Aaron Enderby was Major Harold Henry Enderby's son (see also Appendix 1). He would go on to join the 4th Battalion, the Royal Fusiliers, that had won the first two Victoria Crosses of the Great War at the Battle of Mons in August, 1914. He then died of wounds at Grevillers, near Bapaume, on August 2nd, 1917, aged twenty-one. He is buried in Grevillers Cemetery, suggesting that he died at either No. 3 or No. 29 Casualty Clearing Station, both of which were in Grevillers at the time (34; 59). By then Captain W.C. Green was wounded at Arras on April 13th, 1917. A Second Lieutenant Charles Layton Green also served with the 24th Battalion for a time before transferring to the Royal Flying Corps in 1916 (see also Appendix 1). He went on to killed on June 19th, 1917, and is buried in Bailleul Communal Cemetery Extension. Lieutenant W.G. Perkins was wounded on the Ancre on November 13th, 1916. Second Lieutenant Henry Thomas Gillman Blaauw was also wounded at some point, and had to have his right leg amputated below the knee (see also Appendix 1). Second Lieutenant Ralph Anthony Durand was twice sent back from France suffering from gallstones, and ended the war working in a desk job in Italy. By then Captain Guy Threlkeld Edwards (*Plate 11*) was killed in the Battle of Delville Wood on July 31st, 1916, aged twenty-five, and is commemorated on the Thiepval Memorial (see also below). Second Lieutenant and later Captain Walter Thomas Harold Montgomery, who, like Second Lieutenant Green, had studied Medicine at the University of Edinburgh before the war, survived the war (see also Appendix 1).

An accompanying photograph of the Non-Commissioned Officers included Major and Adjutant Enderby; Regimental Serjeant-Major Morris, Serjeants-Major Finch, Harmer, and Towler; Serjeants Adams, Artis, Axten (Regimental Quartermaster Serjeant), Baines, Burton, Busby (Quartermaster

Serjeant), Challenger (Orderly-Room Serjeant), Clair, Cox, Cronin (Quartermaster Serjeant), Day, Dent, Denton, Drew (Quartermaster Serjeant), Ellis, Essex, Evans, Fairburn, Hadaway, Harvey, Hayward (Provost Serjeant), Heaton, Hurst, Little, May, Morris, Punchard, Remnant, Samuels, Scobell (Quartermaster Serjeant), Shields, Stuart (Quartermaster Serjeant), Tottie, Wakefield, Watson (Pioneer Serjeant), Wellington, Whitfield, and Wilson; and Lance- Serjeants Barr-Hamilton, Bedbrooke, Brock and Mason (*Figure 16*). Regimental Serjeant-Major E.M.S. Morris is also pictured on *Figure 11* (see also Appendix 1). Serjeant Adams is the same man as the Serjeant Adams pictured on *Plate 2*, who played professional football for Southend United and Fulham (see also Appendix 1). Serjeant Evans is the same man as the Serjeant Arthur Nicholas Evans pictured on *Plate 3*, who played professional football for Manchester City, Blackpool and Exeter City (see above). He was reported missing, assumed killed, in the Battle of Delville Wood on July 31st, 1916 (see below). Serjeant Little is the same man as the Serjeant Arthur Joseph - "Mick" - Little who died of wounds sustained in the Battle of the Ancre on November 19th, 1916, aged twenty-four (see below). Serjeant May is the same man as the Serjeant Oliver Bertram May who was killed in the Battles of Arras on April 29th, 1917 (see below). And Serjeant Whitfield is the same man as the Serjeant William Albert Whitfield who was killed at Carency on July 1st, 1916 (see below). It is possible that Lance-Serjeant Bedbrooke (with an "e") is the same man as the Serjeant Duncan Harry Bedbrook (without an "e") who was killed in the Battle of Delville Wood on July 29th, 1916, and who is buried in Delville Wood Cemetery near Longueval (see below). Serjeant William John – "Billy" - Punchard (see also *Plate 12*) had to be sent home on two separate occasions to be treated for "shell shock", but survived the war (see Appendix 1 below).

9

THE GREAT WAR ON THE WESTERN FRONT (1914-18)

In the years leading up to the outbreak of the Great War in 1914, weapons technology had undergone a revolution (9; 84). The world's first true machine gun, the fully-automatic Maxim, had become available in 1884, and indeed had already been put to deadly use in a series of British colonial wars in Africa between 1893-1902, and in the Russo-Japanese War of 1904-05 (84). Moreover, and more significantly, rapid-firing artillery pieces with anti-recoil systems had also become available, and artillery would become the greatest killing machine of the Great War, accounting for almost 60% of all casualties (84). The Great War, the First World War, would be the first modern war, "undisguisedly mechanised and inhuman".

At the outbreak of the war, the British Royal Garrison Artillery had at their disposal a range of medium to heavy guns and – steeply-angled – howitzers of 5-8" calibre, and heavy naval and siege pieces of 9.2-15" calibre, to be deployed to the rear (84). These had ranges of ten to fourteen thousand yards, and rates of fire of one to two rounds per minute. The Field Artillery had lighter 4-4.5" and quick-firing 12-18lb field pieces, for use on the battle-front. These had ranges of up to seven thousand yards, and rates of fire of four to eight rounds per minute (compared to the fifteen to thirty rounds per minute of the famed French 75mm Gun or "*Soixante-Quinze*"). And by early 1916 the Infantry had Garland, 1.57" Vickers, 3" and 4" Stokes, 6" Newton and 9.45" Heavy mortars for use in and around front-line trenches. The German Army could call on an even wider range of light to super-heavy artillery pieces of 5.3cm/53mm (2.1") to 42cm/420mm (16.5") calibre, and *Minenwerfer* or mortars of 7.58cm/75.8mm (3") to 25cm/250mm (9.8") calibre (84). The British would soon come to know the sounds and other effects of rounds from German artillery pieces. 7.7cm/77mm (3") or 10.5m/105mm (4.1") rounds would come to be known as "whizzbangs", and mortar rounds as "Moaning Minnies" (8). And larger calibre, 15cm/150mm (5.9"), 21cm/210mm (8.3"), 28cm/280mm (11"), 30.5cm/305mm (12") ("*Schlanke Emma*") or 42cm/420mm (16.5") ("*Dicke Bertha*" or "Big Bertha") rounds would come to be known either as "crumps" or as "Jack Johnsons", after the immensely powerful African-American boxer who had become the heavyweight champion of the world in 1908 (8). They might leave craters up to twenty or thirty feet wide and ten or fifteen deep. Both sides' artillery shells could be filled with either High Explosive or shrapnel. Or, from 1916 onwards, gas - which was illegal under the terms of the Hague Convention of 1899 (previously, as in the Battle of Ypres, 1915, also known as the Second Battle of Ypres, gas had simply been released from canisters, which was technically legal). Ground-burst High Explosive shells were used against enemy positions, including barbed wire; air-burst shrapnel shells, against personnel. Shells could also be filled with smoke, for the purpose of camouflage. Artillery targets could be identified not only by ground but also by aerial reconnaissance, from balloons or so-called "spotter" aeroplanes (34). As regards heavy machine guns, both the British and German Infantry used modifications of the aforementioned Maxim, which ingeniously used the recoil generated by firing one round to automatically load another (84). The standard-issue British heavy machine gun was the Vickers Mk. I, which was manufactured in factories in Crayford and Erith in Kent (64). The Vickers used belt-fed .303" (7.7mm) calibre ammunition, the same as the standard-issue rifle. It had a rate of fire of around 600 rounds per minute, forty times that of a rifle. And it had an effective range of around 2 200 yards, four times that of a rifle. It was especially renowned for its reliability, which was due in part to its water-cooling system. On August 24th, 1916, during the "Somme" Offensive, one Company of the Machine Gun Corps fired almost exactly one million rounds from ten Vickers machine guns, without a single mechanical breakdown (43). The German heavy machine gun was the Maschinegewehr-08 or MG-08, also known as the Spandau, manufactured either in the Spandau arsenal or in the Deutsche Waffen und Munitionsfabriken (DWM) factory, both in Berlin.

The Spandau used 7.92mm calibre ammunition. It had a rate of fire and effective range similar to those of the Vickers. Its extreme range was around five thousand yards.

The cutting-edge twentieth-century weapons used in the Great War were such as to render any nineteenth-century battlefield tactics, and especially offensive infantry and cavalry tactics, essentially obsolete (9; 34). Tragically, though, it was to take the historically unprecedented losses of the industrial-scale early battles on the Western to force this point home to the belligerents on either side (10; 38; 50). Perhaps most notable among these were the Battle of the Frontiers, and the Battles of the Marne, 1914, the Aisne, 1914, and Ypres, 1914 (also known as the First Battles of the Marne, the Aisne and Ypres, respectively), each of which resulted in hundreds of thousands of casualties. In the aftermath of these battles, trench warfare, or *"Grabenkrieg"*, became the default configuration; although in certain sectors and/or at certain times there was a tacit policy of non-aggression between the supposed belligerents on either side of No Man's Land, as during the "Christmas Truce" of 1914 (1). The British Army's *Field Service Pocket Book* (91) and *Infantry Training* manual (92), which had been issued in 1914, were soon updated with *Notes for Officers on Trench Warfare,* issued in March, 1916 (93); and *Notes on the Tactical Employment of Machine Guns and Lewis Guns* also had to be issued in 1916. The 1914 *Field Service Pocket Book* contained as much content on latrine trenches as on fire trenches, and as much on recipes - including one for chupatties – as on either (91). In contrast, the opening chapter of the 1916 *Notes for Officers on Trench Warfare*, on "Special Characteristics of Trench Warfare", began, "The importance assumed by trench warfare and the progress made in ... the science of the attack and defence of elaborate systems of trenches, have rendered necessary special instruction in the details of trench construction and trench fighting", adding, "It must, nevertheless, be clearly understood that trench fighting is only a phase of operations, and that instruction in this subject ... is only one branch of the training of troops. To gain a decisive success the enemy must be driven out of his defences and his armies crushed in the open" (93). The following chapters dealt with "Siting and Construction of Trenches", "Occupation and Relief of Trenches and General Trench Routine", "Organization of a Trench Line and Action in Case of Attack", and "Notes on the Attack in Trench Warfare" (see also 102). From 1916, simple trenches became complex trench systems, arranged in two or more lines (17; 76; 102). The front line typically consisted of fire, support and reserve trenches, connected by communications trenches, supported by strong-points, and further protected by outposts and barbed wire entanglements in No Man's Land. Fire-steps in fire trenches enabled troops to shoot through loop-holes in the – sandbag - parapet (*Figure 17*). Fire and support trenches were traversed, and reserve and communications tranches zigzagged, "to give protection from enfilade fire and to localise the effect of shell bursts" (*Figure 18;* see also *Figures 21 & 23*). Dugout shelters, below the levels of the trenches, were also provided for large groups of men. And "funk-holes" were commonly hollowed out of trench walls by individual soldiers, in which they could lie full length "like the recumbent effigy of some crusader in a church at home" (77). A number of surviving British trenches, dugouts and associated battlefield features have recently been excavated using the latest forensic archaeological techniques, for example at Thiepval Wood, Beaumont Hamel and Serre on the Somme, and on the Ypres Salient in Flanders (76). French features have also been excavated on the Somme. And German ones on the Somme, and on the Hindenburg Line near Cambrai. The uncovered artefacts have enabled a more complete and detailed understanding of all aspects of trench warfare and everyday life (and death). Those from Beaumont Hamel included not only hundreds of fired and unfired rounds of British ammunition from the Allied "Somme" Offensive of 1916, and a button belonging to a New Zealander who had been stationed in the area during the German "Spring" Offensive of 1918, as might have been expected, but also over a thousand French *Lebel* rifle rounds from 1914-15. A number of the bodies uncovered in archaeological excavations on the Somme have now been individually identified on the basis of subsequent research. These include that of a German soldier, *Wehrmann* Jakob Hones of the 121st (Alt Wurttemburg)

13

Infanterie Regiment, who had been killed at the *"Heidenkopf"* (Quadrilateral) on June 13th, 1915. Jakob Hones's body was re-interred in Labry Military Cemetery, near Metz, in 2004, in a formal ceremony attended by his grandson.

Around the turn of 1915/1916, when the 24th Battalion was deployed to the Western Front, the war there was essentially static, and positions thoroughly entrenched (10; 38; 50). The front line extended some five hundred miles from the Belgian coast in the north, right through France, to the Swiss border in the south, allowing no room for out-flanking manoeuvre (17; 18; *Map 1*). The Germans were "dug in" in generally higher, drier (that is to say, better drained), and more readily defensible ground to the east, and the Allies to the west (25). The defensive tactics and weapons employed in the ensuing trench warfare of 1916 and 1917 would generally prevail over the offensive ones (34). The resulting continuing deadlock would not be broken, and the war would not return once more to one of movement and manouvre, until 1918.

At this time, on the German side, the line was held by a number of armies under the overall command of *Chef der Grosser Generalstab* (Chief of the Great General Staff) *General der Infanterie* (Lieutenant-General) Erich von Falkenhayn, who had replaced *Generaloberst* (General) Helmuth von Moltke after the latter's failure on the Marne to execute the pre-war "Schlieffen Plan" designed to ensure a swift victory over France.

On the Allied, or Entente, side, the line was held in the north, as far south as the Somme, in Picardy, by Belgian and by British and Empire armies. The British and Empire armies were under the command of General, later Field-Marshal, Douglas Haig, who on December 12th had replaced John French after the latter's failure at Mons (67). The line was held in the south, as far north as the Somme, by French and Empire armies under *General* and later *Marechal* (Field-Marshal) Joseph Joffre.

Significantly, the front line was neither entirely straight nor smooth. There was a particularly prominent bulge or salient in the north, around Ypres in Belgium. And another at the mid-point, around the symbolically important fortress-town of

Verdun in the Meuse *departement* of France, close to the border with Germany, which meant that the French garrison there was surrounded by Germans on three sides.

Life on the Western Front

The typical British soldier - the "Tommy" - in the trenches and dugouts on the Western Front was "either frightened to death or bored to tears", as George Hawes of the Royal Fusiliers put it (31; see also 26; 29; 39). Captain Llewelyn Wyn - known as Wyn – Griffith, of the Royal Welch Fusiliers, wrote, "fear, boredom, boredom, fear - we swung from one to the other, with a growing fatigue as we drew nearer to the night of relief, and our minds became as muddied as our clothes" (35). And Private Frank ("Dick") Richards, also of the Royal Welch Fusiliers, wrote, "Some men were perfect philosophers under heavy shellfire, whilst others used to go through severe torture and would cower down, holding their heads in their hands, moaning and trembling. For myself I wasn't worrying so much if a shell pitched clean amongst us: we would never know anything about it. It was the large flying pieces of shell bursting a few yards off that I didn't like: they could take arms or legs off or, worst still, rip our bellies open and still leave us living; we would know something about *them* all right" (75). Death would have been a constant companion, whose cold hand would come to rest upon the shoulder of many. At the same time, though, there was also something of a fatal fascination with the war, at least in certain quarters. As Major Guy Patterson Chapman, M.C. of the 13th Battalion, the Royal Fusiliers put it, in his book *A Passionate Prodigality*, " ... in that fascination lies War's power. Once you have lain in her arms you can admit no other mistress. You may loathe, you may execrate, but you cannot deny her. ... . No wine gives fiercer intoxication, no drug more vivid exaltation. Every writer of imagination who has set down in honesty his experience has confessed it. Even those who hate her most are prisoners to her spell. They rise from her embraces, pillaged, soiled, it may

15

be ashamed, but they are still hers" (16). Moreover, as Lieutenant Sidney Rogerson of the 2nd Battalion, the West Yorkshire Regiment put it, in *Twelve Days on the Somme,* "[T]hough the war may have let loose the worst it also brought out the finest qualities in men. In spite of all differences ... , we were comrades, brothers, dwelling together in unity. We were privileged to see in each other that inner, ennobled self which in the grim, commercial struggle of peace-time is all too frequently atrophied for lack of opportunity of expression" (77).

Most of the soldier's time would actually have been spent to the rear of the fighting, or on the move (26; 29; 39). Here, the strong bonds of comradeship forged by shared danger in the front line were further tempered around camp fires, or on long marches, often to the accompaniment of bawdy, nostalgic, or bleakly sardonic songs such as *Mademoiselle from Armentieres,* *Keep the home fire burning,* and *Hanging on the old barbed wire* (8). Here too, as well as the hardships and inevitable fatigues, there might also have been organised football or boxing matches, or camp concerts, or *impromptu* card, dice, coin or other gambling games ("Nap", "Crown and Anchor", "Two Up"). Second Lieutenant Siegfried Sassoon of the Royal Welch Fusiliers, one of the most famous of the so-called war poets, wrote in his fictionalised autobiography of the comparatively carefree nature of such times, as follows, "What I felt was a sort of personal manifesto of being intensely alive – a sense of physical adventure and improvident jubilation; and also, as I looked at the signs of military occupation around me, a feeling that I was in the middle of some interesting historical tale. I was glad to be there, it seemed ... . Wonderful moments in the War, we called them, and told people at home that after all we wouldn't have missed it for worlds. But it was only one's youngness, really, and the fact of being in a foreign country, with a fresh mind". The soldier would also have designated, more prolonged periods of "rest and recuperation" to the rear, and of home leave (26; 29; 39). Much in-country down-time - and shilling-a-day back-pay - might have been spent in *estaminets* - "just-a-minutes" in the evocative vernacular (8). Some of these were respectable establishments catering to soldiers' staple requests for egg and chips washed down with watery beer or white wine (*vin blanc* or "plonk"); some others, less so.

Some of the soldier's time, though, would have been spent in action in the front line (26; 29; 39). And on occasions, he would have had to go "over the top" on a night-time wiring or reconnoitring mission or trench raid, or into a set-piece battle. Going into a battle, at least in the early stages of the war, he would have had to carry with him a rifle and bayonet, two hundred rounds of spare ammunition, two Mills bombs (grenades), an entrenching tool, one day's rations of food and water, and a basic first-aid kit -in all, at least sixty-six pounds of equipment, and in many cases even more, owing to the addition of a pick or shovel, or a box containing a carrier pigeon, or high(er)-technology communications equipment (15). A Mark I Steel Helmet ("tin hat"), weighing a further 2½lb, became standard issue in May, 1916. The helmet was colloquially known as the "Brodie", after the man who had come up with the design on which it was based. It would offer some protection against shrapnel balls or shell fragments coming down from above, but not against higher-velocity machine-gun or rifle bullets.

As well as the risk of death or life-changing injury in action, there was also that of debilitating or potentially fatal disease, which could strike at any time (26; 29; 39). The squalid conditions that the troops endured on the Western Front led to their own particular range of diseases, including "Camp Fever", "Trench Fever", "Trench Foot" and "Trench Mouth", not to mention dysentery. "Camp Fever" and "Trench Fever" (forms of Typhus) were caused by the bites of infected body lice. Lice were everywhere on the front, where they were known as "chats", and where the shared communal experience of removing them from clothing was known as "chatting". Private Richards wrote, "[W]e were lousy as rooks", and "in our shorts, pants and trousers were whole platoons of crawlers" (75). Incidentally, Richards also wrote, of the similarly ubiquitous rats, "They had a good picking ... [of dead bodies] ... and were as fat as prize porkers"; another man, that "If they were put in a harness they could have done a milk round". And Montague, "the rats are pretty well unimaginable ... , and, wherever you are, if you have any grub about you that they like, they eat straight through your clothes or haversack to get at it as soon as you are asleep. I had some crumbs of army biscuit in a little calico bag in a greatcoat pocket, and when I awoke they had eaten a big hole through the coat from outside and pulled the bag through it, as if they thought the bag would be useful to carry away the stuff in. But they don't actually try to eat live humans" (60). "Trench Foot" (Immersion Foot Syndrome) was caused by prolonged immersion of inadequately-protected feet in cold water, such as in the bottom of a poorly-drained trench: if left untreated, it could lead to Gangrene and amputation. "Trench Mouth" (Infectious Stomatitis or Acute Necrotising Ulcerative Gingivitis) was caused by poor oral hygiene. And dysentery was caused by poor sanitation. There was also, from the late spring of 1918 onwards, "Spanish Flu" (a particularly virulent strain of Influenza). Over the course of the year, "Spanish Flu" resulted in the hospitalisation of 313 938 British soldiers (34). In the November, it caused the deaths of six members of the 23rd (1st Sportsmen's) Battalion, five of them after the formal cessation of hostilities on 11th (30; 98). It would eventually cause the deaths of some fifty million people worldwide - many more, in fact, than the fighting of the Great War.

Most of the time, most soldiers' thoughts would almost certainly not have been about such high ideals as the defence of freedom, or of the Empire, which was what the Great War was actually being fought for (26; 29; 39). Rather, they would probably have been about their comrades and about their rations - and not necessarily in that order. Rations, incidentally, tended to be monotonous, with some of the staples being tainted Tea, Army Biscuits ("so hard that you had to ... smash them with a stone"), Maconochie's Meat and Vegetable Stew, and Tickler's Plum and Apple Jam – Raspberry or Strawberry only on red-letter days. But at least supplies were sufficiently plentiful that large numbers of improvised bombs could be made out of empty jam-tins, filled with "shredded gin cotton and ten penny nails, mixed according to taste" ("Insert a No. 8 Detonator and a short length of Bickford's Fuse. Clamp up the lid. Light with a match, pipe, cigar or cigarette and throw for all you are worth"). In such rare quiet introspective moments as the men would have had, their concerns might have turned to their loved ones at home, and to when the next loving letter, or comforting parcel of candles or chocolate or warm woollen socks, might arrive from home. All too many would never make it home.

Little of any of this would have been known to many of those on the Home Front, who received only censored letters from the troops in the trenches, and few home visits (26; 29; 39). Their principal sources of information as to what was happening would have been the oftentimes sanitised and sentimentalised – even romanticised - accounts, sometimes amounting to little more than propaganda, in the newspapers and on the newsreels. A substantial minority, though, would have seen Geoffrey Malins's comparatively - if not completely – realistic film, "*The Battle of the Somme*" which came out in August, 1916 (44). And not a few would have been shocked by the grainy images of actual as well as staged battles, and of dead British soldiers, pale on the grey-scale ground (100).

DEPLOYMENT TO THE WESTERN FRONT (1915)

According to the wartime diary kept by Private Charles William Stanley – known as Stanley – Spencer, the 24th Battalion, the Royal Fusiliers was deployed to the Western Front on November 15th, 1915 (*Plate 13*; see also Appendix 1). Private Spencer wrote, "On the morning of 15 November we marched out from Candahar Barracks for the last time and entrained for Southampton which we reached at about 1.00 pm. We heard that because there were enemy submarines in the Channel we would not be able to leave the port until after dark, so we remained sitting about on the platform until 5.30 pm when we went on board. The transport was the "Mona's Queen", built in 1885 for the Isle of Man service. ... . We were very crowded and I lay on the wood floor most of the night and by so doing probably escaped seasickness. At about 3.00 am we ran into the estuary at Le Havre and disembarked at 7.30 am. It was cold and bleak as we lined up on the quay and as we marched through the town to the 'Rest Camp' it began to snow heavily" (81; see also 89). Private Sidney Richard – known as Richard - Worger wrote in one of the surviving letters to his "Beloved", his wife Gertrude, that "We had a beautifully smooth [Channel] crossing" (30; see also Appendix 1). What had followed, though, had been less pleasant: "48 hrs in a rest (!) camp (12 men in a tent in a sea of mud), + arrived here after 24 hours in ... trucks [each marked "*Hommes 40, Chevaux 8*", and hence known as a "Homforty": 8]". Where "here" was not specified: "not knowing exactly what one is permitted to write shall save all descriptions + impressions till we meet ... ".

The Battalion moved to Annequin, midway between Bethune and La Bassee, on November 28th, "for instruction in trench warfare under 5th I.B.", on the same day officially joining 5th Infantry Brigade of 2nd Division, which was one of the recognised "top-notch" divisions (89). At this point, the chain of command extended from the Major-General commanding the Division; through the Brigadier-General (Brigade); Lieutenant-Colonel and subordinate Major (Battalion); Captain (Company); Lieutenant or Second Lieutenant (Platoon); and Serjeant or Corporal (Section); to the Private soldier. A Division generally consisted of three Brigades, or approximately 9 600 men; a Brigade, four Battalions, or 3 200 men (later, three Battalions, or 2 400 men); a Battalion, four Companies, or eight hundred men; a Company, four Platoons, or two hundred men; a Platoon, four Sections, or fifty men; and a Section, ten to fifteen men. At the turn of 1915/1916, 2nd Division consisted of 5th, 6th and 99th Brigades, the 99th effectively replacing the 4th (Guards) Brigade, which had transferred to the Guards Division. Fifth Brigade consisted of the 2nd Battalion, the Highland Light Infantry, the 2nd Battalion, the Oxfordshire and Buckinghamshire Regiment, and the 17th (Empire) and 24th (2nd Sportsmen's) Battalions, the Royal Fusiliers, and also included a Machine Gun Company (a Trench Mortar battery would be added in March, 1916). Sixth Brigade consisted of the 13th (West Ham) Battalion, the Essex Regiment, the 1st Battalion, the King's (Liverpool) Regiment, the 17th (1st Footballers') Battalion, the Middlesex Regiment, and the 2nd Battalion, the South Staffordshire Regiment. And 99th Brigade consisted of the 1st Battalion, the King's Royal Rifle Corps, the 1st Battalion, the Royal Berkshire Regiment, and the 22nd (Kensington) and 23rd (1st Sportsmen's) Battalions, the Royal Fusiliers. Each battalion of eight hundred men was responsible for approximately eight hundred yards of front. The successive officers-in-command of the 24th Battalion while it was on active service on the front, leastwise those signing the entries in the *"Battalion War Diary"* (89) were, in January, 1916, Major H.U. Cradock; in February, 1916, Lieutenant-Colonel Francis Alexander Chetwood Hamilton; in March-July, 1916, Lieutenant-Colonel Henry Ernest Walshe (see also Appendix 1); in August-October, 1916, Lieutenant-Colonel L.J. Ashburner; in November, 1916, Major J.C. MacSwiney; between December, 1916-September, 1918, Lieutenant-Colonel Robert Henry Pipon, D.S.O., M.C. (see also Appendix 1); and finally, in October-November, 1918, Major Cyril

21

Alexander Knust, M.C. (see also Appendix 1). Lieutenant-Colonel Walshe was placed on extended sick leave in August, 1916.

"First Taste of the Trenches"

Private Alfred John Westlake of the 24th Battalion wrote in a letter to his home-town's newspaper, *The Dartmouth Chronicle*: "Within a fortnight of our landing [i.e., by the beginning of December, 1915] we had our first taste of the trenches ... . Fritz sent over a little reception in the shape of a whizzbang, which set our nerves tingling and sent our heads below the parapet. ... To be so close to our friends the enemy for the first time naturally made some of us curious to see what the front was like! One peep over the parapet was quite sufficient, for we were greeted by a hail of snipers' bullets [it transpired that the sector of the front that the Battalion was in was infamous for sharp-shooters or snipers, and in particular for one known as "Ginger Fritz"]. A quiet chuckle from our companions of a regular regiment at our evident newness brought us to our senses, and we set to work with our spades and pickaxes - thinking hard. It is surprising how quickly one gets used to the continuous shellfire, and in a few days we reckoned ourselves amongst the cool-headed "veterans". One soon learns to distinguish between the shrill note of the light but dangerous whizzbang, and the heavier shells known as "coal boxes" and "Jack Johnsons" used by the Germans, and consequently to give them each due respect, according to their proximity to one's dug-out or duty post. It is impossible to run into safety from a shell: the only thing to do is to duck, or even fall flat in the bottom of the trench. This practice soon becomes second nature. Trench mortars are spiteful little creatures to deal with, for they are thrown high into the air and drop (if well aimed) right into an opposing trench and explode with a loud detonation, and have effect over a considerable distance, but there is this advantage; one can hear these customers coming, and therefore one is able to make oneself scarce. Snipers' bullets are treated with contempt - as long as one's head is below the parapet. The most trying experience our company had was on the night before Christmas Eve when (with another battalion) we were in the firing line at the time the German artillery commenced a very heavy bombardment of our trenches. I can tell you we had the most exciting time of our lives, for shells were dropping thick and fast around us, though almost miraculous to relate, the sole result was one casualty in the company. To add to the "enjoyment" of the bombardment it rained in torrents the whole night, and throughout the following day (Christmas Eve). The welcome order came to stand to at about 10am, and we knew our relief was due - we should be in billets for Christmas Eve. Alas! Owing to the terrible state of the trenches the company detailed to relieve us took nearly four hours to get to the firing line through thick mud – in some places three feet deep. We knew our fate by the appearance of the newcomers, who were literally covered from head to foot in Flanders mud. At last came the order to retire, but it was easier said than done, and it was only after three and a half hours' struggle that we emerged from the communications trench on to terra firma. We arrived in billets at seven o'clock in the evening thoroughly done in, but very glad to spend Christmas Day in comparative peace and enjoying the contents of welcome parcels from thoughtful friends at home. So many days at rest in the trenches; so many at rest in the billets. This is the programme with little variation, but plenty of excitement, and of course at the price of danger, but the infectious chumminess of each and every man compensates for the necessary discomforts and hardships of trench warfare ... . We spend our time out of the trenches in fairly comfortable barns, with straw for beds and the luxury of a fire and blankets. We are now back some fifteen miles behind the firing line for some days rest, and sports of various kinds are indulged in, in the village schoolroom, all of which tend to recuperate the men who have had a fair share of the shot and shell of the trenches". Private Westlake would go on to transfer to the Suffolk Regiment. He then died of wounds sustained at the Battle of Ypres, 1917 (also known as the Third Battle of Ypres or as the Battle of Passchendaele) on September 27th, 1917, aged twenty-seven (see also Appendix 1). He is buried in

Lijssenthoek Military Cemetery in Popering(h)e in Belgium ("Pop" to the troops: 8). The *"Battalion War Diary"* entry for December, 1915 is missing, and it is not known exactly where the Battalion was over the course of this month (89). Private Worger was only allowed to write in another of his letters to his wife that at this time he was "somewhere in France" (30). In that letter, he also wrote of the terrible conditions in the trenches - the mud, the misery, the discomfort, and the danger. The danger was highlighted when he was wounded in the foot by a piece of shrapnel in December, 1915 (he was later wounded again at Bernafay Wood on the Somme on July 26th, 1916). Private Spencer recorded in his diary on December 4th that the Battalion was "moved from Annequin to Le Preol" (81). And he went on to record on December 6th, "[W]e went into the front line for the first time. ... . It was raining hard and we had to wait in Harley Street ... until it was dark enough to go forward as the HLI [Highland Light Infantry] reported that the trenches were flooded and impassable so that we would have to reach the front line over the top. Just after dusk we started off ... and slithered and slid and stumbled over the shell-torn, corpse-strewn wilderness known as the 'Valley of Death', where the English Guards had met and defeated the Prussian Guards many months before. It ... soon became inky dark and impossible to see even the ground under our feet except when a star shell went up. ... . Once Billy Haigh dropped on hands and knees in the slime and as a light went up found he had put his hand into the decomposing face of one of the enemy dead". And later, "We came out of the trenches into Harley Street at Cuinchy and marched ... back to billets on the far side of Bethune. ... We spent ... four days at Bethune ... [and] ... [o]n 14 December moved up ... to Harley Street". Cuinchy lay on the front line immediately west of La Bassee, which had been in German hands since the battle there in the "Race to the Sea" in October, 1914 (16). Second Lieutenant Edmund Blunden of the Royal Sussex Regiment, another of the so-called war poets, would later write, lyrically, of it, in *Undertones Of War*, "Who that had been there for but a few hours could ever forget the sullen sorcery and mad lineaments of Cuinchy? A mining sector, as this was, never wholly lost the sense of hovering horror. That day I arrived in it [in June, 1916] the shimmering arising heat blurred the scene, but a trouble was at once discernible, if indescribable, also rising from the ground. Over Coldstream Lane, the chief communication trench, deep red poppies, blue and white cornflowers and darnel thronged the way to destruction; the yellow cabbage-flowers thickened here and there in sickening brilliance. Giant teasels made a thicket beyond. Then the ground became torn and vile, the poisonous breath of fresh explosions skulked all about, and the mud which choked the narrow passages stank as one pulled through it, and through the twisted, disused wires running mysteriously onward, in such festooning complexity that we even suspected some of them ran into the Germans' line and were used to betray us. Much lime was wanted at Cuinchy, and that had its ill savour, and often its horrible meaning. There were many spots mouldering on, like those legendary blood-stains in castle floors which will not be washed away" (6).

On December 15th, 1915, Private Spencer wrote in his diary, "[W]e had our first fatal casualty. I was standing ... outside our billet when a small party went past to fetch the tea dixies from the cookhouse further along towards Woburn Abbey [the ruined church in Cuinchy]. As they were returning a few minutes later a shrapnel shell burst right over them and one man was killed. Part of the shell whizzed past my leg and hit a large stone behind me. I picked it up and found it still hot; it was about one inch thick and two inches long" (81). This fatality was to be the first of only too many sustained by the 24th Battalion over the course of the Great War. Incidentally, the 23rd Battalion sustained its first casualty on December 19th, 1915, when Private Archie Joseph Bury Palliser of London was shot dead by a sniper, also in the Cuinchy sector (98). There followed an order to the Battalion to the effect that any attempts at fraternisation with the enemy over Christmas, such as had taken place in 1914, would be punished by court-martial (30). Nonetheless, at least in parts of the British sector of the front, "The soldiers who were out of danger and lucky enough to be out of the line and off duty kept Christmas as far as possible in traditional style. Regimental funds had been

25

ransacked and in many battalions they were subsidised by officers to ensure that the Tommies had a good Christmas dinner. Turkeys were scarce and only for the fortunate few, but pigs were slaughtered wholesale and they were more than happy with roast pork. There were nuts and sweets and apples and almost a surfeit of plum pudding. So many had been sent by public benefactors as well as families and friends that some soldiers were eating them for days" (53).

According to the "*Battalion War Diary*", on January 26th, 1916, the 24th Battalion moved into trenches in the front line at Rue-du-Bois, near Festubert (89). The town of Festubert had been almost entirely destroyed in 1915, essentially nothing remaining of it "except one thing – a cross with the crucified Christ nailed to it *alone* survived". The effective destruction of the drainage system in the surrounding area, and the consequent high water-table and constant risk of flooding, prevented the more-or-less standardised digging out of trenches in this area, and instead forced the improvised building up of breastworks (93; 102). The "*Battalion War Diary*" recorded on January 27th, "A large amount of work was done on repairing the breast work" (89). It added, "the enemy fired a rifle grenade into ... [the] ... trenches, killing 3 men and wounding 2", and "a patrol reconnoitring enemy wire were fired on and the corporal in charge was missing on their return" (89). The following day, January 28th, "the enemy [again] fired a rifle grenade into ... [the] ... trench, which [this time] killed 2 and wounded 1" (89). One of the men killed on this day was Private James Benjamin Thomson, aged twenty-two, who is buried in Brown's Road Military Cemetery in Festubert (see also Appendix 1). The other was Private Siegfried Wedgwood Herford (*Plate 14*), aged twenty-four, who had evidently just finished writing a letter to his sister May, reading in part as follows, "The day itself passed fairly quietly, just the usual amount of strafing on either side. ... . We have nothing to do except sit tight in our little island [outpost] and keep a watchful eye through the periscope at which a German is taking some sporting shots - We come out on Sunday night" (86; see also Appendix 1). Like Thomson, Herford is buried in Brown's Road Military Cemetery. Having been a leading British climber before the war, he is also commemorated on the Fell & Rock Climbing Club war memorial at the summit of Great Gable in the Lakeland Fells (23; 86). The memorial records the names of nineteen men from the Club who lost their lives in the war, out of a membership of sixty-eight, including not only Herford but also Stanley Ferns Jeffcoat, sometime of the 24th Battalion (see below; see also Appendix 1). It was unveiled on June 8th, 1924 - coincidentally, the same day that Herford's sometime climbing partner George Herbert Leigh Mallory was lost on Mt Everest. The unveiling ceremony included a eulogy by Geoffrey Winthrop Young, who had lost a leg in the Great War while serving with a volunteer ambulance unit formed by the Society of Friends (but who would nonetheless go on to climb the Matterhorn). It was brought to a close by two boy buglers from St Bees School Cadets sounding the "Last Post", as "damp grey mist drifted silently ... over to Central Buttress on Scafell" (86).

On February 1st, 1916, while the Battalion was behind the lines at Le Touret, according to the "*Battalion War Diary*", "a hostile airoplane (*sic*) dropped a bomb close to 'C' Company's billets ... and killed 2 horses" (89). And on 5th, when it was back at the front near Festubert, "Pte. J.B. SMITH was killed bullet wound in head" (89). Private James Geddes Baird-Smith, as he is properly known, is buried in Brown's Road Military Cemetery in Festubert. On February 23rd, "Pte. F.E. SOUTHGATE died heart disease in his billet". Private Frank Edward Southgate, who was forty-three when he died, is buried in Lillers Communal Cemetery (see also Appendix 1).

On March 6th, by which time the Battalion was in the front-line trenches near Petit-Sains, somewhat to the west of Lens, the "*Battalion War Diary*" recorded "enemy ... troublesome with rifle grenades and T.Ms. [Trench Mortars] and killed one and wounded 4 of our men" (89). The man killed was Private Jack Harry Vincent, who is commemorated on the Arras memorial (see also Appendix 1). And on 8th, "enemy fired a good many rifle grenades and a few trench mortars ... . We had one man killed ... by a rifle grenade" (89). The man killed was Private Frederick William Dey, who is buried in Bully-Grenay Cemetery (see also Appendix 1). On March 17th, the

"*Battalion War Diary*" recorded "The usual exchange of trench mortar + rifle grenades, the day being cloudy little aireal (*sic*) activity one of our aircraft though when fired at by hostile machine guns approached German line and replied to their fire with its machine gun a pretty plucky action" (89). In what might be characterised as chatty vein, it added, "It is noticeable that the men spend a short portion of each day examining their shirts for the little fellows who cause one's skin to irritate, the writer is free at present" (89). The "little fellows" were, of course, lice. And on 19th, "Captain (*sic*) RADCLIFFE ... was killed, probably by a German sniper, being hit in the head by a bullet. This is a serious loss to the Battalion. He was a good officer and very popular with all ranks. He was buried at BULLY GRENAY [Communal Cemetery, French Extension] this evening" (89). Lieutenant David Radcliffe was only twenty-one (*Plate 15*; see also Appendix 1). At the time of his death, he had been notified of his promotion to Captain, but had not yet been gazetted. Over the course of the month, Private Spencer spent twenty-one days in the trenches without any relief - other than that provided by "occasional doses of Extract of Coca ... that Father had sent out to me in the form of gelatine capsules made by Savory & Moore Limited" (81). This was despite the fact that "[t]he usual routine was four days in the front line, four ... in the support line, four ... in reserve and then back ... to the front".

On April 7th, while the Battalion was in the rear at Clarques, it took part in a Brigade field day, at which "General JOFFRE was present and watched the manouvres" (89). And on April 21st, when it was back in the front-line trenches in front of Bully-Grenay, Second Lieutenant George Tudor Webb, aged twenty-six, was killed by shell-fire, and buried in Tranchee de Mecknes Cemetery in Aix-Noulette (see also Appendix 1). Also in April, Private Spencer wrote in his diary, "We spent Easter weekend in the support line. ... . Patches of flowers could be seen on some of the hillsides and larks rose high and sang even over No Man's Land. At about 4.00 am on Easter Sunday [April 23rd] ... I went ... with a carrying party to fetch water in petrol cans from Bully Grenay village. ... [A]s we had plenty of time we went first to the little 'confiserie' where Madame and her daughter still lived ... and sold oranges, chocolate and biscuits to the troops. It was a lovely day and everybody felt cheerful. After a really good wash (the first for many days) ... at the back of the house we went in and ate a tremendous breakfast. I had six eggs, chipped potatoes, many slices of bread and butter and several basins of coffee. .... We always enjoyed and remembered little trips like this" (81).

On May 7th, when the Battalion was stationed around a crater in front of Bully-Grenay, "Enemy bombarded the crater and hit bombproof shelter killing 4 men" (89). One of those killed was Private Richard Frederick Arthur Westphal, aged nineteen (see also Appendix 1). Like Second Lieutenant Webb, Private Westphal is buried in Tranchee de Mecknes Cemetery. He is also commemorated in Fairfield Moravian Church in Manchester, where he worshipped before the war (his father was a Moravian missionary in Jamaica). On May 11th, when the 24th Battalion was in billets at Bully-Grenay, Private Worger wrote a letter to his wife describing a "most providential escape from death" that he had experienced the previous day, when they had been under trench-mortar- and high-explosive shell- fire in the front-line trenches, and had sustained a number of casualties (30). As he put it, "I was seated just inside my shelter reading a short story in the "Novel" mag, in which I was very interested as it was written by one of our boys (Hylton Cleaver), when at 8 o'clock I was warned to go on guard ... ; when I returned at 9 to finish the story I found my shelter had been blown to smithereens by a trench mortar". The incident evidently made Worger aware of his mortality, although not fearful of death (he went on to be killed at Delville Wood on July 31st).

Later, during the night of June 3rd/4th, when the Battalion was in the trenches near Berthonval, "2nd Lt. Crookes, who joined the Battalion on the 6th May 1916, was killed by rifle fire while in charge of a working party in the front line" (89). Second Lieutenant Ronald Orme Crookes, who was only eighteen, is buried in Zouave Valley Cemetery in Souchez (see also Appendix 1). And on June 11th, when the Battalion was back in the rear at Camblain(e) l'Abbe or Camblaine Chatelain ("Charlie Chaplin"), Private Denis Stuart Mitchell, also only eighteen, was killed accidentally, and buried in Cabaret Rouge Cemetery in Souchez (*Plate 16*; see also Appendix 1). On June 27th, the Battalion moved back into the front line near Carency in Artois, a little to the north of Arras, and west of Vimy Ridge. On this occasion, Private Spencer wrote, "The route up to Carency was really charming, the hillsides ... covered with huge patches of bright-red poppies – millions of them. Carency itself was a wreck without a complete house standing ... . The section of front line we were to take over consisted of a series of connected and numbered advanced posts. ... . Also about this time, night and morning, we heard the peculiar roll and thunder of hundreds of guns farther south in preparation for the Somme offensive. The sky was continuously lighted up by innumerable flashes, the earth shook and the air seemed to quiver with ... restless rumbling and muttering that constantly rose and fell, and rose and fell again ... " (81).

At some point in early 1916, Corporal Robert Stuart Hawcridge wrote one of his many letters to the school at which he was a master in Batley, describing a typical working party, as follows, "For three days we have been sending up working parties to the trenches. I'd better explain at once that there is practically nothing of the fighting of the illustrated paper type going on here. During one's period in the trenches, one is increasingly trying to repair the damage done by the enemy's guns and to improve the fire trenches. On these parties we carry simply a rifle, and anti-gas helmet and so many rounds of ammunition, the rifle being wrapped in everything available to guard it from the mud".

The 24th Battalion went on to fight in the Battles of the Somme in July-November, 1916; in the Battles of Arras in April-May, 1917; in the Battle of Cambrai in November-December, 1917; in the First Battles of the Somme, 1918, in March-April, 1918, during the German "Spring" Offensive; and, during the Allied "Hundred Days" Offensive that eventually won the war, in the Second Battles of the Somme, 1918, in August-September, 1918, the Battles of the Hindenburg Line, in September-October, 1918, and the Final Advance in Picardy, in October-November, 1918 (*).

(*) The terminology I have used is broadly in line with that enshrined in the official Report of the Battles Nomenclature Committee of 1921. What I have referred to as the First and Second Battles of the Somme, 1918, others have referred to, similarly arbitrarily, as the Second and Third Battles of the Somme.

It is worth noting at this point that the great battles of the Great War, unlike those of most previous wars, would seldom be decisively won and lost over the course of a single day, with the victors commanding the field at dusk, and the vanquished in retreat. And that still larger-scale   operations or offensives would go on for weeks and months, and even then often end in indecisive stalemate, at a cost of tens or hundreds of thousands of casualties. A soldier on the ground might not even be aware that an action   he had fought in had officially ended. The fighting, and the daily wastage of men, might seem to him to be carrying on regardless.

ALLIED "SOMME" OFFENSIVE (CHIEFLY 1916)

Germany launched a full-scale attack on the Verdun Salient in February, 1916, that over the next few months was to result in some 320 000 French and 280 000 German casualties (10; 38; 50). It was one of the worst battles of the war. *The* worst was yet to come.

As the situation at Verdun worsened, and the French began to fear that their army might bleed to death, Joffre cajoled Haig into agreeing to relieve the pressure there by advancing the launch date of the previously planned combined French and British - and Empire - offensive on the Somme from August 1st (3; 11; 33; 37; 52; 68; 79; 80; 88). The "Somme" Offensive was rescheduled to commence on June 29th, and eventually actually - because of bad weather – commenced two days late, on July 1st. The French also had the Italians launch an offensive against the Austro-Hungarians on the Isonzo River on the Southern Front in March (9). And in turn, the Italians had the Russians launch two offensives against the Central Powers in present-day Poland, Belarus and Ukraine on the Eastern Front, the first against the Germans in May, and the second against the Austro-Hungarians in June (9). Such was the initial success of the second Russian Offensive - improvised by General Aleksei Brusilov - in the east, that it was only halted by seven German divisions that were meant to have been sent to Verdun in the west. It was partly as a consequence of this that the French had already begun to wrest the upper hand at Verdun from the Germans by the end of June.

The original plan for the British involvement in the "Somme" Offensive, in the sector north of the river, was drawn up by the officer-in-command of the British Fourth Army, General Henry - "Rawly" - Rawlinson, a skilled infantry tactician, with the assistance of his chief-of-staff Brigadier-General Archibald Armar Montgomery (3; 34; 67).

Rawlinson's so-called "bite-and-hold" plan had the comparatively limited objective of bombarding and then capturing the trench systems and village-strongpoints of the German front line on a front of around twelve and a half miles, or twenty-two thousand yards, preparatory to bringing the artillery up and to bear on the second line. The plan was based on a mathematical calculation of what was realistically achievable given the available manpower and firepower. The firepower included some four hundred aircraft of the Royal Flying Corps, which was a sufficient number to ensure air superiority - at least in the early phases of the Offensive. Critically, though, it included under fifteen hundred mostly light to medium artillery pieces, spaced on average over fifteen yards apart, and mostly firing shrapnel rather than High Explosive, which was a barely sufficient number to destroy the enemy's defensive positions and barbed wire. In submitting his plan to Haig, Rawlinson expressly stated the opinion that any more ambitious objective would, "under the conditions that obtain, involve very serious risks and ... be in the nature of a gamble" (50). In his private diary, though, he wrote that "I daresay I shall have a tussle with him [Haig] over the limited objective for I hear he is inclined to favour the unlimited" (50; 67). In the event, Haig, by background a bold cavalryman of the old school, did indeed reject Rawlinson's plan in favour of one with much more ambitious but riskier objectives. Haig's modified version of Rawlinson's plan involved bombarding and then capturing both the German first and second lines in one single rather than in two separate actions, and then breaking out into supposed open country miles beyond to the north and east, making extensive exploitative use of the cavalry and field artillery (34; 67). By the time of the actual launch of the British Offensive, though, there would be a third German defensive line under construction.

The plan ultimately failed, and at great human cost, and so the Offensive as a whole failed, and ultimately ended not in a victory, not even a Pyrrhic victory, but essentially in a bloody stalemate, with both sides worn down almost to the point of being worn out (3). A calculated 419 654 British and Empire troops were killed, wounded or captured in the Offensive, that is, essentially one for every inch of the seven miles of ground gained, alongside 204 253 French troops, adding up to 623 907 Allied casualties (11; 20). And at least 437 000 - and indeed possibly as many as 500 000 or even 600 000 – Germans were also killed, wounded or captured, bringing the total number of casualties on both sides to more than a million men (11; 80). The poet John Masefield, who had worked as an orderly in a military hospital on the Western Front, was moved to write, "The field of Gommecourt is heaped with the bodies of Londoners; the London Scottish lie at the Sixteen Poplars; the Yorkshires are outside Serre; the Warwickshires lie in Serre itself; all the great hill of the Hawthorn Ridge is littered with Middlesex; the Irish are at Hamel, the Kents on the Schwaben, and the Wilts and Dorset on the Leipzig. Men of all the towns and counties of England, Wales and Scotland lie scattered among the slopes from Ovillers to Maricourt. English dead pave the road to La Boiselle, the Welsh and Scots are in Mametz. In gullies and sheltered places, where wounded could be brought during the fighting, there are little towns of dead in all these places: Jolly young Fusiliers, too good to die. The places where they lie will be forgotten or changed, green things will grow, or have already grown, over their graves. .... . There are three places, in that wilderness of the field, which should be marked by us. One is the slope of Hawthorn Ridge, looking down the Y Ravine [near Beaumont-Hamel], where the Newfoundland men attacked. Another is that slope in Delville Wood [near Longueval], where the South Africans attacked. The third is all that great expanse from Sausage Valley to the windmill [near Pozieres] which the Australians won and held. Our own men lie as it was written for them. But over the graves on these places it should be graven, that these men came from many thousands of miles away to help their fellow-men in trouble, and that here they lie in the mud, as they chose" (55). To add insult to injury, the minimal ground gained by the Offensive, at such cost, was immediately rendered strategically valueless by the German withdrawal to the Hindenburg Line in February-March, 1917 (see below).

The reasons for the ultimate failure of the Offensive, from the Allied - and in particular the British - perspective, are many, and have been much debated (3). Principal among them was probably the ineffectiveness of the preparatory artillery barrage in destroying the protective wire entanglements in front of the German lines, and the deep dugouts beneath and behind, most notably in the First Phase. This was in turn caused in part by Haig's effective dilution of Rawlinson's already weak concentration of artillery power, which could have been foreseen as problematic; and in part by a high percentage of "dud" shells, which could not (67). There was also a general inflexibility in offensive tactics, even when they were demonstrably not working, resulting in the repeated ordering of futile frontal assaults against enemy strong-points, in both the First and Second Phases (34).

Set against these British failures were some at least partial successes, most notably in the Third Phase (3). These included the use of surprising new tactics, such the so-called "creeping barrage" (34); and new weapons, such as the Livens Projector and, especially, the Mk. I Tank (84). At this stage of the war, though, the creeping barrage was still experimental, and its practical use sub-optimal (34). And the tank was not deployed in sufficient numbers as to result in any decisive impact (84). It also suffered from the technical limitations of slowness and proneness to mechanical breakdown. It was in fact little more than an armed and armoured version of the caterpillar-tracked vehicle used in place of large teams of horses to tow heavy artillery pieces over soft ground - although it had at least been given a distinctive rhomboid profile to allow it to negotiate trenches up to ten feet wide without ditching. The arms in the so-called "male" version included two quick-firing Hotchkiss 6lb guns, and in the "female" version, four Vickers heavy machine guns, mounted in side sponsons. Both "male" and "female" versions also came equipped with Hotchkiss light machine guns. The armour comprised quarter- and half-inch (6mm and 12mm) steel plate.

There were also undoubtedly many German successes during the Battles of the Somme (3; 27). German Intelligence was generally first-rate, with ample evidence in German archives of captured British plans and orders, transcripts of interrogations with captured soldiers and of eavesdropped telephone communications, and so on. This enabled a high degree of defensive preparation, of a system of "defence in depth" ("*Verteidigung in der Tiefe*"), or "elastic defence", with multiple trench lines behind the front running not only parallel but also perpendicular to it, each with multiple deep dugouts, and surface strong-points and machine-gun and trench-mortar posts. The extent of the German defensive system was grossly underestimated by British Intelligence. And German defensive tactics, although initially rigid, became flexible, essentially as a means of conserving dwindling manpower. German troops would no longer be ordered to fight *in* their front line, where they could be accurately targeted by British artillery fire. Instead, they were to fight *for* their front line, from improvised temporary positions such as shell holes, to the rear, side or even front (that is, in No Man's Land). There, it would be almost impossible to see them either from the ground or from the air, such that the British would not know where they were, or where their fire was coming from. Moreover, German troops were no longer ordered to hold on to their positions at all costs, as per Falkenhayn's earlier edict. Rather, if they did lose positions, they were to regain them by counter-attack. Germany's by then highly evolved counter-offensive and offensive tactics would stand it in good stead in the Battle of Cambrai in 1917 and in the First Battles of the Somme in 1918, in which specialised *Sturmtruppen* or storm-troopers would figure prominently (36).

There remains the contentious question as to the longer-term effect on both sides of the "wearing-down" battle or *Zermurbungskrieg* (3; 27; 65; 80). On the German side, *Generalfeldmarschall* (Field-Marshal) Rupprecht, Crown-Prince of Bavaria, the officer-in-command of Army Group Rupprecht, acknowledged that "What remained of the old first-class ... infantry had been expended on the battlefield [of the Somme]" (80). And *Kapitan* (Captain) von Hentig of the Guard Reserve Division described the Somme as "the muddy grave of the German field army" (80). In contrast, on the British side, Captain Charles Carrington of the Royal Warwickshire Regiment, argued that "The British Army learnt its lesson the hard way, during the ... Somme battle, and, for the rest of the war, was the best army in the field" (80). And, in his last despatch, on March 21st, 1919, Haig claimed, not without justification, "It is in the great battles of 1916 and 1917 that we have to seek the secret of our victory in 1918".

The Battles of the Somme
(July-November, 1916)

First Phase

Immediately preparatory to the launch of the First Phase of the "Somme" Offensive, the Allies subjected the Germans to a week-long artillery barrage, described by them as *"Trommelfeuer"* or drumfire (3; 11; 33; 37; 52; 68; 79; 80; 88). The First Phase proper began at 0720 on July 1st, 1916 with the detonation of a series of mines under the German lines. It proceeded at 0730 with the advance of contingents from - eventually – seventeen British and five French divisions along a twenty-five mile front extending from a point near Gommecourt, midway between Arras and Albert ("Bert") in the British sector to the north of the Somme, to a point near Bray in the French sector to the south. They were opposed by only six German divisions. For the most part, the British moved forward at a walking pace, rather than in repeated "platoon rushes", under covering rifle-grenade- and Lewis Gun- fire, such as would afterwards become standard practice (34). This was because it had been assumed that the German trenches would be taken without a fight, with both the barbed wire and dugout defences, and the defenders, having been wiped out by the preparatory artillery barrage. As intimated above, though, it turned out that the German defences had remained substantially intact, one German soldier, Karl Brenner, writing, "They [the British] had thought that none of us could have survived the 166-hour artillery bombardment, but even the foremost dug-outs survived undamaged". So, as soon as the barrage was lifted, the defenders were able to emerge to man their posts, and, much to their chagrin, the attackers found themselves facing withering fire. According to official statistics, there were a total of 57 470   British casualties on the first day on the Somme alone, of whom 19 240 were killed, 2 152 missing assumed killed, 35 493 wounded, and 585 captured – a casualty rate of the order of   45%   (57).   Among the casualties were a disproportionately large   number of 2 438 officers. This suggests deliberate targeting by the Germans of men wearing distinctive uniforms, complete with shiny Sam Browne belts and cross-straps, and baggy riding breeches, and carrying service revolvers. Two Brigadier-Generals and forty-five Lieutenant-Colonels were killed or wounded. Sadly, bad though it was, July 1st, 1916 was not the worst day of the Great War in terms of loss of life. That most dubious of distinctions belonged to August 22nd, 1914, when the French army engaged the enemy in a series of actions in the Battles of the Frontiers, and sustained a total of some 27 000 fatailities.

The First Phase was to continue until July 13th, with   the main thrust of the Allied attack directed   to the area to the south, where the most ground had been gained on 1st.   Here, French troops, south of the Somme, had seized most if not all of their first-phase objectives on 1st. And British   troops, north of the Somme, had also seized their first-phase objectives around Montauban ("Monty Bong") in   the southern part of their sector, on 1st, but not those on the high ground between Pozieres and Thiepval in the central part, or on the other side of the Ancre between Beaumont-Hamel and Serre in the northern part. (In the event, Pozieres would only be secured, by the 1st Australian Division of the Australian and New Zealand Army Corps, in August; Thiepval in September; Beaumont-Hamel in November;   and Serre on February 25th,   1917, during the German withdrawal to the Hindenburg Line).   Between July 2nd-13th, the British launched forty-six   significant, although essentially un-coordinated,   attacks, in the southern part of their sector, dismissed by Joffre as "a series of disconnected actions, both costly and unprofitable" (34; 67; 80).   The end result was the capture of little more ground than on July 1st, at the cost of some   25 000 additional casualties. Between 7th-12th, Mametz Wood was captured, by 38th (Welsh) Division, at the cost of four thousand casualties.   One of those casualties was Private Watcyn Emil Owen Griffith of the 15th (1st London

Welsh) Battalion of the Royal Welch Fusiliers, a Runner, killed on July 10th. Private Griffith's brother, Captain Wyn Griffith, from the same Battalion, later wrote of his anguish at not being able to give him a proper burial, as his body was never found (he is commemorated on the Thiepval Memorial). Captain Griffith also wrote movingly of the word of the death of many a loved one rippling out to a "quiet village in Wales, ... a grey farmhouse on the slope of a hill running down to Cardigan Bay, or ... a miner's cottage in a South Wales valley" (35). "They captured Mametz Wood, and in it they lie".

Multiple battalions of the Royal Fusiliers were in action in the First Phase of the Battles of the Somme (62; 99). The 2nd Battalion was in action on July 1st, in the strongly-defended northern sector of the front, a little to the south of Beaumont-Hamel (11; 37; 57; 68; 79; 80). There they sustained 561 casualties attempting to rush the so-called Hawthorn Crater, created by the detonation of a mine under the Hawthorn Redoubt, and were unable to advance further. Even their commanding officer, Lieutenant-Colonel A.V. Johnson, was wounded – by a British shell. The 11th Battalion was also in action on July 1st, in the southern sector, a little to the north of Carnoy (57; 68). Over the course of the day, they were able to advance well over a mile, and to capture Pommiers Trench, Pommiers Redoubt, and eventually White Trench, between Mametz and Montauban. Private J. Nicholson distinguished himself in the action by knocking out a machine gun and shooting six snipers (68). Private G.R.S. Mayne wrote of his role in it, "Out of breath and to gather my wits and strength I dropped into a shell hole just in front of the German wire. I peeped over the edge, fired a shot at a round hat on a German head that suddenly appeared, rushed the last few yards and jumped into the German trench. I saw nobody there, friend or foe. ... . I then went on to the second-line trench and jumped in to see a German soldier lying on the parapet. With fixed bayonet I approached him, then saw his putty-coloured face which convinced me he was mortally wounded. The German brought up an arm and actually saluted me. ... [T]he poor chap kept muttering two words, *Wasser, Wasser*" and "*Mutter, Mutter*". It took me a minute or so to realize he wanted a drink of water. The second word ["Mother, Mother"] I could not cotton on to. I am glad to this day that I gave him a drink from my precious water" (57). The 8th Battalion was in action late in the day on July 1st, at Albert; and the 8th, 9th, 10th and 13th later in the First Phase, along the road between Albert and the high-point of Pozieres (37; 68). Thirty-sixth Brigade of 12th (Eastern) Division, comprising the 8th and 9th Royal Fusiliers, the 7th Royal Sussex, and the 11th Middlesex, was involved in an attack directed towards Ovillers (la Boisselle) on July 7th. The attackers captured three German trenches and well over a thousand prisoners, although they also sustained heavy casualties of their own, and eventually had to withdraw from the third trench. According to an account given by Corporal Arthur Razzell of the 8th Battalion, "When we got back ... I saw our regimental serjeant major ... . As soon as he saw me, 'Fall out the 8th Battalion!' I went to him and I said, 'I'm the only one left!' ... . Next day ... we had a roll call. Apparently the colonel was killed, the adjutant was killed, all four company captains were killed, no officers came back, ... ; there was one NCO, that was myself, ... one lance corporal and sixty-three privates" (37). All of the 9th Battalion's officers were also either killed or wounded.   Their commanding officer, Lieutenant-Colonel Albermarle Cator Annesley D.S.O., was wounded in the wrist and ankle, rallying his men by waving his swagger stick in the air, before being mortally wounded by a bullet to the chest, just as they reached their objective. Serjeant Charles Robert Quinnell, M.M. recalled in a later tape-recorded interview, "The objective was 250 yards away. ... . As soon as the [British] bombardment started the Germans' retaliation came and for four hours we had to sit there and take everything he slung at us. We lost twenty-five per cent of our men before we went over. ... . The first wave went over and as soon as they had gone I gave the orders to 'Advance!' Up the ladders, over the top. When I got through our wire, the first wave were down, two machine guns played on them and they were absolutely wiped out. Everybody was either killed or wounded. ... .   We got half way across [No Man's Land] and then the two machine guns found us. They traversed, they played on us like spraying with a hose. At the finish I was the only man standing ... " (37). The 13th Battalion, the Royal Fusiliers were able to advance half a mile towards Ovillers on 8th, although the town would only be finally secured on 16th (37; 68). And on July 9th, as the Germans began to fall back, the 10th Battalion were able to begin to advance beyond La Boisselle towards "Sausage Valley" (79). Here, on July 10th, Lance-Corporal Rupert Whiteman of the 10th Battalion was given the "nauseating job" of commanding a   burial detail tasked with the disposal of large numbers of corpses that had begun to rot after having been left out in the open for days, under a hot sun.   He then found himself buried in the mass grave he had just ordered to be dug by the blast from an enemy shell, and "breathing ... suffocating fumes of High Explosive", with "strange things under me, warm and terribly soft". He was eventually dug out, "trembling ... from head to foot". The 10th Battalion went on to take part in an attack on the German lines between Contalmaison and Pozieres on July 15th, in which they were held up by wire and bloodily repulsed, sustaining some 250 casualties (11; 79).   Lance-Corporal Whiteman was everafter haunted by images of "dead men hanging in the entanglements like half-filled khaki chaff sacks with arms trying to reach the ground", and "bundles in the grass: those who attempted to crawl through" (79).   On finally entering Ovillers on or around July 16th, one Major Henry Hance of the Royal Engineers encountered "the worst sight I saw in the whole war", that of British dead "lying ... in hundreds, most belonging to the 8th Division who had fallen on July 1st" (3). He noted that those in No Man's Land in "Mash Valley" "had been bayoneted ... thro' the neck", and that those on the barbed wire "had the backs of their heads bashed in", and cited this as evidence that "German patrols at night had either murdered our wounded or mutilated our dead".   Hance's   allegation of atrocity remains unsubstantiated.

Also during the First Phase, the 24th Battalion was stationed in the Carency sector in Artois, some distance north of the main fight on the Somme in Picardy on July 1st (89). However, the Battalion did see some action, in particular on the evening and night of July 3rd/4th, when the Twins mine at the southern end of Vimy Ridge, immediately north of Thelus, was blown, the

41

resulting crater captured by a small party of bombers from "C" Company, and the position consolidated by around thirty further men from "C" and "D" Companies (16; 89). Private Spencer was one of the bombers from "C" Company who captured the crater, and wrote of the action in his diary, "After allowing a minute or two for the tons of earth and rock to fall from the sky where they had been blown, we rushed up to the front and scrambled up the great heap of new loose earth to the edge of the crater. The scene was extraordinary and I remember it vividly. The eight of us were spread out a few yards apart along the edge of what appeared in the fading daylight to be a huge chasm. We could not see the far side at all or judge the depth" (81).

Seven members of the Battalion were killed while it was at Carency, and one died of wounds sustained there (89). Private William Stephenson was killed by shell-fire on July 1st, while in the middle of writing a letter to his wife, enquiring as to the health of his newborn daughter, expressing the wish that he might soon be granted leave to see her for the first time, and, commenting, ominously, that the "shelling made him get the wind up" (30; see also Appendix 1). Serjeant William Albert Whitfield (pictured on *Figure 16*) was also killed by shell-fire on July 1st (see also Appendix 1). Private Edwin Wilfred – known as Wilfred or Fred - Wrayford May was killed in the already mentioned consolidation of the Twins crater, on July 3rd/4th (*Plate 17*; see also Appendix 1). Private Arthur Linsdell was killed on 4th, aged twenty-two; Private Herbert George Marshall on 11th, aged twenty-three; Lance-Corporal John Allen Bowen on 12th, aged thirty-two; and Private Walter G. Knight also on 12th (see also Appendix 1). And Second Lieutenant Francis Stanley Mott died on July 23rd, of head wounds suffered on 10th, aged twenty (*Plate 18*; see also Appendix 1). Private Stephenson, Private Linsdell, Private Marshall, Lance-Corporal Bowen and Private Knight are all buried in Cabaret Rouge Cemetery in Souchez, named after a red-bricked and red-tiled *estaminet* that had stood on the site at the outbreak of the war, but that had been destroyed by shell-fire in March, 1915. Serjeant Whitfield and Private May are buried in Zouave Valley Cemetery, also in Souchez.

And Second Lieutenant Mott is buried in Lapugnoy Military Cemetery, indicating that he may have died at No. 18 Casualty Clearing Station in Lapugnoy, near Bethune (59). Incidentally, Zouave Valley was so named in honour of the French North African colonial troops or zouaves who had fought and died nearby in the Battles of Artois in 1914-15 (61). French North African colonial troops are also commemorated on the memorial to the Moroccan Division on nearby Vimy Ridge.

The 23rd Battalion also sustained a number of casualties at Carency, including its Commanding Officer, Lieutenant-Colonel H.A. Vernon, D.S.O., who was wounded while on a visit to inspect the front-line trenches (98).

Second Phase

The Second Phase of the "Somme" Offensive began on July 14th, and ended on September 9th (3; 11; 33; 37; 52; 68; 79; 80; 88). It began with the Battle of Bazentin Ridge, the largest and best-planned operation since July 1st, which lasted from 14th-17th (34; 67). The opening attack of the battle came at 0320 – before dawn - on July 14th, after a steady three-day artillery barrage followed by an intense five-minute "hurricane" bombardment that featured firepower over twice as concentrated as on July 1st. It caught the Germans essentially entirely by surprise, and achieved its primary objective of seizing the villages of Bazentin-le-Peit and Bazentin-le-Grand on the Bazentin Ridge, immediately north-east of Mametz Wood, later on the morning of 14th. Remarkably, that same afternoon, it even achieved its stretch objective of seizing the high point of High Wood, atop the Longueval Ridge, although ultimately this proved impossible to hold on to for long, and eventually had to be relinquished on the night of 15th/16th (it would only be secured on September 15th). Incidentally, the one and only use of the cavalry on the Somme was in a charge on High Wood. This involved a three-hundred strong detachment from the 7th Dragoon Guards and 20th Deccan Horse, both at the time part of the 9th (Secunderabad) Cavalry Brigade of the 2nd Indian Cavalry Division of the Indian Cavalry Corps (61). Although much heralded in the newspapers from London to Bombay and beyond, the action only resulted in the deaths - at lance-point – or capture of around a hundred Germans. And what the newspapers did not report was that over a hundred of the cavalrymen themselves were killed or wounded, alongside well over a hundred horses. The Battle of Bazentin Ridge was followed by the Battle of Delville Wood, which lasted from July 14th-September 3rd. And the Battle of Delville Wood was in turn followed by the Battle of Pozieres, between July 23rd-August 7th, the Battle of Guillemont, between September 3rd-6th, and the Battle of Ginchy on September 9th. Over the two-week course of the Battle of Pozieres, the Australian and New Zealand Army Corps sustained some 22 900 casualties - almost as many as in eight months at Gallipoli. The so-called "Fighting for Mouquet Farm" ("Moo-Cow" or "Mucky" Farm) began on the same day as the Battle of Pozieres, July 23rd, but only ended on September 26th. By the first week of August, it had become apparent that a significant Allied breakthough was unlikely (80). The fighting over the course of the following six weeks would essentially be directed toward the continuing attrition of the enemy, and the straightening of the line, preparatory to the next planned "big push" on September 15th (65). It is probably fair to say that the supposed benefits of the costly - and seemingly haphazard - line-straightening operations were by no means always obvious to those who took part in them.

Delville Wood consisted of around 160 acres, that is, only a quarter of a square mile, of chiefly oak and birch trees, with dense hazel thickets, but also with open grassy clearings and cleared rides – the rides coming to be known by the Allied troops as "Rotten Row" etc. It was situated at the apex of a dangerous salient, a "Bloody Angle", on strategically important high ground, which was nonetheless often water-logged, even in summer, the Chalk bedrock here being overlain by a superficial deposit of clay-with-flints essentially impervious to drainage (25). Lieutenant-Colonel Graham Seton Hutchison, at the time serving with the Argyll and Sutherland Highlanders, wrote that "anywhere between Les Boeufs and Rancourt [immediately adjacent to Delville Wood],

... men sank waist, even breast, deep beneath the surface of the oozing mud, trenches were water-logged, a pitiless rain descended" (42). Mark Plowman wrote that the mud on the Somme was "all but impassable, and now sunk in it up to my knees, I have the momentary terror of never being able to pull myself out. Such horror gives frenzied energy, and I tear my legs free and go on" (29). And L.W. Kentish wrote of having seen men stuck in the mud on the Somme "dead from exhaustion from their efforts to get out", and in Flanders, having to be "dragged out" to be saved from drowning (33). Even the *Official History* momentarily forgets itself in its description of the mud on the Somme, and admits simile and even something approaching hyperbole: "[It] took on an aggressive, wolf-like guise, and like a wolf could pull down and swallow the lonely wanderer in the darkness" (20). In it, "the infantry abode in conditions which might be likened to earthworms, rather than of the human kind".

The wood - "Devil's Wood" - was the scene of some of the worst fighting and most hellish scenes of the war. A British officer, Captain S.J. Worsley, of the North Staffordshire Regiment, wrote, in a piece published in *Everyman* Magazine: "Every semblance of a trench seemed full of dead-sodden, squelchy, swollen bodies. Fortunately the blackening faces were invisible except when Verey lights lit up the indescribable scene. ... . [W]e stood and lay on putrefying bodies and the wonder was that the disease did not finish off what the shells of the enemy had started. ... . There was hand-to-hand fighting with knives, bombs and bayonets; cursing and brutality on both sides such as men can be responsible for when it is a question of 'your life or mine'; mud and filthy stench; dysentery and unattended wounds; shortage of food and water and ammunition". And a German officer wrote "Delville Wood had disintegrated into a shattered wasteland of shattered trees, charred and burning stumps, craters thick with mud and blood, and corpses, corpses everywhere. In places they were piled four deep. Worst of all was the lowing of the wounded. It sounded like a cattle ring at a spring fair" (87).

During the Battle of Delville Wood, on July 15th, the South African Infantry Brigade of 9th (Scottish) Division, under

Brigadier-General Henry Timson Lukin, managed to capture almost all of the wood (14; 87). Even more remarkably, although heavily outnumbered and repeatedly counter-attacked, they then held on to it for six days, until they were finally relieved on 20th. In so doing, they sustained an appalling total of 2 408 casualties out of a force of 3 163 (a casualty rate of 76%). The casualties included a total of 766 fatalities, that is, killed, assumed killed, or died of wounds. There followed repeated costly attempts to capture the remaining parts of the wood between July 21st and August 25th, when it finally fell to 14th (Light) Division.

Multiple battalions of the Royal Fusiliers were in action in the Second Phase (62; 99). The 20th Battalion was in action in High Wood on July 20th, 1916, where it sustained some 390 casualties, and again in Delville Wood on August 24th. Second Lieutenant Edward Chapman of the 20th Battalion wrote in a letter in August, "I hate all this business from the bottom of my soul. It has turned a beautiful country into a desolate waste. All this area is one vast cemetery. Dead bodies taint the air wherever you go. It has robbed thousands and thousands of men of life, and thousands more of the things that made life seem worth living. ... . I am sorry ... , but I cannot always look at the war from a Bairnsfather point of view [a reference to Bruce Bairnsfather, whose cartoons in *The Bystander* portrayed the humorous side of life on the Western Front]". Acting Captain – as he was by then - Chapman went on to be wounded in the aftermath of the Battles of Arras, on May 20th, 1917, and took no further part in the war. The 17th (Empire) Battalion was just behind the front line in a communication trench called Longueval Alley on July 27th (14). Their history recorded that day's fighting as follows: "The 27th was ghastly in the extreme. 17/R Fusiliers were not one of the attacking battalions, but it is an open question whether they would have suffered more than they did in Longueval Alley. For when 99 Brigade attacked the wood the enemy's guns opened fire on the whole area and on Longueval Alley especially, or so it seemed. All communications with the wood were quickly broken as high explosive and shrapnel lashed the trenches in which the fusiliers crouched, trying to take cover from that awful storm. At 2 pm

46

... [two] ... Companies of the 17th ... moved up to Delville Wood. ... On the way up the shell fire was terrific and B Company lost several men, although Angle Trench was a fairly safe approach to the wood. ... The front line at this period was a chain of shell holes and blown-in trenches just inside the far edge of the wood. The horrors of that place were now everywhere evident. The fearful havoc created by our barrage of the early morning, when no less than 369 guns of all calibres had poured a continuous storm of shells upon the unfortunate enemy, had piled destruction upon destruction. Branches of trees had been thrown about in all directions; the thick undergrowth of the wood was pitted with shell holes into which the enemy had crept for shelter – the whole place was in a state of indescribable confusion – to the attackers it was almost like creeping through a jungle, not knowing where the enemy was lurking or at what minute he might be encountered. The dead were everywhere – equipment littered the ground; and, above all, in the momentary pauses between one shell-burst and another, the moans or agonised cries of the wounded, calling for water or assistance, lent a final touch to an altogether ghastly scene". An anonymous account described what happened the following day: "[O]n the 28th ... the 17 Middlesex reinforced the depleted forces and further ammunition arrived; the counter-attack launched by the enemy was cheerfully and successfully dealt with. A timely artillery barrage cut off a large body of Germans who were practically wiped out by bombs [that is, Mills bombs, or grenades] and rifle and machine-gun fire. During the succeeding lull the 9th Essex relieved the 17th Royal Fusiliers, the last of whom left the dreadful wood at 11 am on the 29th".

The 22nd (Kensington) and 23rd (1st Sportsmen's) Battalions both went into action – the 23rd for the first time - in Delville Wood also on July 27th (14; 30; 62; 90; 98). Major N.A. Lewis, D.S.O., M.C. of the 23rd Battalion wrote of how "for two days before the fight the Battalion occupied some trenches near Bernefay [Bernafay] Wood, and sustained a number of casualties from shell-fire", and of how "for some hours before ... , the Huns shelled the area with gas shells. Fortunately, however, just before 11 p.m., the time for starting, a breeze

47

sprang up, and we were able to move without wearing gas masks". He added, "The move up was not pleasant. The area had been much fought over, it had been impossible to bury the dead for ten days, and it was a hot July! Our artillery was firing to cover our move up. Just after passing Longueval one of our shells dropped, unfortunately, near the platoon which, with the C.O., I was following. As luck would have it, though, only one man was badly wounded. ... . We took up our position in a trench at the edge of the wood. This was all that remained after the South Africans had been beaten back, and our attack was to start at dawn on the following morning. This attack was in two parts, two companies to take the first objective, a trench in the centre of the wood, and two companies to capture the far edge, and dig themselves in there. ... . The waves formed up in position shortly before dawn, and it was our first experience of going over the top as a battalion. The men, however, were quite cool and cheerful" (98). As to the actual attack, Lewis wrote, "At zero our barrage started, and our first waves were off ... . The whole wood was immediately full of machine-gun bullets. There must have been hundreds of machine guns - up in trees, hidden in the undergrowth, in fact all over the place. The Hun artillery came down on all the approaches to the wood, but not on the wood itself so long as any of their own men were in it. Owing to the position of the wood, however, at the apex of a captured triangle of ground, we received fire from both flanks, and also from our right rear, as well as from the front. The first objective was quickly taken, and then there was a pause before the advance to the second. A large number of prisoners came in, and were herded up near Battalion headquarters' trench. We then found that we were up against the Brandenburg Regiment, which had been specially sent up to hold the wood. ... . The advance to the second objective started promptly, but the Hun fought hard for a time, and held us up. Every bush seemed to contain a machine gun, and a redoubt on our left front caused us many casualties. ... . As soon as the C.O. received news of this check he sent up two reserve Lewis guns. These worked round the redoubt, and, finding an opening, killed most of the garrison, and then rushed it. The survivors fled, but Sergeant Royston found one of their own guns was still in action, and finished them off with it. ... . The final objective was quickly reached and consolidated, and for a while our men had a pleasant time dealing with counter-attacks from the front. The field of fire was good, and they quickly dealt with all the attempts made to push us back. ... . Then the Hun artillery got busy on the wood, which was, of course, an ideal mark. For the rest of the day they simply poured heavy shells in. It was pretty terrible. Trees were torn up by the dozens, and fell blazing. By the end of the day there was nothing but shattered stumps. The Medical Officer had a busy time, and owing to the barrage could not evacuate his wounded. The aid post was filled, and the overflow had to be put in shell-holes round about. The consequence was that many of them were killed as they lay there. Owing to the barrage, too, the sending of messages back to Brigade headquarters and the companies in front became almost impossible. Out of sixteen headquarter runners no fewer than fourteen became casualties before mid-day. One message was sent back by carrier pigeon, and a message received from the Brigadier read: 'Hold on. Reinforcements are being sent'. ... . As the day wore on many efforts were made to get round our flanks and turn us out. Bombing parties crept up, and had to be dealt with by our bombers. It was in one of these tussles that Jerry Delan[e]y ... was killed. At one time word came from our comrades on the right that the Hun had broken through. So we sent over a party to their assistance, and finally repelled the attackers. We spent the whole of the afternoon and evening in this way, but when our relief came up that night we handed over the wood intact. The scene at night was awful, the wood being ablaze in many places. I read messages and wrote out the relief orders by the light of a blazing tree, which had fallen across the shell-hole then being occupied by Battalion headquarters. ... . We were relieved by the 6th Brigade, and at dawn returned to our quarters ... - that is to say, those of us who were left. Our casualties were nearly 400, over 60 per cent of those who went in. Out of eighteen officers who went into the wood, thirteen became casualties, every company commander being included in this number ... . As I was making out our casualty return in our headquarters' shell-hole by the light of the blazing trees, our Quartermaster appeared with the rations. He threw a newspaper down to me, with the remark: 'You'll find something interesting in that.' I opened the paper, and found a full column describing how the South Africans took Delville Wood! When we were moving back into support, I noticed a horrible smell, and found it was due to the fact that almost every man was smoking a Hun cigar, large quantities of which had been found in the trenches ... " (98). The aforementioned Corporal Jeremiah – "Jerry" – Delaney, M.M. from Bradford, was a famous boxer, the lightweight champion of England, and a contender for the world title (30). He is commemorated on the Thiepval Memorial (48). Another of the 23rd Battalion's casualties on July 27th was Private Arnold Russell Garcia, aged twenty-one, who had previously seen service with the 24th (see also Appendix 1). Private Garcia's missing body was finally found in 1929, and buried in Serre Road No. 2 Cemetery.

The 24th Battalion was in "Happy Valley" on July 23rd-24th, Bernafay Wood on 25th-27th, and Trones - correctly, *Troncs* - Wood on 28th, and in the trenches around Delville Wood on 29th-31st (62; 89; *Maps 2-4*). At this time, it had not received any specialist training in fighting in woods, and indeed it would not until May 31st, 1918. While in "Happy Valley" on July 23rd-24th, it witnessed the unnerving sight of the survivors from another battalion from another regiment marching back from the front – there was only one officer and about forty other ranks. And while in Bernafay Wood between July 25th-27th, it sustained several casualties of its own, from shell-fire, including from gas shells. Private Edward Bowes was killed on July 26th, and Privates David Allen Cole and Cecil Dobie Murray White (*Plate 19*), aged twenty, on 27th, and, having no known graves, all three men are commemorated on the Thiepval Memorial (see also Appendix 1). Also on July 27th, Second Lieutenant Cyril Alexander Knust was awarded a Military Cross "for conspicuous gallantry": according to his citation, "He went out over the open some 50 yards to assist a wounded man, and, with the aid of two men, carried him to a shell hole, where he bandaged his wounds. Later, he succeeded in bringing him into safety. The party were under heavy shell and machine-gun fire the whole time". The following day, July

28th, by which time the Battalion was in Trones Wood, Private Spencer wrote in his diary, "Two of our men were blown to pieces and just disappeared in fact. Part of a boot of one was found afterwards but nothing else" (81). Among the total of eighteen men from the 24th Battalion known to have died on July 28th were Serjeant James Matthew Armstrong, aged forty-one, Private Frederick Noel Bond, aged nineteen, Private William John – "Willie" - Coulson, aged twenty-six, Private George Harrop Fish, aged twenty-one, and Private David Bruce McKechnie, aged twenty-seven, whose bodies were never found, and who are commemorated on the Thiepval Memorial (*Plates 20-22*; see also Appendix 1). Private Randolph Spencer Loibl, aged twenty-one, died the same day, and is buried in Dive Copse British Cemetery in Sailly-le-Sec, suggesting that he may have died of wounds at the nearby XIV Corps Main Dressing Station (*Plate 23*; see also Appendix 1). Also on 28th, Private Spencer wrote: "[W]e moved up into close reserve in 'Longueval Alley', a trench that ran ... on to the remains of Longueval village and Delville Wood. Longueval Alley was in an awful state. It was a German trench had been shelled to pieces. It was extremely wide and shallow and was soaked in gas and blood and the acrid smell of high explosive. It was full of dead men ... [who] ... now formed part of the floor on which everyone walked. One man had had his head and shoulders blown away and the rest of his body and internal organs lay about the trench while odd hands and legs of others lay just by. ... . The day on which we went up was very hot and the combined smells were almost overpowering. Some of the bodies under the floor of the trench had swollen and the result was a springy, cushiony feeling when walking along which gave us a ... very unpleasant sensation. On the way up near Hell Corner we picked up boxes of Mills bombs and our job was to carry them ... to the front line ... . A few minutes after we got back from the fatigue Haveridge [*sic*] was ... hit by a piece of shrapnel and died almost immediately. He was buried ... in a shell hole just outside the trench, and a small wooden cross was ... put up to mark the spot" (81). Corporal Robert Stuart Hawcridge, who was twenty-nine, is commemorated on the Thiepval Memorial, his original grave, at the site at which he was killed, having been lost (*Plate 24*; see also Appendix 1). Tragically, written orders for his immediate return to England to train as an officer did not reach the Battalion until the day after he was killed. In one of his surviving letters to Batley School, Hawcridge described a near-miss he had experienced on a previous occasion, as follows, "The day before yesterday I had the liveliest ten minutes of my life. While I was waiting with a working party at a busy corner of the road, a German gun got the range and dropped between twenty or thirty shells around us. Ragged chunks of metal and bricks flew all over the place, men scuttled to sand-bagged cellars, ducking and jumping at every explosion. One shell took the corner clean off a big house. The next fell through the roof and exploded inside, bursting a wall outwards. Most of the others fell all but harmlessly on the road or open ground near, with great fussy explosions and columns of black smoke and splashing earth. But of the hundred men standing there not one was touched. After that little episode it felt very safe to get back into the trenches again ... ".

On July 30th, a contingent of well over a hundred men from "C" ("West Country") Company of the 24th Battalion was terribly cut up in a failed frontal assault on an enemy trench-line six hundred yards east of Waterlot Farm, which was part of a wider attack on the strategically important section of front around the village-strongpoint of Guillemont (62; 82; 89; see also *Map 4*). Evidently, "Such was the price paid for co-operation in the attack on Guillemont" (62). Unbeknownst to the attackers, the German defensive positions were substantially intact, and substantial numbers of German defenders were waiting for them, despite the supposed "softening-up" by the British artillery. "C" Company's advance over No Man's Land was slowed by disorienting thick early morning mist, and by deep mud following days of rain. It was met not only by annihilating artillery, machine-gun and volley rifle fire from directly ahead of it, but also by enfilade fire from the German-occupied northeastern corner of Delville Wood ahead and to the left, and from Leuze Wood ("Lousy Wood") ahead and to the right. And, in the event, from Guillemont ("Gilly Mong") to the right, which had not been simultaneously captured as planned by 89th and 90th Brigades of 30th (Lancashire) Division, as they, too, had incurred heavy losses (33; 37; 68; 79; 80; 82). Brigadier-General Ferdinand Charles Stanley of 89th Brigade – the younger brother of Edward George Villiers Stanley, 17th Earl of Derby, the originator of the idea of "Pals Battalions" – later wrote, "About our new venture, which was to take place on 30th, I must confess that we were not happy, and we expressed ourselves on these lines to the division ... . It was not for us to criticise the plans of those above us, but we one and all recognised the enormous difficulty of the task which had been allotted to us. Our own particular job depended too much upon what happened on our flanks. If one or both of them did not succeed ... then the success of our operation would be out of the question" (37). The attack had gone ahead regardless, and Company Serjeant-Major William John George Evans, a Londoner serving with the 3rd Manchester Pals (the 18th Manchesters), who were part of 90th Brigade, had won a Victoria Cross for his courageous actions in it, as a runner, in the course of which he had been wounded and captured (82). In the aftermath of the attack, "Many of the bodies of the dead lay, unrecoverable, in machine-gun-raked No-Man's Land, until they were reduced to skeletons by the depredations of rats and the intensity of the August sun. Some, submerged and buried under the continually shell-shattered earth, were not discovered until more than a decade after the war" (33). The action was later likened to that of "1 July all over again", albeit on a smaller scale (80). This time, the effectiveness of the preliminary British artillery bombardment was further reduced by the novel German defensive tactic of "thinning out their positions and holding shell holes, rather than lines of trenches which ... were easily located" (80).

According to the 24th Royal Fusiliers *"Battalion War Diary"*, "The attack was unsuccessful owing to the wire not having been cut ... . Of the 3 Officers + 114 other ranks who made the attack, 1 officer (wounded) [Second Lieutenant C.L. Dunn, S.H. Gore or H. Laidley] + 11 other ranks got back [in time for roll-call on the evening of July 30th]. Capt. C.S. MEARES was killed on the German wire, leading his men"

(89). And as O'Neill put it, in his regimental history, "'The king of the war' as the French called barbed wire, exercised its sovereignty once again" (62). Captain Cecil Stanley – known as Stanley - Meares, who was killed on July 30th, aged thirty-three, is buried in Delville Wood Cemetery near Longueval (*Plate 25*; see also Appendix 1). It seems that the decision to have Captain Meares lead the attack had been based on the toss of a coin (81). The lucky loser of the coin-toss, incidentally, was one Captain Green (the same man as the Lieutenant W.C. Green pictured on *Figure 15*), who went on to be wounded at Arras on April 13th, 1917. Besides Captain Meares, two other men were reported in the "*Battalion War Diary*" as having been killed in the attack on July 30th, namely Lance-Corporal George Hague Hatfield, aged twenty-nine, and Private Arthur Alexander Stokes, aged twenty-two (89). Private Stokes was killed outright, and has no known grave, but is commemorated on the Thiepval Memorial (*Plate 26*; see also Appendix 1). On July 18th, twelve days before he was killed, he had written in a letter to his sister Marjorie that he was "pretty well and manage to pull along all right ... with a lot of grumbling etc. – that's only natural for a Tommy. I hope that the war will be over before the winter, as I shouldn't like another one out here. ... . I am your affectionate Bro., Art xxxx". Lance-Corporal Hatfield is buried in Abbeville Communal Cemetery, suggesting that he might actually have died of wounds in one of the Stationary Hospitals which were situated nearby (see also Appendix 1). A Private William Stewart Becher was reported in the "*Battalion War Diary*" as having died on July 30th, of wounds suffered on 28th, aged forty-seven, and he is also buried in Abbeville Communal Cemetery (see also Appendix 1).

A total of 102 men were reported in the "*Battalion War Diary*" as "missing" after the action on July 30th - on 31st (89). According to the Commonwealth War Graves Commission's database, forty-three of these men were either killed or officially assumed to have been killed in the action (Roy Hemington, CWGC, personal communication). The body of one man, Private George Ernest Burston, was found in Caterpillar Valley, near Delville Wood, and is buried in Caterpillar Valley Cemetery (see also Appendix 1). The bodies of fifteen further men were found also near Delville Wood, and are buried in Delville Wood Cemetery near Longueval, alongside Captain Meares, 1 920 other individually identified men, and 3 593 unidentified men. These men were Private Sidney Bertram Clarke, Lance-Serjeant Frederick Cross, Lance-Corporal Charles Ford, M.M., Private Frederick John Geary, Private Francis Idris Greenwood, Serjeant Eric Gordon Hutchins, Private Percy Johnson, Private Walter Misson, Private James Peduzzi, Lance-Corporal Arthur Tipton, Private Albert Edward Turner, Private George Charles Vickery, Private Edwyn Cyril Wellicome, Lance-Corporal Frederick Harold Wescott, and Private Henry William Wyatt (Private Peduzzi's body, incidentally, was found east of Ginchy). Lance-Corporal Ford was twenty-three, Private Geary forty-one, Private Greenwood twenty-one, Private Hutchins twenty-nine, Private Peduzzi thirty, Lance-Corporal Tipton twenty-two, Private Wellicome twenty, and Lance-Corporal Wescott, twenty-one (see also Appendix 1). It is not known how old Privates Clarke, Cross, Johnson, Misson, Turner, Vickery or Wyatt were (but see Appendix 1). The bodies of twenty-seven of the "missing" men from the 24th Battalion were never found, as was all too often the case under the prevailing circumstances. These men are commemorated on the Thiepval Memorial, which altogether bears the names of 72 195 "missing" of the Somme, who have no known grave (48). Among these men were Serjeant Arthur Nicholas Evans, aged twenty-nine, and Second Lieutenant Francis John Eathorne, aged twenty-four (*Plates 3, 27*; see also Appendix 1). Also among them were Privates Richard James Carpenter, aged twenty-one, William Henry Fortnam, aged twenty-two, Willis Rees Lloyd, aged twenty-three, Sidney Charles Richards, and Robert Massingberd Rogers, aged twenty-three (see also Appendix 1). And Private Percy Bishop, whose body, identified by means of associated effects - including a paybook, a will, and a personal letter - was evidently found by the Germans on July 30th, before becoming lost (see also Appendix 1). His death was recorded by them on a *"Todesnachweis"* ("Proof of Death" certificate) and *"Totenliste"* ("List of Dead"), both of which still survive in the historical archives of the

International Committee of the Red Cross. Also according to the ICRC's database, and other sources, a further forty-seven men were captured in the action on July 30th (for more on the conditions encountered by Allied Prisoners-of-War in the Great War, see section on "The Battles of Arras ... ", and Appendix 3, below; see also 47). Four of the captured men, namely Privates Charles William Gammicott Burston, Frederick Grundy, Bernard James Mahoney, and Tom Wood, had been wounded when captured, and had died of wounds or disease in captivity (see also Appendix 1). Private Grundy died somewhere behind the German lines, although still in France, on September 2nd, 1916, aged twenty-five, and was probably originally buried in St Martin Military Cemetery in St Quentin in 1916, and certainly subsequently reburied in St Souplet Cemetery near Le Cateau in 1918, where he lies today. Private Wood died in a Prisoner-of-War camp in Niederzwehren near Cassel (now Kassel) in Hesse in Germany on September 14th, 1916, aged twenty-two, and is buried in Niederzwehren Cemetery. Private Burston also died in Niederzwehren, on January 27th, 1917, aged twenty-seven, and is also buried in Niederzwehren Cemetery. Private Mahoney died in a Prisoner-of-War camp in what was Schneidemuhl in Prussia – and is now Pila in Poland - on October 17th, 1918, aged twenty-six, and, having originally been buried in Schneidemuhl Prisoners-of-War Cemetery, is now buried in Berlin South-Western Cemetery, which opened in 1922-23. It appears that he had been put to work in a salt mine. At least three of the other captured men, Corporal Frederick Pearce Hancock, Corporal Sidney George Hindom, and Lance-Corporal Edgar James Smith, had also been wounded when captured, and, being too badly wounded either to work for the Germans or fight against them, were subsequently released and eventually repatriated, well before the end of the war (see also Appendix 1). It is evident that only twelve of the 102 men both survived the action and evaded capture - perhaps by sheltering in shell-holes in No Man's Land until it was safe to return to their trenches. Private Bell and Private Howarth were later recorded as having been killed, and Private Ebdon as wounded, in the Battle of the Ancre on November 13th, 1916

(89). Lance-Corporal Millar was recorded as having been killed at Arras on April 28th, 1917 (89). Privates William Corrie, Leonard Gauntlett and Bertram Charles Stone were subsequently recorded as in receipt of Army pensions. Gauntlett and Stone were also recorded as having been discharged from   the Army on medical grounds, in 1916 and 1917 respectively.   1916, and subsequently granted a pension. And as having been given Silver War Badges to wear on their civilian clothes to demonstrate that they had been honourably discharged.   And Lance-Corporal William Austin McCready was recorded as having returned to his pre-war position in the Northern Bank in Ireland in 1919 (*Plate 28*; see also Appendix 1).

On July 31st, again according to the "*Battalion War Diary*", "Battn. was relieved at 3.15 a.m. ... . Captain G.T. EDWARDS [pictured on *Figure 15* and on *Plate 11*] was killed during the relief + there were several casualties" (89). One of the fatal casualties on 31st was the previously mentioned Private Sidney Richard Worger, by now aged forty-one, who was killed in a tireless effort to help retrieve the many wounded men from the wood (30). One Private Peter Cassidy of the 2nd Highland Light Infantry found Worger's body, and arranged for the return of his personal effects to his widow, who worked as a nurse in Colchester Military Hospital.   In a letter to her, Cassidy assured her that her late husband's body had been buried with as much respect as the circumstances of the ongoing battle had allowed. In the event, Worger's grave was later lost.   He is, though, commemorated on the Thiepval Memorial. A large number of letters that Worger wrote to his wife are now in the Imperial War Museum in Kennington. A number of letters of condolence that his comrades and friends wrote to his widow are also there. One, from Hylton Reginald Cleaver (*Plate 29*), reads in part as follows: "Your husband ended his life with the utmost gallantry and crowned a long succession of deeds of great bravery and consistent grit; up to the very last he was tending the wounded under heavy fire, and it was whilst carrying a comrade away on a stretcher that he fell. He was killed, I think, instantaneously, and I feel sure he did not suffer pain". Further Battalion fatalities on July 31st

included Privates Henry George Purver, Louis Lawrent D'Abadie, Oswald Baron, Balfour Jackson, Francis Austin Elliott Paget, William George Miller Parsons and William Hadwen Peake, and Corporal Alexander Robertson. Private Purver (pictured on *Plate 4*) was killed on 31st, aged twenty-five, and is commemorated on the Thiepval Memorial (see also Appendix 1). Private D'Abadie (*Plate 30*) was also killed on 31st, aged thirty-eight, and is commemorated on the Cenotaph in Port-of-Spain in his native Trinidad, which at the time was part of the British West Indies, as well as on the Thiepval Memorial (48; see also Appendix 1). Incidentally, at least five British West Indians of Black African descent are also known to have served with the Royal Fusiliers in the Great War – and many thousands in other units, including some sixteen thousand in the British West Indies Regiment (see also 61). One, David Louis Clemetson of Jamaica, served as a Private soldier in the 23rd (1st Sportsmen's) Battalion, the Royal Fusiliers, and went on to be become a Second Lieutenant in the Pembroke Yeomanry, and later a Lieutenant in the 24th (Pembroke and Glamorgan) Battalion, the Welsh Regiment (*Plate 31*). Lieutenant Clemetson was killed in action near Peronne, on the Somme, on September 21st, 1918, and is buried in Unicorn Cemetery in Vendhuile. Returning to the 24th (2nd Sportsmen's) Battalion, the Royal Fusiliers, Private Jackson, aged twenty-four, Private Parsons, aged only eighteen, Private Paget, aged twenty-five, and Private Peake, aged forty-three, were all killed on July 31st, 1916, and are all commemorated on the Thiepval Memorial (see also Appendix 1). Private Baron, aged nineteen, and Corporal Robertson, aged thirty-nine, are both recorded as having died on 31st, and are buried in Corbie Communal Cemetery Extension, which was situated some twelve miles behind the front at the time (*Plate 32*; see also Appendix 1). It is possible that they died of wounds at No. 5 or No. 21 Casualty Clearing Station, which were both located in or near Corbie at the time of their deaths (59).

According to the "*Battalion War Diary*", the 24th Battalion's total casualties - that is, officers and other ranks killed, wounded or missing - for July were 364 (89). This was by some distance the highest monthly total of the war. Private

Spencer noted in his diary that the Battalion marched out of Delville Wood only some two hundred strong on July 31st. He also wrote, "We received large reinforcements of men and officers and moved back for what we hoped was our long-promised rest" (81). Montague wrote, "not to that battalion returned the spirit of delight in which it had first learnt to soldier together" (60).

Later, towards the end of the Second Phase, the 24th Battalion was in the trenches in the Beaumont sector on August 23rd-29th and again on September 4th-10th, and under intermittently heavy shell-fire. The 24th Battalion's total casualties for August were forty-nine (89). One of them was Private Bernard Warth, who died at No. 8 Stationary Hospital in Boulogne on August 23rd, of wounds received on the Somme on July 27th, aged twenty-nine, and who is buried in Wimereux Cemetery (*Plate 33*; see also Appendix 1). Another of the 24th Battalion's casualties for August was a Private Charles Sutherland, who reportedly committed suicide on 7th, and who is buried in Bray Military Cemetery (see also Appendix 1). It is impossible to know, but not unreasonable to speculate that Private Sutherland may have been suffering from "shell shock", now known as Post-Traumatic Stress Disorder (96). Eight men were recorded in the casualty lists in the "*Battalion War Diary*" as suffering from "shock" or "S.S." ("shell shock") in July, 1916, six of them between 28th-31st, during the Battle of Delville Wood (89). And no fewer than 501 men were reported in 2nd Division's medical records as suffering from one or other of the manifestations of the condition between July 26th-August 11th, accounting for 17% of the division's total number of wounded of 2 945 (24). The 24th Battalion's total casualties for September were eighteen, including two deaths in German captivity (see also above). One of the fatalities for September was Private Harold Victor Barnes, who was killed on 2nd, while the Battalion was receiving specialist training at Coigneux, and who is commemorated on the Thiepval Memorial (see also Appendix 1). Another was Private Frederic Thomas Horne, aged forty-four, who was killed on 5th, by which time the Battalion was back in the trenches in the Beaumont sector, and who is buried in Euston Road Cemetery in Colincamps (see also section on "The 24th Battalion ... " above; and Appendix 1 below).

Major Coxhead of the 9th Battalion, which had been in action in the First and Second Phases of the Battles of the Somme, wrote in his diary on October 19th, 1916, "It was fine seeing the places where all the heaviest fighting had been, *e.g.*, Guillemont Station, the sugar refinery [Waterlot Farm], etc., both now a pile of ruins of course. ... . The appearance of the country was lamentable. All trees are stripped of leaves, and Bois des Trones [Troncs] presents the most awful ruins I have ever seen – dead horses, battered trees and trenches, ammunition, huge shell holes, all in one huge jumble. ... . Having crossed that, we were soon in the neighbourhood of Guillemont. ... . Our walk took us back *via* the sugar refinery, where the enemy white flag of surrender is still flying" (62). Major Coxhead went on to be killed in the Third Battle of the Scarpe, one of the Battles of Arras, on May 3rd, 1917.

Incidentally, the defence of Guillemont was later acknowledged by British authorities as "the finest performance of the war by the German army" (3; 27). It was vividly recounted by *Leutnant* (Second Lieutenant) Ernst Junger of the Rifle Regiment of Prince Albrecht of Prussia (the 73rd Infantry Regiment), part of the Hanoverian 19th Division, in his book *Storm of Steel* (45). As day broke after his night-time arrival on the outskirts of Guillemont in late August, 1916, Junger wrote that his position "proved to be little more than a series of enormous craters ... ; the country around, as far as they eye could see, ... completely ploughed by heavy shells. ... . The churned-up field was gruesome. In among the living ... lay the dead. When we dug foxholes, we realised that they were stacked in layers. One company after another, pressed together in the drumfire, had been mown down, then the bodies had been buried under showers of earth sent up by the shells ... . And now it was our turn. ... . The village of Guillemont seemed to have disappeared without trace; just a whitish stain on the cratered field indicated where one of the limestone houses had been pulverised. In front of us lay the station, crumpled like a child's toy; further to the rear the woods of Delville, ripped to splinters". Later the same day, "a fire-storm was directed at ...

us. ... . As the storm raged ... , ... the men ... stood stony and motionless, rifle in hand .... Now and then, by the light of a flare, I saw steel helmet by steel helmet, blade by glinting blade, and I was overcome by a feeling of invulnerability. We might be crushed, but surely we could not be conquered". Only a matter of days afterwards, though, in early September, Junger suffered a shrapnel wound in the lower left leg, and had to be evacuated to an improvised hospital in St Quentin in the rear. As he arrived there, " ... all the window-panes were jangling; it was exactly the moment when the British, with maximal help from their artillery, were taking Guillemont".

Third Phase

The Third Phase of the "Somme" Offensive began on September 15th, and ended on November 18th (3; 11; 33; 37; 52; 68; 79; 80; 88). It began with the Battle of Flers-Courcelette, which lasted from September 15th-22nd, and which witnessed the first deployment of the Allies' secret weapon, the Mk. I Tank (34; 67). Such was the initial success that an observer-pilot was able to report that "A tank is walking up the High Street of Flers with the British Army cheering behind it". However, none of the thirty-two tanks originally deployed was still in operation after the third day, September 17th, most having ditched or broken down, and a few having been incapacitated or destroyed by enemy machine-gun- or shell-fire. And, after a week, the Army, which included not only British but also Canadian and New Zealand troops, found itself bogged down after heavy rain. One of the casualties of the battle was Lieutenant Raymond Herbert Asquith of the Grenadier Guards, the son of the British Prime Minister Herbert Henry Asquith. He was killed in action near Ginchy on September 15th, and buried in Guillemont Road Cemetery, with the epitaph, taken from Shakespeare's *Henry V*, "Small time but in that small most greatly lived this star of England". The Battle of Flers-Courcelette was followed by the Battle of Morval, between September 25th-28th, the Battle of Thiepval Ridge, between September 26th-28th, the Battle of the Transloy Ridges, between October 1st-November 11th, and the Battle of the Ancre Heights, also between October 1st-November 11th. The Third Phase culminated with the Battle of the Ancre, orchestrated by General Hubert Gough, which began on November 13th and ended on 18th, as the first snow of winter fell (67).

During the Battle of the Ancre, the fortified village of Beaumont-Hamel, or what was left of it, was finally captured by troops of 51st (Highland) Division under Major-General ("Uncle") George Harper, although only at the cost of some 2 200 casualties – and then not on the first day of the battle, as per the plan, but on the 136th, November 13th, 1916 (13; 19; 74). However, to the north, what C.R.M.F. Cruttwell called "the sinister ruins" of Serre, and A.H. Farrar-Hockley, "the last of the cruel Somme fortresses", would not yield, and would exact a bloody toll from 3rd and 31st Divisions - as it already had from 31st on July 1st.

Attacking between Beaumont-Hamel and Serre, on the left flank of 51st Division and the right of 3rd, 2nd Division, including the 24th Battalion, the Royal Fusiliers, also incurred heavy losses. Serjeant Sibley, of the Machine Gun Corps Company attached to 99th Brigade of 2nd Division, wrote, "The signal to go over was a mine going up [at Hawthorn Crater]. The morning was very foggy, a good job for us too, as Fritz didn't expect us. We collared some of them asleep and without boots on, we got the first three lines easy, but had to fight mighty hard for the rest. The ground was awful, lots of our fellows got stuck in the mud and we had to leave them to die" (37). Lieutenant Edgar Lord of 32nd Division, who relieved 2nd Division on November 16th, wrote, "The mud was so bad ... we found two English soldiers up to their armpits ... , one dead, the other ... stark mad. We ... got him out as soon as we could, but he died. They had been stuck for 48 hours" (37). And Captain Arthur Acland of 19th (Western) Division, positioned somewhat to the right of the 51st, on the far bank of the Ancre, in front of Thiepval, wrote that it was "a horror quite apart, quite unlike anything else in this war! Imagine a man, wounded ... , struggling ... , overcome by the sucking ooze, sinking, sinking inch by inch, in full view of willing friends, not one of whom can do a thing to help him; sinking and sinking, until, although he calls and calls for help, he realises no help can come – and he begs his own people to end his horror with a bullet" (37). As Lieutenant Sidney Rogerson of the 8th Division, in front of le Transloy, put it, the mud was "the arbiter of destiny" (77).

The 24th Battalion, the Royal Fusiliers was in the trenches in the Redan sector, between Beaumont-Hamel and Serre, on September 16th-19th, October 6th-8th, October 23rd-25th, November 7th-9th and November 12th, again under shell-fire, which did a great deal of damage to the trenches; and in action on 13th (89; *Maps 2, 5-6*). Blunden wrote of the immediately adjoining Thiepval sector at this time, "[T]he days were melancholy and the colour of clay. ... . [O]ne ... entered a land of despair. Bodies, bodies and their useless gear heaped the gross waste ground; the slimy road was soon only a mud track which passed a whitish tumulus of ruin with lurking entrances, some spikes that had been pine-trees, a bricked cellar or two, and died out. ... The shell-holes were mostly small lakes of what was no doubt merely rusty water, but had a red and foul semblance of blood. ... . Of the dead, one was conspicuous. He was a Scottish soldier, and was kneeling, facing east, so that one could scarcely credit death in him ... . Death could not kneel so, I thought, and approaching I ascertained with a sudden shrivelling of spirit that Death could and did" (6).

According to the *"Battalion War Diary"*, on October 24th-25th, "Battn Headquarters was heavily shelled" (89). In the aftermath, Private Eric Montagu, aged around twenty, found himself trapped in the entrance, and forced to cut off his own arm in order to free himself, and to allow two seriously wounded men buried behind him to be rescued (*Plate 34*; see also Appendix 1). Private Montagu was swiftly sent back to the U.K., where he was treated at Mile End Military Hospital, and eventually fitted with an artificial arm at Queen Mary's Hospital in Roehampton, which had come to specialise in such procedures (51; 78). He was one of 115 280 soldiers to be fitted with a prosthestic limb between 1920 and 1929 (78). After being invalided out of and pensioned off by the Army, he was able to secure civilian employment, as a senior clerk for a scientific instrument maker. Like Privates Gauntlett and Stone (see above), he was also given a Silver War Badge to demonstrate that he had been honourably discharged, as "permanently physically unfit". Also in October, Private Spencer wrote in his diary "my reports on the progress of the artillery in cutting the enemy wire [preparatory to the attack scheduled for November] were noticed at Divisional HQ to differ very materially from the reports of the artillery observers themselves. They said that it was well cut, while I reported that it was still extremely thick, especially in front of the enemy ... 'strongpoint' known as The Quadrant [Quadrilateral]. One day General Walker ... came up to ... our observation post in Valois trench himself ... to get first-hand information on this most important point. ... . The General then said he thought it would be best not to attack the Quadrant itself but to try to nip it out by advancing on either side" (81). He later added, "I believe this was ultimately done. If this was so our persistent reports did some good in saving the useless sacrifice of many lives".

On November 12th, Second Lieutenant Walter Barrington – "Wat" – Medlicott of the 24th Battalion, a family man in his forties, wrote to a letter to his wife that read, in part, as follows: "Well, darling ... tomorrow we advance on a large front. This letter won't go off till 6 a.m., so by that time we shall be ... over the Boche and sitting in a new line. This attack has been hanging fire for a long time but weather has postponed it. I don't call it perfect yet, but we must get forward. I shall be all right, but whatever happens – it is right. Others are writing to solicitors to forward – I prefer to write to you Darling – you are a soldier yourself, and can bear a command to carry on whatever happens. I had a great sleep last night and feel as fit as ever. I meant to write to ... [illegible] ... , but can't – as we must move at once – and Dad and all – but give them my love – and all to you and Bet.- yr. husband, Wat" (11). The tone of the letter contrasts markedly with that of many written in the earlier phases of the war, as it is one not of over-the-top enthusiasm, but rather of steady determination, to get the job of winning the war done. Medlicott went on to be seriously wounded in action in the Battle of the Ancre the following day. However, he recovered from his wounds, and survived the war (see also Appendix 1).

On November 13th, the first day of the Battle of the Ancre, "The Battalion took part in the[general] attack on the German lines, between SERRE + BEAUMONT-HAMEL. ... Objectives allotted to the Battn. the German trenches from [Trench Map Grid Reference] K 35 C 24½ , ... to K 35 C 94½ [Beaumont Trench] ... . The Battalion formed up in our lines in accordance with orders + at 5.15a.m. the Coys in our front line trenches went over + formed up in NO MAN'S Land, about 50 yds clear of our trenches. At 5.45 a.m. the whole advanced according to orders. Owing to the broken nature of the ground + the fog the various lines became mixed up + the whole advanced in one mass. The leading troops were within 20 yds of the [creeping] barrage, all along the front allotted to the Battalion. A few casualties were caused by our own barrage but the advantages gained in getting into the enemy's trench immediately the barrage lifted far outweigh the loss occasioned. On the barrage lifting the line advanced at a walk into the enemy's front line trench, where the Germans were found to be emerging from their dugouts. These men all surrendered. The enemy's wire was found completely demolished + formed no obstacle. The advance proceeded in accordance with orders, until the green line [the primary objective, Beaumont Trench] was taken [on schedule, at 0615]" (89; see also *Map 6*). Apparently, "composite groups ... [then] ... attempted to advance towards the secondary objective, ... [Frankfort or] Frankfurt Trench ... [and] ... heavy fighting ensued ... [until] ... those that were able to made a retirement [towards Beaumont Trench or the intermediate Munich Trench]" (74; see also 68). Later, "The Coy. Commanders realised ... that the assault on the left flank had not succeeded [and it was "in the air"] + took steps to block all the trenches leading N. ... . The remainder of the day was spent in consolidating the position + in beating off ... bombing attacks from the N." (89). The following day, November 14th, "orders were received to withdraw to a central position in the German first and second lines", and on 15th, "The coys continued to hold the positions indicated above, until relieved by part of the Machine Gun Company of the 112th Infantry Brigade", and "The Battalion then proceeded to hutments at

BERTRANCOURT". O'Neill wrote, in his regimental history, "The advance, though not spectacular, was useful in the general scheme of things; and it had not been achieved without considerable losses" (62). One of the Regiment's casualties, incidentally, was Lance-Serjeant Hector Hugo Munro of the 22nd Battalion, a sometime writer, better known as "Saki", who was killed at The Quadrilateral on November 14th.

According to the *"Battalion War Diary"*, the 24th Battalion's total casualties for September were eighteen, including two deaths in German captivity (see also above); those for October, also eighteen; and those for November, 251; bringing the total for the Battles of the Somme between July and November to seven hundred (89). One of the fatalities for October was Private John Prior, who was killed on 7th, when the Battalion was in the trenches in the Redan sector, and who is commemorated on the Thiepval Memorial (see also Appendix 1). One of the fatalities for November was Private Francis Caleb Fowler, aged twenty-six, who was killed on 3rd, when the Battalion was receiving specialist training at Arqueves, and who is also commemorated on the Thiepval Memorial (see also Appendix 1). Another was Second Lieutenant Andrew William Burnham, aged twenty-nine, who was killed on 13th, when the Battalion was in action in the Redan sector, and who is commemorated on the Thiepval Memorial (*Plate 35*; see also Appendix 1). Other soldiers from the 24th Battalion killed on the action on November 13th included Private Ernest William Cross, aged twenty-six, Private Arthur Gilbert Decimus Dorman, aged twenty, Private Horace George Dunham, aged twenty-four, Private Fred Howarth, Corporal Norris Ridley Johnson, aged twenty-five, and Private Sydney Herbert Kirby, also aged twenty-five, who are also all commemorated on the Thiepval Memorial (*Plate 36*; see also Appendix 1). Also Private Joseph Edmund Alexander Anderson, aged twenty-four, who is buried in Canadian Cemetery No. 2 near Neuville-St. Vaast; Private William John Bell, aged thirty, who is buried in Redan Ridge Cemetery No. 3, near Beaumont-Hamel; Lieutenant Frederick Sidney Bracey, aged twenty-seven, Private Cyril Christopher David Bradberry, Corporal Ernest Albert Firstbrook, M.M., aged thirty, a bandsman, who had

66

been shot in the head while carrying a stretcher, and Private
Arthur Stanley Robinson, aged thirty-two, who are all buried
in Redan Ridge Cemetery No. 1, also near Beaumont-Hamel;
and Second Lieutenant Stanley Harris Gregory, aged twenty-
seven, Lance-Corporal Charles Alfred Hicks, aged twenty-one,
and Serjeant Geoffrey Leonard Hughes, who are all buried in
Munich Trench Cemetery (*Plates 37-38*; see also Appendix 1).
Private Bell, like Private Howarth, had earlier survived the
attack on Guillemont on July 30th. He had last been seen alive,
although severely wounded, in a shell-hole on November 13th,
and his parents were later notified that he had been "missing"
since. His body was finally recovered at the beginning of 1917,
and, as noted above, buried in Redan Ridge Cemetery No. 3.
His gravestone was one of thirteen later destroyed by shell-fire,
and so had to be replaced by a special memorial plaque.
Among the many men of the 24th Battalion reported as
"missing" on November 13th were Private Charles Frederick
Brinklow, Private Francis Robert Clayton, Private Thomas
Cordwell, Private Edward Minty Miller, Lance-Corporal John
Cecil Pickering, and Private Yorke Smith. Private Brinklow,
who was twenty-six, was later found dead, and is buried in
Serre Road Cemetery No. 2 (*Plate 39*; see also Appendix 1).
The body of Private Clayton, who was thirty-four, was also
later found, and buried: his grave still later lost, he is
commemorated on the Thiepval Memorial (*Plate 40*; see also
Appendix 1). The bodies of Private Cordwell, aged twenty-
two, Private Miller, aged thirty-four, Lance-Corporal
Pickering, aged twenty-two, and Private Smith, aged twenty-
eight, were never found, and all four men are also
commemorated on the Thiepval Memorial (*Plates 41-42;* see
also Appendix 1). Private John Wilcock was killed on
November 14th, aged twenty-eight, and he too is
commemorated on the Thiepval Memorial (see also Appendix
1). Second Lieutenant William Henry Liddon Parry was
reported as having died on November 29th of wounds sustained
on 13th, aged twenty-six, and is buried in Le Treport Cemetery,
which at the time was in use by No. 3, No. 16 and No. 47
General Hospitals (see also Appendix 1).

The 23rd Battalion was in action immediately adjacent to the 24th in the Battle of the Ancre (62; 90; 98). Here, on November 13th, their "'B' and 'D' Companies ... carried the German second line"; and on 14th, "'A' and 'C' Companies proceeded to Crater Lane, and later to Wagon Road", and "'B' and 'D' Companies took up position in Lager Alley" (98). And, according to O'Neill, in his regimental history, the 22nd Battalion "went up to form a defensive flank to the 5th Brigade [on November 13th], but such were the difficulties that this subject was not achieved until 9 a.m. on ... 14th. But when the line was ... taken ... it was firmly held, despite a persistent and very accurate shell fire throughout the day. It was nervous and wasting work, but the battalion bore it so well that, on the 15th, they were able to leap forward and seize the Quadrilateral" (62).

Aftermath

In the aftermath of the Third Phase, the 24th Battalion spent late November and December, 1916 in comparative quiet in the rear, some of it in the village of Cornehotte, close to the site where the Battle of Crecy took place in 1346. It does not appear to have sustained any further casualties until January, 1917, when there were three, including one death in German captivity (89).

On November 19th, Private Spencer wrote in his diary of the news of the deaths of a number of his comrades and friends from "D" Company of the 24th Battalion, including "old Cupid" (Sergeant Hicks), Sergeant Morris, Sergeant Little, Private Anderson, Private Bradbury [sic] and many others" (81). As noted above, Private Anderson is buried in Canadian Cemetery No. 2 near Neuville-St. Vaast, and Private Bradberry in Redan Ridge Cemetery No. 1 near Beaumont-Hamel. Serjeant Joe Leslie Hicks, aged twenty-two, was reported as missing on November 13th, and was never found, and he is commemorated on the Thiepval Memorial (see also Appendix 1). Serjeant Arthur Joseph Little (pictured on *Figure 16*), aged twenty-four, died of wounds on November 19th, and is buried in Warlincourt Halte Cemetery near Saulty (see also Appendix 1). It is

68

possible that he died at No. 20 or No. 43 Casualty Clearing Station, both of which were located in Warlencourt at the time of his death (59).   As regards Private Spencer's "Sergeant Morris", there was a man of that name and rank   in the 24th Battalion (pictured on *Figure 16*), but there is no record of his having been killed.   There was also a Company Serjeant-Major Ernest John Morris, who was wounded on November 13th, and died on 21st, aged twenty-two, and who is buried in Nunhead Cemetery (see also Appendix 1).

On Sunday December 3rd, church services were held at 12 noon, on "C" Company's parade ground for the Anglicans, in the local parish church for the Roman Catholics, and in a barn for the "Presbyterians and Non-Conformists", immediately after a lecture entitled "History of the Royal Fusiliers and *Esprit de Corps*" - and bayonet practice (89).   Later in the month, the Battalion was even able to play a number of football matches in the Brigade League. On 11th, they played "away" against the 17th Royal Fusiliers (winning 3-2); on 13th, "at home" against the 5th Machine Gun Company; on 14th, "away" against the 2nd Highland Light Infantry (winning 2-0); on 16th, "away" against the 2nd Oxfordshire and Buckinghamshire Light Infantry (losing 2-0); and on 18th, "away" against the 5th Trench Mortar Battery (winning 8-0). Also on 18th, one man was sentenced to ten days "F.P. [Field Punishment] no. 2" for "Drunkenness near billets". This would have consisted of his being kept fettered or handcuffed for the duration of the sentence, and having his pay docked.   Later, on March 10th, 1917, another man was sentenced by a Field General Court Martial to three months Field Punishment No. 1 for "When on Active service, Losing by Neglect his Rifle, Bayonet and Equipments". This was more serious, and would also have included being "attached for a period or periods not exceeding two hours in any one day to a fixed object" – for which, read "shackled spread-eagled to a cartwheel".   Additionally, in this case, the man concerned had to "pay for the cost of the articles deficient".   On December 25th, 1916, Private Spencer described his "really jolly good" Christmas dinner in some detail in his diary, as follows, "We served up a good piece of beef from our rations and plenty of vegetables. We bought a duck and a bottle of rum from Abbeville, two lots of preserved cream and a lot of cigarettes from the BEF canteen. We were issued with a ... goose and a large tinned Christmas pudding. Our ... cook, Corporal Catchpole, made fancy dishes with buns, jam, whipped cream etc. Altogether we had a very good time" (81). An a few days later, he wrote "Simonite and I tried some yellow, syrupy looking drink ... served ... in small coffee cups half full at 50 centimes a cup. ... . We rather liked it, had four cups each and then ... collapsed ... and could not get up again. ... . We found out the next day that we had been drinking yellow Chartreuse".

The "Actions of Miraumont" (February, 1917)

The 24th Battalion began 1917 as it had ended 1916, to the rear, and only returned to the front, between Pozieres and Courcelette, between January 12th-16th. On 15th, Private Percival Biddlecombe, aged nineteen, was killed, and is buried in Regina Trench Cemetery in Grandcourt, which was first used in the winter of 1916/1917, and considerably extended after the end of the war in 1918, when bodies were brought in for reburial from scattered groups of graves around the Courcelette Road, near Miraumont, and around Miraumont itself (see also Appendix 1). And on 16th, Private W. Willett was wounded. These were the only two casualties sustained by the Battalion in the entire month of January. On 18th, at which time the Battalion was billeted in Wolfe Huts near Pozieres, Private Spencer wrote in his diary, "Second Lieutenant Furlong took us up the line to the [abandoned German] West Miraumont dugouts close to Courcelette ... . The ground over which we passed on our way up had been won yard by yard at the cost of enormous casualties during the Battle of the Somme the previous summer. It was so torn and scarred by innumerable shell holes that scarcely a square yard of unchurned soil remained. ... . For the first part of our journey ... we followed the ... road past the ruins of Ovillers (marked by a name board) ... and on through ... Pozieres, which we should never have known was there at all except for the noticeboard by the roadside. At Pozieres we left the roads and walked on a duckboard track ... for a mile and a half, ... bringing us at last to the series of underground galleries known as the West Miraumont dugout. This was the largest ... I ever saw. It had six parallel shafts running down into the ground at a gradual slope and these were all joined up laterally by four long, level galleries ... . Some sections of these galleries had wire beds on either side in two tiers; other sections were widened into rooms and used for Signals, Aid Post etc., and later on as Divisional Headquarters" (81).

The Battalion was in the front line near Courcelette between February 5th-9th and 13th-15th, and near Miraumont between February 28th-March 3rd. At this time, Private Spencer wrote in his diary, "the condition and arrangement of the front line ... was most extraordinary and exceptional. It was also most unpleasant and uncomfortable. There was no trench system at all – none [presumably because the ground was frozen hard]. The whole ... front was held by twenty-one isolated small posts with about six or eight men in each, and there were no support or reserve lines behind them. The men actually in support were accommodated in the huge West Miraumont dugout [see above], and in other smaller dugouts in Courcelette village, and in case of attack would ... have had to deploy in the open. ... . The conditions for the men who held the front posts at this time were very severe. The cold was intense and they had very little room to move about. No hot rations could be got up to them ... . Cases of 'trench feet' were very common and after one spell of extreme cold all the divisional transport had to be sent up to bring down the men ... as hardly any were able to walk. Of my own old D Company in the 24th RF, 'Alec' ... got trench feet very badly and had to have both feet amputated in hospital" (81). The 2nd Royal Welch Fusiliers were near Combles, a few miles to the south-east of where the 24th Royal Fusiliers were, during that long, hard winter, until they, like the 24th, were relieved in the first week of March. Their Private Richards wrote, "It ... snowed very heavily. We used the snow for making tea but it took a mountain of snow to make a quart of water. Our trenches ran into the River Somme, which was soon frozen over a foot thick, except for a small stream in the middle. The whole of this sector was nothing but bleak hills and valleys and the only life around were the wild ducks and moorhens. It was one of the most desolate places that I had been in in France. ... [F]ire-wood was ... scarce; also our charcoal and coke rations were very small. We took the wooden crosses from lonely graves that we found here and there. They were no good for the dead but provided warmth for the living" (75). An Australian serjeant wrote, "I filled my water-bottle at Mametz at midday with boiling hot tea, and ... at 5 pm it was frozen so hard that an ordinary knife made hardly any impression on it" (29).

On February 17th-18th, 1917, the 24th Battalion was peripherally involved in the so-called Actions of Miraumont or Battle of Boom Ravine, one of a series of Operations on the Ancre, and at least arguably the last of the major engagements of the "Somme" Offensive (3). On 17th, Private Thomas Robert - known as Robert – Marchant, attached to the Trench Mortar Battery, was killed, aged nineteen (see also Appendix 1). Like the aforementioned Private Biddlecombe, he is buried in Regina Trench Cemetery in Grandcourt. He is also commemorated on the memorial bell in the church of St Mary in the village of Westham in Sussex, where he had been a bellringer before the war. At least one other man probably had his life saved by a "Dayfield Body Shield – Army Pattern", which was worn over clothing and under equipment. Such body shields offered a certain amount of protection against gun-fire, but were very heavy, and so suffered from the twin drawbacks of being exhausting to wear, and of rendering wearers top-heavy and prone to losing their balance. According to the "*Battalion War Diary*", the 24th Battalion's total casualties for February were six, and for March, nine (89). Among the casualties for March was Private Laurence John Francis Rhydding Ridding, who was wounded at Pys, near Miraumont, on 3rd, and later died of his wounds, and who is buried in Albert Communal Cemetery Extension (*Plate 43*; see also Appendix 1). The cemetery was in use by Field Ambulances at the time. Bernard Henry Limpus died, aged forty-one, on 12th, and is buried in St Michael's Churchyard in Bude Haven in Cornwall (see also Appendix 1). It appears that Limpus died of tuberculosis after having been discharged from the 24th Battalion on medical grounds in 1916.

Like Privates Gauntlett, Stone and Montagu (see above), he had been given a Silver War Badge to demonstrate that he had been honourably discharged.

The 23rd Battalion was also involved in the Actions of Miraumont (30; 90; 98). One of the men from the Battalion, Private C. Clark, wrote an account of the actions that is now in the Imperial War Museum. It appears that the Battalion arrived at the front on February 16th, after a hard slog through melting ice, mud and congestion, to be met with an intense enemy artillery bombardment. It then went into action the following day, February 17th, and was able to get as far as the first German trench without great difficulty, with British shells fitted with the revolutionary new 106 "Graze" fuze having effectively cut all the wire in No Man's Land. However, it was unable to get any further in the face of murderous machine-gun and shell fire. The Battalion would eventually sustain some 240 casualties, many of whom are buried in Regina Trench Cemetery near Grandcourt.

Lieutenant Richard Hawkins of the 11th Battalion wrote of the action on 17th, "It was 6.29 when the biggest bloody barrage I have ever been through suddenly descended upon us. It was obvious that the Germans had wind of our attack. Captain Collis-Sandes, who was commanding B Company, turned up at my side. 'I think this is going to be a pretty awful show'. 'Yes', I replied, 'I think I am going to get a rifle and bayonet', and I collared one from a fellow who was dead. ... . We were still bogged down with the German barrage when ... Collis-Sandes fell dead and I was hit in the shoulder. It was like being kicked by a mule. As the force spun me round, I lost my balance and fell right down the ravine, crashing into some barbed wire at the bottom. I lost consciousness for a while. I awoke as it was beginning to get light, to hear a Cockney voice say, 'Cor blimey, 'ere's Lieutenant Hawkins, the poor so-and-so is dead'. 'No, I'm not', I replied, 'but I soon shall be if you don't get me out of this lot'" (88). The Battalion sustained a total of 281 casualties in the attack (62). It was later confirmed that the Germans had indeed learned of the plan in advance, from a British prisoner.

Incidentally, it was in the action on February 17th that Lance-Serjeant and later Second Lieutenant Frederick William Palmer, M.M. of the 22nd (Kensington) Battalion was awarded a Victoria Cross, actually managing to capture a German trench with a handful of men, and holding it even in the face of constant heavy fire and repeated attacks (62). Some "Recollections of Miraumont" were published in the 22nd Battalion's Old Comradres' Association magazine *Mufti* after the war, which read in part as follows, "Freddy Palmer's exploit has become historic. How he held the flank – a vital position – against repeated attacks by superior numbers and only gave way when his supply of ammunition ran out, only to make his way back to B.H.Q. [Battalion Head-Quarters] for more bombs and men and regaining the strategic line, has become famous, and, as the War Office said, 'it was a deed of heroism which cannot be exaggerated'. Jimmy Carr (who died in the 'flu epidemic after the Armistice) gained the D.C.M. [Distinguished Conduct Medal] and a commission, and decorations were bestowed on others of the little band".

At the end of March, 1917, after the German withdrawal to the Hindenburg Line, Private Spencer of the 24th Battalion wrote in his diary, "I went ... to ... Lonpart [Loupart] Wood ... and saw some of the enemy sunken big-gun emplacements from which they used to shell us at West Miraumont ... , and read one of the range cards giving the range in metres to various places behind our lines" (81).

ALLIED OFFENSIVES (1917)

At the beginning of 1917, in France, the French army was under *General* Robert Nivelle, who at the end of 1916, had replaced Joffre after his success at Verdun, while the British and Empire armies remained under now Field-Marshal Haig (67). Then, in April, 1917, the United States of America entered the war on the Allied side, although it would not be until the following year of 1918 that American troops began to be deployed in large numbers to the Western Front (9). This was shortly after Germany had authorised unrestricted submarine warfare in the North Atlantic, and had been discovered – through the interception of the so-called "Zimmermann telegram" - also to have authorised financial support to Mexico in exchange for an invasion of Texas, New Mexico and Arizona.

The German army was under the overall command of *Chef der Grosser Generalstab* (Chief of the Great General Staff) *Generalfeldmarschall* (Field-Marshal) Paul von Hindenburg, the architect of the famous victory over the Russians at Tannenberg on the Eastern Front in 1914, who had replaced von Falkenhayn after the latter's failure at Verdun. Second in command, and Chief of Operations, was the logistician *Erster Generalquartiermeister* (First Quartermaster-General) Erich von Ludendorff, a brilliant tactician but a less than brilliant strategist. The Germans' first major action of 1917 was "*Operation Alberich*", which took place between February 9th-March 20th (3; 10; 38; 50). This was a master-stroke, a surprise strategic withdrawal to the *Siegfried Stellung* or Hindenburg Line, a much more heavily fortified and readily defensible front than the one on the Somme, that they had constructed - entirely in secret - during the Battles of the Somme. The Hindenburg Line ran more or less southward from just east of Arras in the north, past Cambrai in the centre, to St Quentin in the south. It incorporated into its defences the St Quentin Canal, built by Napoleon at the turn of the eighteenth and nineteenth centuries, in the south, and the Canal du Nord, just west of Cambrai, built so recently that it was not yet filled with water, in the centre, with the dominating feature of Bourlon Wood in between. Besides an outpost line strategically located on high ground a little to the west of the Canal du Nord, and crossing it at Havrincourt, there were three main lines of defence. There was a front line, known as Siegfried I, hidden from sight on a reverse slope around one mile behind the outpost line, and further protected by four rows of wire, ninety-five yards deep in all, which consisted of a system of deliberately wide trenches designed to hinder the progress of tanks. Then there was a support line, around two miles behind it, also protected by wire and with well dug trenches. And finally there was another line, known as Siegfried II, still further back. During their withdrawal to the Hindenburg Line, the Germans took away everything that they came across that they could use in their war effort, including brass memorials from churches, and destroyed everything else. An urbane and – at least when it suited him – humane, German officer, Rudolf G. Binding, commanding a Squadron of Dragoons, wrote, on March 19th, "The withdrawal of the line from the hopeless positions on the Somme has been effected without loss. A fearful zone of deliberately devastated territory has been left as a barrier between us and the enemy. The expulsion of the inhabitants from their little towns and villages was a heart-rending business, more ghastly than murder. The thought that their houses and homes, with all that they had tended through a lifetime, were to be destroyed drove many of them out of their wits. The priest of the little place where I was billeted had a stroke at the news. Women hurled themselves out of the windows, and among the disorderly processions of refugees streaming to the rear one could see cases for whom this fate was as good as death" (5). The Germans left behind them only scorched earth, poisoned water-wells and booby-traps. The 24th Battalion's Orders for March 1st, 1917 included the following: "13/ Great care must be taken in handling any articles left behind by the enemy. Already the Battn. on our right has found a German helmet which, when picked up, set off a bomb and blew a man's hand off".

The Allies began their advance to the Hindenburg Line at the end of March, 1917 (10; 38; 50). The British launched their "Arras" Offensive, which would include the Battles of Arras, on April 9th, partly to pin German troops down in the Artois region, well away from the Aisne and Champagne to the south where the French were to launch their "Nivelle" Offensive on 16th. The "Arras" and "Nivelle" Offensives both failed in May. The British then launched their "Flanders" Offensive, around the Ypres Salient, on June 7th, which eventually failed on November 10th. And their "Cambrai" Offensive Operations, which would include the Battle of Cambrai, on November 20th. After a startling initial success brought about by a co-ordinated attack involving the mass deployment of tanks, this, too, ultimately failed, in December.

The Battles of Arras (April-May, 1917)

The Battles of Arras began on Easter Monday, April 9th, 1917, and ended on May 17th, or later, if associated flanking operations are included (69). The first day was a qualified success from the point of view of the British and Empire armies. On this day, the British Third Army made good progress east of Arras, its artillerymen clearing the way with a heavy barrage, with shells fitted with the 106 fuze continuing to prove effective in cutting the German wire (34). Moreover, in a remarkable feat-of-arms, the four divisions of the Canadian Corps, under Lieutenant-General Julian Byng, seized the high ground of Vimy Ridge, overlooking the Plain of Flanders, that had previously withstood all Allied attacks (12). Only the British Fifth Army, attacking the Hindenburg Line to the south, stalled. However, even around Arras and Vimy, the successes achieved and ground gained were insufficiently swiftly reinforced for them to have proved decisive (69). It was not until the night of April 10th that General Edmund Allenby, who was in overall command of Third Army, realised that he was "pursuing a defeated enemy", and not until the following day, 11th, that he sought to press his advantage by sending in the cavalry. By then, though, the time for action was passed, and the opportunity missed. When the cavalry was eventually sent in, the German 125th Regiment, according to its war diary, "stood up as on a rifle range and, laughing, greeted this rare target with a hail of bullets". An infantry attack on 14th was similarly bloodily repulsed. The "Arras" Offensive had essentially already failed. However, the British continued it well beyond the point where it could realistically achieve any further success, leastwise without great cost. This was partly to relieve the pressure on the French, whose own "Nivelle" Offensive finally failed on May 9th. The average daily British casualty figure during the "Arras" Offensive, at over four thousand men, was the second worst of the war. It exceeded that of the "Somme" Offensive of 1916, and was only exceeded by that of the German "Spring" Offensive of 1918.

According to the *Battalion War Diary*, the 24th Battalion's total casualties for April were 194, and for May, thirty, bringing the total for the Battles of Arras to 224 (89). Second Lieutenant Harry Daft of the 17th Battalion, the London Regiment, who was on attachment to the 24th Royal Fusiliers, was killed on April 13th, aged twenty-two, and is buried in Roclincourt Cemetery (*Plate 44*; see also Appendix 1). Private John Basil Taylor of the 24th Royal Fusiliers was also killed on April 13th, aged thirty-two, and is buried in Bois-Carre Cemetery, near Thelus (*Plate 45*; see also Appendix 1). Lance-Corporal Alfred Frederick Clare was reported as "missing" on 14th, and later confirmed to have been killed, and he is buried in Bois-Carre Cemetery, alongside Private Taylor (see also Appendix 1). Second Lieutenant Cyril Francis Stafford died on April 14th of wounds sustained on 13th, aged either thirty-one or thirty-two (having been born in 1895), and is buried in Haute-Avesnes Cemetery, somewhat to the north-west of Arras, which was widely used by field ambulances (*Plate 46*; see also Appendix 1). Private Alfred Baverstock Dykes was killed on April 14th, aged thirty-eight, Private John Henry Bright – "Bright" - Millar, aged nineteen, on April 28th, Private Arthur Thomas Collins, Private Hubert Henry Marrable and Serjeant Oliver Bertram May on April 29th, and Private James George Simco on May 1st; and Second-Lieutenant Vincent Kendall Barnes and Lance-Serjeant Walter Prince Taylor, M.M. were reported as missing, assumed killed, on April 29th, and were never found (*Figure 15; Plates 47-49*; see also Appendix 1). Lance-Corporal Millar, who had earlier survived the attack on Guillemont on July 30th, had been sniping at enemy positions for several hours when he was killed by a shell at Arras. All eight men, having no known grave, are commemorated on the Arras Memorial. Private Albartus Degens died of wounds on April 16th, aged thirty-three, and Private Frank Allan Urry on May 2nd, aged thirty, and both men are buried in Aubigny Communal Cemetery Extension (*Plate 50*; see also Appendix 1). It is possible that they died at No. 30 or No. 42 Casualty Clearing Station, both of which were based in Aubigny at the time of their deaths (59). Private Patrick – "Pat" - O'Kavanagh was killed on April 21st, and is buried in Achiet-le-Grand Communal Cemetery Extension (see also Appendix 1). Second Lieutenant Douglas Maurice Jacques Ullman, aged twenty-five, was killed on April 23rd, Private George William Pereira, aged twenty-six, on April 24th, Private Frederick William Bates, on April 29th, and Privates Malcolm Cedric Alston, aged twenty-one, William Arthur Spittels, aged thirty-five, and Charles William Edward Wells, on May 1st (*Plates 51-52*; see also Appendix 1). All six men are buried in Orchard Dump Cemetery near Arleux-en-Gohelle. Private Alston is also commemorated on the Cenotaph in Port-of-Spain in his native Trinidad. Private Ernest Arthur Godfrey was killed on April 29th, and is buried in Point-du-Jour Military Cemetery in Athies (see also Appendix 1). Lieutenant Leon David Griffiths was also killed on April 29th, aged twenty, and is buried in Aubigny Communal Cemetery Extension (see also Appendix 1). Second Lieutenant Gilbert Colin Clifford was reported as "missing, believed wounded" on April 29th, and later found to have been taken prisoner and interred in an officers' camp in Karlsruhe (see also Appendix 1). Private Robert Wishart Barrowman was later discovered to have died on May 2nd of wounds suffered on April 30th, aged twenty-four, and to have been buried by the Germans in Douai Communal Cemetery, which was being used by them at this time (*Plate 53*; see also Appendix 1). And Corporal Charles George Moon also died of wounds on May 2nd, and was also buried in Douai Communal Cemetery (see also Appendix 1).

Some of those of the 23rd Battalion who were killed in April-May, 1917 are buried in the aforementioned Orchard Dump Cemetery in Arleux-en-Gohelle; some others in Albuera Cemetery in Bailleul-sir-Berthoult. One Brooks of the 23rd Battalion was taken prisoner on April 28th, near Oppy, and kept an account of his subsequent captivity in his diary (98). He described how at the moment of capture the thought that passed through his mind was "that the question which had been at the back of my mind since a second or two after the first opening of the guns, 'Was this the end?' was about to be answered". He also described how at least at first he was reasonably well treated by his captors, despite being subject to heavy manual labour at makeshift camps at Douai and Lille. And how the "man-handling" only began later, at Phalemphin. His main complaint, though, was not about physical abuse, but rather hunger. He was always hungry, "thinking of nothing but food", being given only soup, dry bread, preserves, preserved meat and raw fish by the Germans, supplemented by whatever he could forage for himself, and whatever the French and Belgian civilians he encountered could surreptitiously smuggle to him. "Willingly they give us all they can spare, and much that they cannot", he wrote, and, if allowed, "they would have given us their souls". Brooks was also always "Waiting with, oh, how many hopes and fears, for that parcel to turn up. Hungrier and hungrier, and with the dread of tobacco running out".

Multiple additional battalions of the Royal Fusiliers were in action in the Battles of Arras (62; 69). Notably, the 10th and 13th Battalions were heavily involved in the capture of the strategically important village of Monchy-le-Preux, a little to the south and east of Arras, on April 10th-11th. Up until this time, the Germans had been able to direct artillery fire onto Arras from elevated positions in and around Monchy, and in the process had damaged the historic *Belfroi* (bell-tower) in the main square. The 10th and 13th Battalions were also involved in the capture of Gavrelle on April 23rd.

The First Battle of the Scarpe

During the first of the Battles of Arras, the First Battle of the Scarpe, the 24th Battalion was moved up to a position in Maroueil Wood, a little to the north and west of Arras, on April 10th, 1917 (89). The following day, April 11th, in unseasonal heavy snow, they moved into the front-line trenches, a little to the north and east of the city, to relieve the 9th Battalion, the Royal Scots, and there established contact with the battalion of Canadian infantry to their left, and the 1st Battalion, the King's Royal Rifle Company to their right (62; 89). It appears that they marched all the way to the front. Many other units, though, were able to get at least some of the way there by way of the extensive network of underground caves, quarries and tunnels in existence in the area around Arras at the time. The quarries had been excavated in the Middle Ages, to provide material for the construction of Arras Cathedral (between the eleventh and fourteenth centuries). The tunnels, though, had been freshly added by specialist tunnelling companies of the Royal Engineers or the Royal New Zealand Electrical and Mechanical Engineers. As to the ancient city itself, incidentally, Major Chapman of the 13th Battalion wrote, "There was a savage snap of cold as the car ran down the route nationale. Snow lay in white masses, threatening the cherry blossoms. At the narrow gate to Arras I stopped the car. .... It was still standing, but how it was shaken. Shop-fronts lay gaping, shutters torn down and swinging. Fronts of houses had fallen away, uncovering intimacies. A staircase hung poised; but none could reach the attics, for the bottom flight had been shattered to a heap of rubble. There was a thunder of gun-fire as we reached the station square; and the enemy was replying. Sharp noises slapped to and fro between streets. Our way became obscure. I dived out and ran into the station. A party of doleful men were struggling to mend the line. A shell fell just outside ... and some of the roof fell tinkling down. I caught sight of a ... square of trees between which lay rows of dead horses. The air moaned. We bundled out and made for a heap of chalk, marked DIV. H.Q. [Divisional Head-Quarters]" (16). And, later, "A cold moon added a colder pallor to those lovely dead gables, windows, and arcades, 'relics of the Spanish domination', said the guide book".

On April 13th, the 24th Battalion was involved in a successful attack on Bailleul-Sir-Berthoult ("Baloo"), south-east of Vimy Ridge; and on the following day, 14th, in an ultimately unsuccessful attack directed toward the village-strongpoint of Oppy, on the way to which objective it found itself surrounded on three sides, and under heavy fire, and unable to advance further (62; 89). According to the "*Battalion War Diary*", on April 13th, "At 3 p.m. a report was received that the Battn. on our right had found the LENS-ARRAS railway unoccupied by the enemy. Orders were accordingly received for an advance on the whole Battalion front, covered by a screen of scouts. The 1st. objectives being the railway line + the second a line from E. edge of WILLERVAL to that of BAILLEUL, covering the SUGAR FACTORY, midway between. At 5 p.m. the leading waves advanced, + reached both objectives, under heavy artillery fire, from which C Coy. on the left suffered most severely. 30 or 40 Germans were seen to have the SUGAR FACTORY as our line approached it. A line of posts was dug on the second objective, where the Battn. remained for the night. A German Naval 6 inch gun was captured in an orchard at the SUGAR FACTORY" (89). And on 14th: "At 1 p.m. orders were received to press forward + gain touch with the enemy + dig in. At 3 p.m. Battn. moved forward on whole front + advanced to 500-600 yards from ARLEUX-en-GOHELLE – OPPY line + dug in a front + support line of posts under heavy artillery + machine gun fire, the flanks being bent back to maintain contact with troops on either flank, who had not moved. Relieved that night by 2nd. Oxf. + Bucks L.I. + proceeded to dug outs in old British + German front lines ... , arriving on the morning of 15th April. Weather wet, snow + sleet". O'Neill wrote, in his regimental history, "the 24th ... , despite heavy artillery and machine gun fire, succeeded in getting to within about 500 yards of the Arleux en Gohelle-Oppy line. This was a formidable sector of the German front, and the 24th had to lie facing it with both flanks refused, since the units on neither side had advanced" (62). The 23rd Battalion was also involved in the action at Bailleul-sir-Berthoult on

April 13th (30; 62; 90; 98). According to O'Neill, "the 23rd Battalion ... advanced with the 24th to the railway, and, pushing further on, occupied Bailleul. A line was established on the east of the village and patrols were sent forward towards Oppy. A platoon of C Company, misinterpreting orders, went out to attempt the capture of Oppy, and was itself captured, after a spirited fight before the village. The 23rd captured four guns in this advance. But they also lost heavily, for, in addition to the platoon cut off at Oppy, Captain Lissmann [Lieutenant and Adjutant Arthur John Lissaman] ... was killed by a shell as he walked with the N.C.O. towards the railway" (62).

On April 16th, Private Spencer of the 24th Battalion wrote in his diary, "I went forward right over the top of Vimy Ridge to find a suitable position on the forward slope for use as an observation post" (81). Later, he wrote, "One of my instructions was to watch ... for the passage of trains on the ... 'Izel-Vitry Railway'. This was the length of line along which troop trains were expected to bring up enemy reinforcements to our section of the line. ... [On]e day while watching through my telescope I counted eighteen trains ... going north along the line in less than an hour. I reported this to Divisional HQ. ... [I]f these trains had come up full of enemy troops it would make a great difference to the big attack we were going to make a few days later. ... . Zero day for the big attack was 28 April ... ".

The Second Battle of the Scarpe

On April 22nd, the 24th Battalion "Relieved the 13th Essex Regt in new line dug 300 yards from GERMAN ARLEUX-OPPY line", and was "shelled during the night" (89). And on 23rd, during the Second Battle of the Scarpe, it was "subjected to heavy shelling at times during the day + night" and "HQs in SUGAR FACTORY intermittently shelled with 4.2s and 5.9s".

The Battle of Arleux

On April 28th-29th, during the Battle of Arleux, the Battalion was involved in attack on Oppy Wood, near Arleux, from which they eventually had to make a tactical withdrawal (4; 62; 69; 89). On 28th, according to the "*Battalion War Diary*", "At 4.25 a.m. an attack on a wide front was carried out. The Bn was in Bn Reserve + at 11 a.m. moved forward to occupy the old British support trenches opposite the front ARLEUX-OPPY WOOD. At 8 p.m. reports were received thro Bde that the enemy had broken through south of OPPY WOOD and the Bn were consequently ordered to form a defensive flank facing S.E. from the Northern outskirts of BAILLEUL to their former right flank in the O.B. support line. Posts were dug on this new alignment and work was still in progress when orders were received that at dawn 2 coys were to cooperate on an attack on the left flank of an attack which would be launched by the 99th. Bde. against OPPY WOOD. A + B Coys were detailed for this attack, C + D Coys following them and mopping up and holding the German front line immediately N. of OPPY WOOD" (89). And on 29th, "Zero hour was 4 a.m. and it was then still quite dark, and to this may be attributed the fact that A + B Coys reached their final objective which was a sunken road running from OPPY VILLAGE to ARLEUX before it became apparent that the troops on their right had not been able to reach their objective through the wood, and that consequently their right flank was in the air. Captain Hooke who was in command of the two Coys had been wounded during the advance in the course of which 64 prisoners had been taken, including 1 officer, and many Germans killed. 2 Lt Barnes and 2 Lt Clifford [see above] were missing, and only 3 officers remained with the two companies, the senior of whom, 2nd Lieut [Harold Howard Linsdell] Kilmister, ... took command. The Coys were exposed to heavy M.G. [machine gun] and rifle fire from OPPY VILLAGE and WOOD and in addition the enemy was making furious bombing attacks on their left front line from OPPY TRENCH which cuts through the road they were holding. The officer in command finding himself far in advance of troops on either flank decided to swing his right flank round to occupy the part of OPPY TRENCH west of the sunken road and gradually to withdraw his men along this trench till they got in touch with Bns on right and left. This was successfully accomplished though many casualties had unfortunately been suffered in the severe fighting in the forward position". The following day, April 30th, the 24th Battalion was "Stationary in position taken up the previous evening. Both lines were heavily shelled throughout the day and were also subject to sniping from the trees of OPPY WOOD on their right flank" (89). And on May 1st, "The front support lines were subjected to heavy shelling at periods throughout the day", although it was "Relieved in the evening ... " and "... moved to dugouts in the Old German Front Line E of ROCLINCOURT". Oppy Wood turned out to be the easternmost point of the entire British advance during the Battles of Arras.

Four other battalions of the Royal Fusiliers were also involved in the attack on Oppy Wood on April 29th, namely, the 7th, 17th, 22nd and 23rd (62). Second Lieutenant Stanley Ferns – "Jeff" – Jeffcoat (*Plate 54*), aged thirty-two, of the 22nd Battalion, although formerly of the 24th, was mortally wounded, and later buried in Roclincourt Military Cemetery (4; 62; 69; see also Appendix 1). For his "sheer personal courage and leadership" in the action, in bombing his way a considerable distance up an enemy trench, he was recommended for - although in the event not awarded - a posthumous Victoria Cross.

The Third Battle of the Scarpe

The 23rd Battalion was involved, as part of a composite unit, in another attack on Oppy on May 3rd, during the Third Battle of the Scarpe (30; 90; 98). On this occasion, according to their *"Battalion War Diary"*, "At 3.45am ... the ... battn advanced ... , captured Fresnoy Trench ... and captured 60-70 prisoners and a machine gun" (90). Later, though, "Heavy counter-attacks were made by the enemy ... , and in view of this and of the retirement of troops on the right, it became necessary to withdraw".

85

Aftermath

According to the "*Battalion War Diary*", in the aftermath of the Battles of Arras, the 24th Battalion spent most of May and June in reserve and in training in the rear (89). The Battalion then returned to the front-line trenches at Cuinchy on July 1st. It remained there or thereabouts until October 6th, when it was marched to billets at Lapugnoy.

The 24th Battalion's only casualty in May and June was Company Serjeant-Major Horace Oliver Stratford, M.C., who died on June 5th of wounds suffered on May 1st, and who is buried in West Norwood Cemetery and Crematorium (see also Appendix 1). The Battalion's total casualties for July, sustained not in any particular set-piece battle but simply as part of the so-called "wastage" of the war, were forty-four; for August, thirteen; for September, six; and for October, twelve (89). Among the casualties for July was one man categorised as "S.I.W." - that is, "Self-Inflicted Wounded" - on 6th. Also among the casualties for July were three men killed and six wounded in a German trench raid by a party of thirty to forty on the night of 9th/10th. Those killed in this raid were Serjeant Charles Richard Collier, Private Ernest John Martin, and Lance-Corporal Herbert ("Bert") Sargant, aged thirty-seven, who are all buried in Cambrin Military Cemetery, near Cuinchy (see also Appendix 1). One of those wounded was Corporal Frank Leonard Patching, who died of wounds on 13th. aged nineteen (see also Appendix 1). His service number, 3963, indicates that he enlisted in September or October, 1915, when he would only have been seventeen. Corporal Patching is buried in Bethune Town Cemetery. He may have died in one of the many hospitals in Bethune, or in No. 33 Casualty Clearing Station, which was also there until December, 1917 (59). There were no casualties in another raid on 12th, preceded by an strafing run by a low-flying enemy aircraft. But seven men were wounded during a gas attack on the night of 12th/13th. Among the casualties for August was Lieutenant and Acting Captain William Herbert Bambridge, who was shot through the head by a sniper on 19th, aged twenty-seven, and is buried in Gorre British and Indian Cemetery, between Cuinchy and Bethune (see also Appendix 1). Among the casualties for September was Private Sidney Southgate, aged forty-one, who died of wounds on 7th, possibly in one of the many hospitals in Calais, and is buried in Calais Southern Cemetery (see also Appendix 1). And among the casualties for October were eleven men wounded in a British trench raid on the night of 2nd/3rd. One of these men, Serjeant Harry Rainford, aged twenty-five, later died of wounds, and, like the aforementioned Corporal Patching, is buried in Bethune Town Cemetery (see also Appendix 1). The raid that he died in was deemed a success, with "identification obtained" from the enemy. Rum and soup had been given to the twenty-five participants beforehand, and three Military Medals, two Military Crosses and a Distinguished Conduct Medal afterwards. One of the Military Medals was awarded to Corporal Thomas Edward – "Tommy" – Isaac (see also Appendix 1).

In September, 1917, the 23rd Battalion was tasked with the instruction of at first one and then another battalion of Portuguese troops, while holding the line at Givenchy (90; 98).

The Battle of Cambrai
(November-December, 1917)

The Battle of Cambrai began on November 20th, 1917, after the "Flanders" Offensive had finally failed, freeing up "fresh" troops – some of whom had to be sent to the Southern Front to help prevent the Italians from being routed after their defeat by the Austro-Hungarians at the Battle of Caporetto (now Kobarid in Slovenia) (9; 10; 50; 67; 70). By this time, it had come to be recognised by Haig and Byng, the newly-appointed commander-in-chief of Third Army, that breaking through the Hindenburg Line and taking the important rail-head at Cambrai would bring the considerable benefits of seriously disrupting both German defences and troop movements (67). Moreover, as forcefully argued out by the officer-in-command of the newly-formed Tank Corps, Brigadier-General Hugh Elles, the ground around Cambrai was constituted of chalk, and firm, and perfectly suited to the mass deployment of the new and improved Mk. IV Tank (34; 67; 84). And furthermore, as pointed out by the officer-in-command of the artillery of 9th (Scottish) Division, Brigadier-General H.H. Tudor, advances in artillery target-acquisition technology together with improvements in accuracy meant that enemy gun positions could be identified and then neutralised immediately before any advance - by so-called "predicted" fire" (34; 67; 84). The developments in technology included "flash-spotting" and "sound-ranging", while those geared towards improved accuracy included factoring in meteorological conditions: all were the work of specialist Field Survey Companies. "Predicted fire" obviated the need for "registration" or "sighting" rounds, and thus re-introduced an important element of surprise.

In detail, the final – expanded - plan was for a two-pronged attack involving three Army infantry corps, supported by over a thousand artillery pieces, and accompanied by nearly four hundred fighting Mk. IV Tanks, and significant numbers of aircraft (34; 67; 70; 84). A further fifty-odd supply tanks would pull sledges, and thirty-odd would carry grapnels with which to clear wire. Most of the tanks would also carry fascines, which were essentially large bundles of brushwood, to be dropped into trenches to provide crossing-points. In the north, IV Corps, accompanied by over a hundred tanks, would take Flesquieres Ridge and Bourlon Wood. And in the south, III Corps, accompanied by over two hundred tanks, were to break in to the Hindenburg Line between the Canal du Nord and Canal St Quentin, and the Cavalry Corps were then to break out to take Cambrai and the important crossings over the River Sensee. As is evident, the plan involved a high degree of co-ordination across and co-operation between service arms, requiring the infantry and tanks to practise joint manoeuvres in advance (34; 67).

As at Arras, the first day of the Battle of Cambrai, November 20th, was a qualified success (70). At 0620 on that day, the planned artillery barrage began and the tanks began to move forward. And by 1200, the outpost and front lines of the

Hindenburg Line had been overrun on much of the attack frontage. Major E. Mitchell of the Tank Corps wrote, "Thus was the famous Hindenburg Line, the much boomed bulwark of the German Army, crossed as easily as a boy jumps over a small stream". The surprise and shock had evidently been too much for many of the German defenders, 7 500 of whom were taken prisoner without a fight. Some 120 German guns were also captured. By the end of the day, some British tanks had advanced almost five miles. When the news made it back to the U.K., church bells were rung for the first time since the outbreak of the war. Any celebrations at this stage, though, were premature. The surviving tanks had outrun the infantry, and the horse cavalry had essentially been stopped in its tracks by machine-gun fire (although a squadron of the Fort Garry Horse, part of the Canadian Cavalry Brigade of the 5th Cavalry Division, had very nearly achieved a breakthrough between Masnieres and Marcoing). And at Flesquieres, a number of tanks had been taken out by the German defenders. As bad luck would have it, the German commander there, *Oberstleutnant* (Lieutenant-Colonel) von Watter, of the 54th Division, had a brother who had been through a tank attack on the Somme in 1916, and had warned him what to expect. And von Watter had in turn trained his men to remove their 77mm guns from their gunpits and to engage with tanks with them using direct fire, to great effect. German troops also came to discover that tanks could also be taken out of action by having their caterpillar tracks blown off by grenades. Or by having their crews blown up by grenades dropped through the manholes in their rooves. *Leutnant* (Second Lieutenant) Miles Reinke of the 2nd Guards Dragoons recalled in an interview screened as part of the BBC television series *The Great War*, "When the tanks passed the first line, we thought we would be compelled to retreat towards Berlin. ... . Some of the boys soon discovered they could stop the tanks by throwing a hand grenade into the manhole on the top. ... . I was shocked and felt very sorry for those fellows in the tanks, because there was no escape for them. Once a man was on top of the tank it was doomed ... , and the poor fellows were not able to escape. The fuel would start to burn and after an hour and a half or two hours we saw only burning tanks in front and behind us. Then ... the attack came to a standstill" (85). If the break-in had largely succeeded, the break-out had failed, although again, as at Arras, the British continued with offensive operations beyond the point where they could achieve further success without great cost (70). A cautious Byng had advised against doing so after forty-eight hours, but an over-confident Haig had countermanded him. He, Haig, believed the intelligence that he had been given that the Germans had become "soft" as a result of the wearing-down battles of the preceding two years, and that they had become prone to "a disposition to retire". He also continued to believe in the disproved myth of the breakthrough by the cavalry.

Inevitably, on November 30th, the Germans counter-attacked along the Bourlon-Moeuvres Ridge, by this time a dangerous salient in the British line held by tired troops (40; 70). Here, the British faced a number of separate German attacks, followed by a more prolonged period of continuous fighting over two days, resulting in their eventually having to withdraw, although not before inflicting heavy casualties. By the end of the battle on December 5th, the British had been forced even further back, ultimately losing most the ground they had gained in the opening exchanges of the battle, with the exception of a reduced salient around Flesquieres and Havrincourt. There had been 40 000 casualties on both the British and German sides.

In early November, 1917, immediately before the Battle of Cambrai, the 24th Battalion was stationed in Flanders, as the British and Empire Offensive there finally drew to a close. It would play no part in that Offensive, as multiple battalions of the Royal Fusiliers had (62). Between 8th-15th, the Battalion was at Wemaers Cappel, in French Flanders, somewhat to the west of Ypres ("Wipers" or "Eeps"), in Belgium (89). And between 16th-19th, it was in Murat Camp, on the northern outskirts of Ypres (89). Later, the Battalion was moved south to Hermies, half-way along the Bapaume-Cambrai road, between November 20th-28th, 1917, and thence towards the Hindenburg Support Line on November 30th, and into trenches and consolidated shell-holes near Bourlon Wood, immediately west of Cambrai, on December 1st (40; 62; 70; 89). There the Battalion was immediately in action, helping to defend a concerted enemy counter-attack. Such was the strength of the German attack, and its success in infiltrating the British line, that they were eventually forced to retire to a position near Graincourt on the night of 4th/5th, and then to near Demicourt on the night of 6th/7th.

According to the "*Battalion War Diary*", on November 30th, "Enemy attacked heavily on 3rd Army front, including the 2 Brigades of 2nd Div. in the line [99th and 6th Brigades]. At 1030 a.m. Batt ordered to get ready to move as quickly as possible. Batt moves off to support of 2nd Div at approx 1230 p.m. ... Batt ordered to relieve the 17th Bn R. Fus. in the line in [Trench Map Grid Reference] K.22.C + d (Map sheet 57C 1/40000) ... . Relief completed about 1030 p.m." (89). It was on this day and on this part of the front that Captain Walter Napleton Stone of the 17th (Empire) Battalion was awarded a Victoria Cross "for valour" (40; 62). Captain Stone ordered most of his troops to retire from their position, in the Hindenburg Support Line, just east of Lock No. 5 on the Canal du Nord, which had become untenable. But he stayed there himself to form part of a covering rearguard, and to telephone observations on enemy movements to Battalion Headquarters, all the time under heavy fire. The rearguard was eventually surrounded, and Captain Stone was shot through the head and killed. The citation for his – posthumous - Victoria Cross read, in part, "The extraordinary coolness of this heroic officer and the accuracy of his information enabled dispositions to be made just in time to save the line and avert disaster". Captain Stone's body was never recovered, but he is commemorated on the Cambrai Memorial in Louverval. Incidentally, two further Victoria Crosses were awarded to men from the Royal Fusiliers on November 30th, 1917, one to Lieutenant-Colonel Neville Elliott-Cooper of the 8th Battalion, and the other to Captain Robert Gee of the 2nd.

Again according to the "*Battalion War Diary*", on December 1st, "Considerable machine gun activity during the night along the whole Battalion front, causing casualties" (89). On 2nd, "During the morning considerable enemy shelling of Batteries in rear, and of the factory in E.29.a. At about 11.30

A.M. 6th Brigade reported main enemy trench in E20 and 21 and EAST towards BOURLON full of enemy. Battalion "Stood to" while artillery dealt with situation. Stood down at 1.35 P.M. as situated reported normal. Remainder of day passed quietly, machine guns at night again showed considerable activity, and 3 men were wounded". On 3rd, "Battalion Headquarters moved back to [German] concrete dugout in Hindenburg Line ... . About 5 P.M. 99th Brigade reported enemy massing in E.22.b. Battalion "Stood to", but nothing materialised and situated clear at 6 P.M.". On 4th, "Orders were received that the Bourlon Salient would be evacuated during the night ... . The withdrawal [to a position near Graincourt] was successfully made, without casualty". On 5th, at 9.45 A.M., "An enemy patrol on about 6 men were observed entering out front support lines ... moving cautiously – evidently our evacuation had been discovered"; and at 1.30 P.M., "Enemy seen in large numbers ... advancing ... . Gunners informed and fired excellently. Battalion Lewis Gunners did considerable execution". At 2 P.M., "Enemy seen massing ... and advancing in large numbers ... towards Graincourt"; and at 2.25 P.M., "Enemy seen entering ANNEUX village". On 6th, at 6.15 A.M., "The enemy attacked our bombing post at junction of HINDENBURG LINE with KANGAROO TRENCH [Kangaroo Alley] ... but after a sharp hand to hand fight lasting ½ an hour were driven off. Enemy thought to have suffered heavily from our Lewis Gunners and Bombers during this fight. ... Sergt. A.F. WOOD, ... Sergt. E. TARLTON, and ... L/C. G. [George] DAY showed admirable skill and courage for which they were awarded the Military Medal. During the morning it was ascertained that owing to a gap in the covering line near GRAINCOURT parties of the enemy had worked their way through into the village of GRAINCOURT and to within a short distance of Battalion Headquarters. For confirmation of this, ... Sergt. D. McCABE was sent out with 2 men ... and by skilful and daring handling of his patrol located positions of the enemy and inflicted casualties upon them [Serjeant McCabe was awarded a Military Medal on December 24th, along with a Lance-Corporal William King and a Private H.D. Blount, who were presumably the "2 men" in question]. German occupation of GRAINCOURT having been established, one company of 1st K.R.R.C. [King's Royal Rifle Corps] was despatched to the Battalion to form a defensive flank". On the night of 6th/7th, "the Battalion withdrew to trenches and dugouts in K.14b and D [near Demicourt]". The withdrawal was described as "entirely successful and no casualties", although one man was killed and eight wounded over the course of the day. And on 7th, "Except for occasional shelling ... , the day was quiet", although a further two men were killed and five wounded. The Battalion was relieved by the elements of the South Staffordshire Regiment on the night of December 8th-9th. Bourlon Wood turned out to be the easternmost point of the entire British advance during the Battle of Cambrai.

Two other battalions of the Royal Fusiliers were in action at Bourlon Wood on December 4th, namely the 17th and 23rd (62). On that day, "early in the afternoon a very heavy attack was delivered on a front a mile west of Bourlon Wood. This was beaten off except on the extreme right of the 2nd Division, where the 1st Royal Berks [Royal Berkshire Regiment] lay on the right of the 17th Royal Fusiliers. Three posts were there lost ... . A company of the 23rd Royal Fusiliers were sent up, and, by a sharp counter-attack, re-established the Royal Berks' line. Another company assisted the 17th Battalion later in the day; and at 10 p.m. the battalion were relieved by the 24th Royal Fusiliers. The strength of the 17th Battalion on leaving the line was 20 officers and 351 other ranks".

The 24th Battalion's total casualties for November are not known, there being no casualty list for that month in the "Battalion War Diary", but those for December were fifty (89). The casualties for December included Lance-Corporal Edgar Murdock, aged thirty-eight, who was killed on 1st, and who is buried in Mouevres Communal Cemetery Extension (see also Appendix 1). They also included Private William Waymark, who was recorded as "missing, believed Prisoner of War" on 2nd (see also Appendix 1). And Private Harry Hayes, aged twenty, and Lance-Corporal Walter Tichbourne Irons, aged twenty-two, who were both killed on 6th, and who are both commemorated on the Cambrai Memorial in Louverval, having no known grave (see also Appendix 1). (Confusingly, there were two men named Harry Hayes who served in the 24th Battalion, the Royal Fusiliers in the Great War.   The other, more formally John Henry Hayes, transferred to the 17th Battalion, the Royal Welch Fusiliers in December, 1916, and was killed, aged twenty-eight, on the first day of the Battle of Ypres, 1917 - also known as the Third Battle of Ypres or as the Battle of Passchendaele - on July 31st, 1917: *Plate 55*; see also Appendix 1).   Also commemorated on the Cambrai Memorial are Private William John Black, formerly of the 24th Battalion, and latterly of the 9th, who was killed on November 30th, and numerous men from the 23rd Battalion   (*Plate 56*; see also Appendix 1).   The 23rd Battalion's casualties for November were seventeen, and for December, seventy-six (90; 98).

The 24th Battalion's total casualties for January, 1918, were one, and for February, 1918, sixteen (89).

GERMAN "SPRING" OFFENSIVE (SPRING, 1918)

The year of 1917 had gone badly for the Allies (9). In addition to the failures in the field, there had been widespread mutiny in the ranks. Large numbers of French troops had mutinied in the May and June, after the failure of the "Nivelle" Offensive, and in counter-moves designed to maintain discipline, the authorities had ordered the executions of 629 mutineers, and had actually executed forty-three, by firing squad. And British and Empire troops had mutinied at Etaples ("Eat Apples") Camp, near Boulogne, in the August and September, and one of the British ringleaders had been shot as an example. He was one of only three British and Empire soldiers executed for mutiny over the entire course of the Great War on the Western Front (97).

All this was, though, was overshadowed by the full-scale revolution in Russia in October/November, 1917, which was actively encouraged - and even covertly assisted - by Germany (9). And, even more ominously, by the withdrawal of Russia from the war, and of the Russian army from the field, following the signing of an armistice with the Central Powers at Brest-Litovsk, in present-day Belarus, on December 15th, 1917 (and a peace treaty, also at Brest-Litovsk, on March 3rd, 1918).

This provided the German General Staff, under the command of Hindenburg and Ludendorff, with an opportunity to transfer large numbers of troops from the eastern to the western front, and to plan and mount a mass-attack there designed to destroy the remaining Allied armies (10; 38; 50; 66). At the same time, there was a realisation on the German side that there was considerable risk attached to the opportunity, especially as regards timing, although they had no real choice other than to take it. They would have to make a decisive breakthrough before the large and growing American Army had been trained to a point of battle-readiness, which point was calculated to be some months distant. Their mass-attack would be known to them as the *"Kaiserschlacht"* ("Kaiser's Battle"), and would come to be known by the Allies as the German "Spring" Offensive. Ludendorff's detailed plan for it comprised five distinct offensive operations. The first, codenamed *"Operation Michael"* and commencing in March, was to be directed at the comparatively weakly-defended Somme in the centre; the second, *"Operation George/Georgette"*, in April, at the Lys to the north; the third, *"Operation Blucher-Yorck"*, in May, at the Aisne to the south; the fourth, *"Operation Gneisenau"*, in June, at Noyon-Montdidier, again in the centre; and the fifth, the *"Marneschutz"*, in July, at the Marne to the extreme south. His principal objective was to "beat the British" in the centre and north, thereby turning the northern flank of the front, and forcing the French to capitulate.

On the allied side, in France, the French army remained under the command of *General* Robert Nivelle, although he was to be shortly to be replaced by *General* and later *Marechal* (Field-Marshal) Philippe Petain after his failure at Chemin des Dames; and the British and Empire armies under Haig (67). Effective from March 26th, 1918, though, in response to the enemy Offensive, all the Allied armies, British and Empire, French, Italian and American, were placed under a single Supreme Commander. That man was the Frenchman *Generalissime* (Supreme General) Ferdinand Foch, who had a reputation as a master-strategist.

The First Battles of the Somme, 1918 (March-April, 1918)

The battles that took place during the first operation of the German "Spring" Offensive, *"Operation Michael"*, would come to be known by the Allies as the First Battles of the Somme, 1918 (11; 54; 57; 71). They included the Battle of St Quentin (which lasted from March 21st-23rd), the First Battle of Bapaume (March 24th-25th), the Battle of Rosieres (March 26th-27th), the Battle of Arras, 1918 (March 28th), the Battle of the Avre (April 4th), and the Battle of the Ancre, 1918 (April 5th).

Initial Phase

The first of the First Battles of the Somme, 1918, the Battle of St Quentin, began on March 21st, and ended on 23rd, or a little later, if associated actions at the Somme crossings are included (11; 54; 58; 71). It involved a three-pronged German attack on a fifty-mile front. The first prong, involving the Eighteenth Army under General von Hutier, recently returned from the Eastern Front, pierced toward St Quentin in the south; the second, involving the Second Army under von der Marwitz, toward Albert in the centre; and the third, involving the Seventeenth Army under von Bulow, toward Bapaume in the north.

Immediately preparatory to the launch of the battle, the Germans unleashed the largest artillery bombardment of the Great War, according to a detailed plan put together by a staff artillery officer of the Eighth Army, *Oberst* (Colonel) Georg Bruchmuller, nicknamed *"Durchbruchmuller"* ("Breakthrough Bruchmuller") – "the man who synchronized fire and maneuver" (58; 103). The first of the seven phases of the bombardment, beginning at 0440, and ending at 0640, was mainly directed at British artillery positions to the rear, and also caused no end of destruction to communications, even of telephone cables laid six feet underground (103). The second to sixth phases, beginning at 0640, and ending at 0935, ranged to and fro over forward and rearward trench systems and associated defensive positions. And the seventh, beginning at 0935, and ending at 0940, delivered "saturation fire" on front-line positions. Over the course of the five hours between 0440 and 0940, the Germans sent over some 3 200 000 shells from 6 608 guns and 3 530 mortars. Of those three million and odd shells, one million and odd were gas-shells, being either *Gelbkreuz* or "Yellow Cross" shells filled with a newly formulated mustard gas, or *Buntkreuz* or "Mixed-Colour Cross" shells filled with phosgene (which was essentially a mixture of chlorine and carbon monoxide) and diphenylchloroarsine (which contained chlorine and arsenic). For those five hours, one shell fell every second on every square mile of the fifty-mile-long by three-mile-deep battle-front. A German infantryman who had helped manoeuvre a 28cm or 11" gun into place, *Gefreiter* (Lance-Corporal) Wilhelm Reinhard, of the 109th Baden Life-Grenadier Regiment, wrote, "Someone shouted '*Feuer frei*' ['fire at will'] and then the gun went off with a great crash. We all fell over on our backs and the gunners laughed at us. The gun settled down to fire steadily after that – about one shell a minute I would say – but we didn't stay long" (58). A field artillery officer, *Leutnant* (Second Lieutenant) Herbert Sulzbach, of the 9th Division, wrote that "I'd like to wrote volumes about this day; it really must be the greatest in the history of the world. So the impossible thing has been achieved; the break-through has succeeded! The last night of the four years of static warfare passed ... in the greatest possible excitement ... . The darkness begins to lift, very, very slowly; we stand at the guns with our gas-masks around our necks, and the time until 4.40 crawls round at a dreadfully slow pace. At least we're there, and with a crash our barrage begins from thousands and thousands ... of gun-barrels and mortars, a barrage that sounds as if the world were coming to an end ... . In the middle of this booming I have to take a break in my fire control duties, since I just can't carry on with all the gas and smoke. The gunners stand in their shirt sleeves, with the sweat running down and pouring off them. Shell after shell is rammed into the breach, salvo after salvo is fired, and you don't need to give fire orders any more, they're in such good spirits, and put up such a rate of rapid fire, that not a single word of command is needed" (83). On the receiving end, a British machine-gunner, Lance-Corporal William Sharpe, wrote that it was as if "the bowels of the earth had erupted, ... [and] ... there was one long and continuous yellow flash", and that "such HELL makes weaklings of the strongest and no human's nerves were ever built to stand such torture, noise, horror and mental pain". The four terrified raw recruits who were with him he never saw again.

Following the preparatory bombardment, over seventy German divisions moved forward, under a creeping barrage, accompanied by twenty German A7V and an additional number of captured British tanks, covered by over seven hundred aircraft (some dedicated to ground attack, others to air defence), and screened by smoke and fog (58). The German plan called for spearheading *Sturmtruppen* or storm-troopers to rapidly break through comparative weak points in the British defences, as around St Quentin, and for supporting troops to exploit the breakthroughs (36). The storm-troopers would be armed with specialised weapons, and they would be trained in specialised infiltration tactics. The weapons would include light mortars and machine guns; Bergmann Maschinenpistole-18 or MP-18 sub-machine guns; *Eierhandgranaten* or egg-grenades, which had a longer range than the more familiar *Stielhandgranaten* or stick- or "potato-masher"- grenades; and *Flammenwerfer* or portable flame-throwers. Facing the Germans were under thirty divisions of the British Fourth and Fifth Armies, armed with under three thousand artillery pieces and Mk. IV and Whippet tanks, although also covered by over seven hundred aircraft of the Royal Flying Corps (later known as the Royal Air Force). Incidentally, the first time that the tanks from the opposing sides would fight each other would be on April 23rd, near Villers-Bretonneux or "Bret". On this occasion, three British Mk. IVs engaged with three German A7Vs, which fired armour-piercing bullets. Two of the Mk. IVs were soon damaged and forced to withdraw. However, the third, under the command of Lieutenant F. Mitchell, managed to knock out one of the A7Vs and drive the other two from the field, before ditching in a shell-hole – it was No. 1 Tank, No. 1 Section, A

Company, 1st Battalion, Tank Corps. A fourth A7V then appeared on the scene, but was in turn seen off by seven British Whippet tanks. Lieutenant Mitchell was awarded a Military Cross for his role in the action.

By the end of the first day, the Germans had broken through the British lines along a front forty miles wide, and five miles deep. And the British had begun a long and lengthy fighting retreat through the wilderness of the previous battlefield of the Somme, where so many of their comrades lay, and in the direction of the Channel ports. A total of some 17 500 British troops had been killed or wounded, and a further 21 000 captured. It was the second-worst day of the war for the British in terms of losses (only the first day of the Allied "Somme" Offensive was worse). At the end of the third day, the Germans began shelling Paris, some seventy-five miles to the south-west, with their long-range *Kaiser Wilhelm* Guns, also known as Paris Guns.

During the Battle of St Quentin, having been behind the front line on March 21st, the 24th Battalion was ordered to move up to the front on 22nd-23rd, as part of a move to counter the enemy attack (62; 89; *Map 7*). According to the "*Battalion War Diary*", on March 21st, "Bn. warned for general move ... in view of enemy offensive" (89). On 22nd, at 4.30 a.m., "2nd. Div. concentrated in BARASTRE-HAPLINCOURT area - Bn. at BARASTRE"; at 1.40 p.m., "5th Bde. in readiness at BERTINCOURT"; and by the end of the day "5th Bde. attached as reserve troops to 17th Div. at HERMIES. 24 R.F. in BDE. RESERVE on CANAL DU NORD, S.W. of HERMIES". On 23rd, at 6.30 a.m., "Bde. moved back to GREEN LINE, N. of BERTINCOURT, 24 R.F. astride the BERTINCOURT-VELU ROAD, and dug in at once. Enemy reported in BEAUMETZ. Bde. no longer with 17 Div.". At 2 p.m., "17th Div. retired through GREEN LINE, this becoming the front line. 5th Bde. to put up an all-round defence. Enemy approached as far as S. edge of VELU WOOD. 2 Coys. 24 R.F. withdrew to reserve positions S.W. of BERTINCOURT". And at 10 p.m., "Enemy attacked Bn. H.Q. troops and remnants of 1st K.R.R. Regt. just N. of BUS. Attack was beaten off, 2 reserve coys. of 24 R.F. forming a defensive flank N.E. of BUS (63rd Div., thought to be holding YTRES, had apparently withdrawn)". A more personal account of events was written by Private W.A. Hoyle of the 24th Battalion, and given by him to a Nurse Russell, treating him for his wounds at a hospital in Cranbrook in Kent on his repatriation to the U.K., and later by Nurse Russell's husband to the Imperial War Museum (10; 30). Private Hoyle's narrative tells of the 24th Battalion coming under heavy artillery and aerial bombardment as it attempted to advance to the front on March 21st-22nd, and of it being passed on the way by thousands of British troops and hundreds of heavy and later light artillery pieces retreating to the rear. It goes on to describe the battalion's own eventual retreat, during which scores of men went missing. By March 23rd, the situation in the field had evidently become extremely confused, at least from the British point of view. According to O'Neill, in his regimental history, "Many battalions ... had the same feeling of complete isolation, as though no one was fighting and prepared to fight but themselves. The 2nd Division were operating very close to the area of the 7th Battalion [at Lechelle, just south of Bertincourt], and to the Fusilier battalions included in it the retirement of the 63rd (Royal Naval) Division appeared inexplicable and tended to make their own position untenable. The central control of the operations appeared to have given way" (62). And according to Edmund Malone of the 7th Battalion, "I was much struck by the lack of interest shown in this great battle. ... . We got a grand view of the Fifth Army on our right, running like hares. Our Army (the Third) was slouching along the road like a crowd leaving a Cup Final – no hurry, all regiments mixed up, some of them singing, some of them looting chocs from abandoned canteens, but no one taking the slightest interest in the War except ourselves. We more or less had to, as we were still a unit" (31). Lance-Corporal William - "Billy" – Bentley of the 24th Battalion was awarded a Military Medal for "courage and resource during an enemy attack", on March 23rd, 1918 (see also Appendix 1). And, either on this or on a separate occasion, he reputedly saved the life of my maternal grandfather, Private Charles Reuben Clements, also of the 24th Battalion (see Appendix 2).

During the First Battle of Bapaume, on March 24th, at 9 a.m., "Under Arty. Barrage, BDE. retired to positions (RED LINE) between BARASTRE and HAPLINCOURT ... " (89). And at 4.35 p.m., "Enemy advanced rapidly, and all troops retired from RED LINE, 24 R.F. to occupy new positions on BAPAUME-PERONNE Road astride the road from VILLERS-AU-FLOS. During this retirement units of 2nd. Div. + other Divs. Were mixed. All troops of the 5th Bde. that could be got together formed a line just S.E. of LIGNY-THOLLY". On 25th, at 10 a.m., "5th Bde. took up front line positions between PYS and LE SARS. Enemy pursued his attack. After a brief exchange of rifle + M.G. [machine gun] fire, our troops retired from N.W. side of LE SARS. 5th Bde ordered to hold on until a fresh Div. got up. About 6 p.m. line was formed and 5th Bde. retired through BEAUCOURT. 24 R.F. occupied positions on spur E. of HAMEL during night 25/26th". According to O'Neill, in his regimental history, "the 24th saw the development of the disorganisation which had begun on the previous day. ... . The 17th Royal Fusiliers were the last to retire, after fighting a stubborn rearguard. They passed through Villers and Beaulencourt to Ligny, where the 24th Battalion joined them in position south of the village. ... . On the night of the 24th, the 17th and 24th Battalions ... withdrew ... south-west along the Bapaume-Albert Road. Between Pys and Le Sars the ... battalions ... took up positions and met the German attack with rifle and machine-gun fire. But at noon [on 25th] fresh attacks were delivered. Grevillers and Bihucourt fell. ... . At 2.10 p.m. the Germans were pushing through Le Sars, and could be seen advancing under cover of a smoke screen on Courcelette. At 4 p.m. the 17th Battalion was ordered to stand at all costs. But ... [after an unsuccessful counter-attack] ... began to retire ... to a spot just south of the Ancre near Hamel. The 24th Battalion had also fallen back to the spur east of Hamel, and in these positions the night was passed" (62). Private Hoyle's narrative (see above) tells of an unusual incident that took place near Beaumont-Hamel, on or around March 25th, in which German troops in British uniforms attempted to lure him and his comrades into an ambush (10). As he put it, "Six men rose out of a trench just in front of us.

They were all bareheaded and wore English equipment and overcoats. They shouted out to us, 'Come on ... .' Our officer yelled, 'Don't fire they are our own men', but a Corporal who was in a trench just in front of us shouted, 'Fire, they are Fritzes, so we cheered and let rip with our Lewis guns and rifles. Those six never got up again".

During the Battle of Rosieres, on March 26th, "During the morning, 5th. Bde. withdrew to line E. of AUCHONVILLERS ["Ocean Villas"]. During the day NEW ZEALAND troops reinforced the line, and 24 R.F. spread out astride the AUCHONVILLERS-BEAUMONT HAMEL road to get into touch on left with NEW ZEALAND troops who were attacking in the neighbourhood of HEBUTERNE ["About Turn"] Enemy approached rapidly and a heavy exchange of rifle and M.G. [machine gun] fire continued during afternoon and evening". That evening, "2nd Division withdrew, leaving the line in the hands of the NEW ZEALANDERS, and passed night of 26/27th bivouacked in MAILLY-MAILLET wood". Later, on March 28th, "Enemy attacked ... front line positions on RLY. EMBANKMENT, W. of [Aveluy] Wood. He enjoyed initial success, but 24 R.F., R.W. Kents [the Royal West Kent Regiment] and 52 L.I. [52nd Oxfordshire Regiment of Foot (Light Infantry)] counter-attacked, + drove enemy off" (89). According to O'Neill, in his regimental history, "on the 26th ... the 17th and 24th Battalions held positions near the final resting place of the 3rd Army front. On the north, however, the Germans crossed the Ancre and took Colincamps in the morning, but the village was retaken by New Zealand troops in the afternoon. ... . In this sector, March 27th again saw heavy fighting. At 8 a.m. the Germans renewed their attempts to force a crossing, but were again driven back by the 9th Royal Fusiliers. ... . [T]he 24th Royal Fusiliers took over positions in close support along the northern edge of Aveluy Wood. On the 28th the enemy attacked the railway embankment west of the wood, but the 24th Royal Fusiliers counter-attacked with two other battalions and drove them back. ... . The 9th and 24th Royal Fusilier Battalions on this front were relieved on the evening of this day, and the battle began to die down" (62).

According to the *"Battalion War Diary"*, the 24th Battalion's total casualties – killed, wounded, missing or captured - for March were 162 (89). Second Lieutenants William John Coppard and Wallace Remington were both killed on March 23rd, and are commemorated on the Arras Memorial. Second Lieutenant Coppard was twenty-one, and Second Lieutenant Remington thirty-four (see also Appendix 1). Private Henry John Morrell and Second Lieutenants William Neate and Dudley Richard Nyren were all killed on March 24th, and are also commemorated on the Arras Memorial. Private Morrell was of unknown age, but Second Lieutenant Neate was twenty-one, and Second Lieutenant Nyren twenty-four (see also Appendix 1). Second Lieutenant Charles Richard Stewart Coppack, was killed on March 25th, aged twenty-seven, and is commemorated both on the Arras Memorial, and in the church of St Mary in Lewisham, near where he was born (see also Appendix 1). Lance-Corporal Arthur William Beard was wounded, and later died of wounds on March 27th, and is buried in St Hilaire Cemetery in Frevent, suggesting that he may have died in No. 6 Stationary Hospital, which was situated nearby at the time (see also Appendix 1). Private Harold Southwell Shearing died on No. 12 Ambulance Train of wounds received in action at Aveluy Wood on March 29th, aged nineteen, and is buried in Etaples Military Cemetery (see also Appendix 1). Company Serjeant-Major Alfred Edgar Arrowsmith died in No. 3 Canadian Stationary Hospital on March 30th, of wounds received in action at Aveluy Wood on 28th, aged twenty-nine, and is buried in Doullens Communal Cemetery Extension No. 1 (see also Appendix 1). Also among the 24th Battalion casualties for March were one unnamed Non-Commissioned Officer reported missing after a German trench raid on 1st.

The 23rd Battalion was also in action during the First Battles of the Somme, 1918, a little to the south of the 24th (30; 90; 98). During the Battle of Bapaume on March 24th-25th, they had "held the position on the flank of Third Army, and after fighting an engagement with both flanks in the air had fallen back to Le Transloy ... " (98). Lieutenant Bird, M.C. was reported to have been killed by a shell on March 25th, and his wife was notified to that effect on April 5th, only to be find out later that he had in fact not been killed, but rather captured (30). The 23rd Battalion's total casualties for March were 310 (90).

One of the highest-ranking British casualties of the German "Spring" Offensive was Brigadier-General Randle Barnett-Barker, D.S.O. and Bar, officer-in-charge of 99th Brigade of 2nd Division, who was killed at Gueudecourt, not far Delville Wood, on March 24th, 1918, and is buried in Albert Communal Cemetery Extension (80). Two years previously, Lieutenant-Colonel Barnett-Barker, as he was then, had commanded the 22nd Battalion, the Royal Fusiliers in their successful attack on Delville Wood, on July 27th, 1916.

Subsequent Phases

On March 28th, the Germans sought to further widen their front by switching their main point of attack towards the fortified town of Arras, in *"Operation Mars/Valkyrie"* (11; 54; 71). There and then, though, they were held, as they were at Amiens on April 4th, and thereafter *"Operation Michael"* essentially ground to a halt. The gamble of the Offensive had nearly paid off for the Germans - nearly, but not quite. In fact, even before the end of March, the Offensive had already begun to run ahead of its supplies and out of steam, and to suffer from what Clausewitz had termed "the diminishing power of the offensive". It had done so, moreover, without further advance in strategically significant areas of the front, but with worrying lapses of military order and discipline. On March 28th, Binding wrote, "Today the advance of our infantry suddenly stopped near Albert [some way short of its objective of Amiens]. Nobody could understand why .... I jumped into a car with orders to find out what was causing the stoppage in front. As soon as I got near I began to see curious sights. Strange figures, which looked very little like soldiers, and certainly showed no sign of advancing, were making their way back out of the town. There were men driving cows before them ... ; others who carried a hen under one arm ... . Men carrying a bottle of wine under their arm and another one open in their hand. ... Men staggering. Men who could hardly walk" (5). Binding later wrote, "It is practically certain that the reason why we did not reach Amiens was the looting at Albert and Moreuil. ... . The two places, which were captured fairly easily, contained so much wine that the divisions, which ought properly to have marched through them, lay about unfit to fight in the rooms and cellars. ... . The ... hunger, thirst, and ... general sense of years of privation, were simply too great and too overpowering. The disorder of the troops at these two places ... must have cost us a good fifty thousand men, apart from the lost opportunity, for the troops which moved out of Albert next day ... were mown down straight away ... by a few English machine-guns, while those who escaped were laid out by French artillery in their next attack". And, "The physical exhaustion of the infantry during the period from April 4th to 10th, not until the end of which was a cessation of the fighting considered necessary ... , was so great that finally the men could hardly fire their rifles; they let themselves be slowly wiped out by the enemy's artillery fire almost without caring, and would hardly move from the spot. They were just like used-up horses which stand fast ... and dumbly take the blows of the whip without a movement. They could not advance; they could not shoot; they could not even get out of the way of the fire; they just stuck there".

The 24th Battalion was forced to continue its retreat to Mesnil on March 29th, and Hedauville on 30th, and eventually ended up at Monts-en-Ternois, half-way to the Channel ports, on April 6th (89).

Subsequent Offensive Operations and Aftermath (April-July, 1918)

The next German Offensive Operation, *"Operation George/Georgette"*, directed at the Lys to the north, began in April (54; 71). For an exceedingly tense, albeit brief, period, it posed a significant threat to the narrow northern hinterland and the strategically vital Channel Ports beyond, the loss of which might have forced the British out of the war.

In May through July, continuing operations – *"Operation Blucher-Yorck"*, *"Operation Gneisenau"*, and the *"Marneschutz"* – were eventually checked by an outbreak of influenza, which ultimately affected over 500 000 German soldiers.

High-Water Mark

On April 11th, Haig issued his famous "Backs to the Wall" Order to All Ranks of the British Army in France and Flanders (54; 71). The Order read, in full, as follows: "Three weeks ago to-day the enemy began his terrific attacks against us on a fifty-mile front. His objects are to separate us from the French, to take the Channel Ports and destroy the British Army. In spite of throwing already 106 Divisions into the battle and enduring the most reckless sacrifice of human life, he has as yet made little progress towards his goals. We owe this to the determined fighting and self-sacrifice of our troops. Words fail me to express the admiration which I feel for the splendid resistance offered by all ranks of our Army under the most trying circumstances. Many amongst us now are tired. To those I would say that Victory will belong to the side which holds out the longest. The French Army is moving rapidly and in great force to our support. There is no other course open to us but to fight it out. Every position must be held to the last man: there must be no retirement. With our backs to the wall and believing in the justice of our cause each one of us must fight on to the end. The safety of our homes and the Freedom of mankind alike depend upon the conduct of each one of us at this critical moment".

According to the *"Battalion War Diary"*, the 24th Battalion was in reserve at Monts-en-Ternois, the westernmost point of its retreat, between April 6th -8th, but advanced eastwards again to hold the line at Bavrincourt, between Arras and Bapaume, between 16th-18th (89). The Battalion then spent the rest of April in reserve at Hendecourt, north-west of Bapaume. And May through July either holding the line at Boyelles and Adinfer, midway between Arras and Bapaume, or in reserve, again at Hendecourt.

The 24th Battalion's casualties for April were thirty-four (89). Private Charles Sidney Ralph died on April 5th, 1918 of wounds received in action at Bullecourt on March 24th, aged thirty-six, and is buried in Etaples Military Cemetery (*Plate 57*; see also Appendix 1). Company Serjeant-Major Frederick Herbert Read, who had been awarded the Distinguished Conduct Medal and Military Medal for his gallantry, was killed at Bavrincourt on April 16th, aged around twenty-five, and is buried in Berles New Cemetery in nearby Berles-au-Bois (see also Appendix 1). Incidentally, Corporal William Henley of the 24th Battalion, who was also awarded the D.C.M. and M.M., and Mentioned in Despatches three times, survived the war (see also Appendix 1). Private Richard Haynes Mintorn, sometime of the 24th Battalion, died of pneumonia in the Royal Herbert Hospital in Woolwich on April 28th, aged fifty-three, and is buried in St Mary's Church in Harrow (*Plate 58*; see also Appendix 1). The Battalion's casualties for May were twenty-six, and for June thirteen. Second Lieutenant Angus Mackay, aged twenty-two, died of wounds on May 10th, and is buried in Bagneux Cemetery near Gezaincourt (see also Appendix 1). It is probable that he died at No. 3, No. 29 or No. 56 Casualty Clearing Station, all of which were located in Gezaincourt at the time of his death (59). Private James Francis Wells, aged thirty-seven, was killed on June 8th, and is buried in Bac du Sud Cemetery in Bailleulval (see also Appendix 1).

The 23rd Battalion's casualties for April were thirty-six (90).

The Turning of the Tide

In late July, German Offensive Operations were reversed by a counter-attack by resurgent French forces, at the Battles of the Marne, 1918, also known as the Second Battle of the Marne. Sulzbach wrote, on July 15th, "At 4.50 the [German] creeping barrage begins, and with it the infantry advance. ... The attack is coming to a halt outside Prosnes: enemy resistance seems to be insurmountable" (83). And on 16th, "We hear that our attack has in fact been repulsed by the French ... , with heavy losses". Binding wrote, also on July 16th, "I have lived through the most disheartening day of the whole War ... . [T]he French deliberately lured us [into a trap]. They put up no resistance in front; they had neither infantry nor artillery in this forward battle-zone, the full use and value of which they had learned from Ludendorff. Our guns bombarded empty trenches; our gas-shells gassed empty artillery positions; only in little hidden folds of the ground, sparsely distributed, lay machine-gun posts, like lice in the seams and folds of a garment, to give the attacking force a warm reception. ... . After uninterrupted fighting from ... morning until ... night, smothered all the time with carefully directed fire, we only succeeded in advancing about three kilometres ... [and] ... suffered heavy losses" (5). Sulzbach wrote on 17th, "Orders to withdraw ... , the craziest night I've ever known: as a reaction to the tropical heat of the last few days, dozens of thunderstorms opened up on us while moving along the road". And on 18th, "Strong enemy attacks in progress". From the Germans' point of view, the Offensive had begun as a tactical success, but had ended as a strategic failure. Its ultimate failure dealt a crushing, and arguably mortal, blow to their morale. The situation can only have been made worse by the news filtering through to the battle front of increasing food shortages and other depredations being endured on the home front, as a consequence of the Allied Naval Blockade of Germany. War-weariness began to seep in, and the willingness to fight and die, for what was coming to be seen as a lost cause, to seep out. The tide of the war was finally turning, in the Allies' favour.

According to the *"Battalion War Diary"*, the 24th Battalion's casualties for July were twenty-three (89).

ALLIED "HUNDRED DAYS" OFFENSIVE (SUMMER-AUTUMN, 1918)

By July, 1918, the manpower and firepower available to the Allies had come to exceed that of the Germans, and they were finally in a position to start planning an Offensive of their own (10; 34; 38; 49; 50; 66; 67). *"Tout le monde a la bataille"* ("everybody to battle"), went up the cry from Foch. The British and Empire armies were to attack in the north; the French in the centre; and the Americans, under General John J. - "Black Jack" - Pershing, fresh from their blooding at Belleau Wood, in the south. According to the *"Battalion War Diary"*, from July 29th-August 8th, the 24th Battalion had the novel experience of holding the line at Adinfer, between Arras and Bapaume, alongside troops of the 1st Battalion, 319th Regiment, of the American Army (89). Some officers from the Battalion were attached to American platoons, and at least one Non-Commissioned Officer and two Privates to every American patrol.

In the British and Empire sector to the north, Rawlinson and his confederates, having learned important lessons from the successes and failures at Cambrai, began to plan closely co-ordinated offensive operations using "all possible mechanical devices" as force-multipliers (34; 67). At 0310 on July 4th, the Australian Corps, under Lieutenant-General John Monash, launched an attack on the village of le Hamel on the Somme, a little to the east of Amiens, involving the advance of comparatively small numbers of Australian - and some American - infantrymen and large numbers of British tanks, under a creeping barrage, while predicted counter-battery fire subdued enemy artillery (67). It was a notable success.

Following on from the success at le Hamel, Rawlinson, taking advice from Monash, came up with a plan for another similar attack on the Somme, a little further to the east of

Amiens (67). Haig and Foch extended the scale and scope of the plan, and ordered Rawlinson to make the line Chaulnes-Roye, midway between Amiens and St Quentin, his objective. This objective might have seemed to some at the time to have been too much of a stretch. However, Rawlinson had at his disposal first-rate Australian and Canadian infantry divisions, over three hundred fighting Mk. V Tanks together with an assortment of infantry-carrying and supply versions thereof, and two thousand artillery pieces (84). That is not to mention nearly two thousand aircraft of the Royal Air Force (earlier known as the Royal Flying Corps). What was to become known as the Battle of Amiens began at 0420 on August 8th, with the infantry and armoured cavalry advancing under creeping and counter-battery artillery barrages (34; 67). Monash wrote, "A great illumination lights up the Eastern horizon: and instantly the whole complex organisation, extending far back to areas almost outside earshot of the gun, begins to move forward: every man, every unit, every vehicle on the appointed tasks and to their designated goals, sweeping on relentlessly and irresistibly". The Battle of Amiens turned into a triumph for the Allies, who were eventually able to advance around eight miles, encountering little serious opposition on the way; and it was an unmitigated disaster for the Germans, who sustained 27 000 casualties (killed, wounded, missing or, in a large number of cases, captured). In the aftermath, Rawlinson remarked that "we have given the Boche a pretty good bump this time". And Ludendorff was forced to acknowledge August 8th as *"der schwarze Tag des deutschen Heeres"* - "the black day of the German Army".

The black day for the Germans would be followed by around a hundred more in August-November, 1918, in an all-out Allied Offensive that would eventually win the war, and go down in history as the "Hundred Days" (67). From the Allied point of view, the war was now at last one of forward movement and momentum. A by now justifiably confident Haig was able to tell his Army commanders "It is no longer necessary to advance in regular lines step by step. On the contrary, each division should be given a distant objective which must be reached independently of one's neighbour, and even if one's flank is thereby exposed for the time being. Reinforcements must be directed on the points where our troops are gaining ground, not where they are checked".

The Second Battles of the Somme, 1918, would take place in late August to early September, the Battles of the Hindenburg Line in mid-late September to early October, and the Final Advance in Picardy in mid-late October to early November.

The Second Battles of the Somme, 1918 (August-September, 1918)

The Second Battles of the Somme, 1918 included the Battle of Albert, which took place between August 21st-23rd, and the Second Battle of Bapaume, which took place between August 21st-September 3rd (11; 72; 73). The Third and Fourth British Armies captured Albert on August 23rd, and Bapaume on 29th. At Bapaume, twenty-three British and Empire divisions roundly defeated thirty-five German ones, and captured over 34 000 men and 270 guns, with a prominent role being played by the New Zealand Division, under Major-General Andrew Hamilton Russell. The 2nd Australian Division of Monash's Australian Corps, under Major-General Charles Rosenthal, then took Mont St Quentin on September 1st; and the 5th Australian Division, under Major-General Joseph John Talbot Hobbs, took Peronne on 2nd (67). And the First and Third British Armies took the Drocourt-Queant Switch, well to the east of Arras, in Artois, on September 3rd, with a prominent role being played here by the Canadian Corps, now under Lieutenant-General Arthur Currie (67). Under this relentless Allied pressure, the Germans were forced further and further back, and by the middle of September, far sooner than Ludendorff had hoped, as far back as the Hindenburg Line.

112

The Second Battle of Bapaume

During the Second Battle of Bapaume, between August 21st-25th, the 24th Battalion was in action a little to the north and west of Bapaume (62; 89). On August 21st, "99th. Brigade stormed German First positions in conjunction with Brigades of other divisions on flanks" (89). On 22nd, "2nd. Division ordered to attack from the ARRAS – ACHIET-LE-GRAND Railway Line on morning of 23rd., ... 5th. Brigade objectives being the capture of BEHAGNIES and SAPIGNIES". On 23rd, "at 9-30 A.M. the Battalion moved forward in Artillery formation [in files with open ranks, each man at least 6' from the next] to the Railway Embankment - ARRAS – ACHIET-LE-GRAND Railway. The attack, with Tanks, started at 11 A.M. under the cover of a barrage. Heavy enemy artillery fire was encountered at once and crossing the ... Railway small arms enfilade fire was brought to bear on the Battn. from isolated posts S. of the advance. GOMIECOURT was passed on our right and the advance continued by the Battalion swinging to the right and pressing forward in face of exceedingly heavy fire from machine guns and guns of all calibres up to 8". The uninterrupted M.G. [machine gun] fire from the left flank ... was especially telling from the high ground left unaccounted for between the advances of the 6th. and 5th. Divisions. The barrage was traversed though not without heavy casualties and the advance pushed on in a determined manner the drill-like precision, steady bearing and unfaltering pace of the troops under the prolonged ordeal, being wholly admirable. The enemy commenced hurriedly to move his guns, but one of the leading Coys pushed forward a Lewis Gun team which was quickly in action, the enemy gunners being shot down and 2 Field Guns captured. The two leading Companies, with those of the H.L.I. [Highland Light Infantry], had reached the ridge West of BEHAGNIES and this position was consolidated and held. Headquarters was established in a bank N.W. of BEHAGNIES, where a Field Gun, limber and 8 horses were captured with much valuable booty and documents. The enemy withdrew his troops to BEHAGNIES and patrols of the Battalion were pushed out to ascertain the enemy's dispositions. A further advance proved out of the question without an artillery preparation, in view of the completely open valley to be crossed, the intense machine gun fire, and the presence of enemy positions on the flanks. Remainder of the day was spent consolidating the positions won" (89). On 24th, "Coys. recorganised and preparations were made for continuing the attack. Two Coys of 2nd. Ox. & Bucks placed under command of Comdg. Officer 24th. R.F.". And on 25th, "At 1-30 A.M. orders were received for the Battalion, in conjunction with the H.L.I., to take BEHAGNIES. Two Coys were allotted to the assault proper, 1 Coy to Support as Moppers up, and to form a defensive right flank, and 1 Coy in reserve. At 3-30 A.M. the attack commenced under cover of a barrage and was a complete surprise for the enemy and a success for us. Many nests of Machine Guns were overcome and the teams killed or made prisoners. The village was held in strength by the enemy with many machine guns, officially estimated at 110, but the Battalion followed so closely to the [creeping] barrage that the resistance was in most cases overcome before the enemy had time to man his defences. Many of the enemy were discovered asleep in their dugouts and surrendered without a struggle, and those attempting to escape were shot down. The leading Coys pushed forward to their objective, the ridge some 300 [yards] E. of BEHAGNIES, where work of consolidation and preparation for any counter-attack was thoroughly organized. The Support Coy, whose task was to Mop up the village, quickly accounted for all enemy stragglers and did their work most effectively before swinging round to guard the southern approaches to the village. By 6 A.M. BEHAGNIES was reported to be completely in our hands, with the Battalion in strong positions, of its own choosing, E. of the village and prepared for all eventualities. 200 Prisoners alone were taken in the operation, this total almost approximating the entire casualties sustained by the Battalion in the two days fighting. Altogether it was a proud day for the Battalion, the operation in its conception thoroughly outwitting the enemy, the Officers and N.C.Os. leading the men in a manner beyond all praise, and the men, many of whom were young untried soldiers in their first fight,

going forward in full confidence that they could beat the enemy
and when they had so thoroughly beaten him, proud and elated
to have seen him so thoroughly outmanoeuvred and outfought.
Work on consolidation proceeded apace and by 9 A.M. the
62nd. [2nd West Riding] Division was in line with B.H.Q. and at
9-30 A.M. advanced through our forward positions.
BEHAGNIES was heavily shelled all day and at 5 P.M. an
intense barrage was put down in the village and Bn. H.Q.
heralding the imminence of a counter-attack. This was
developing from FAVREUIL WOOD, and artillery was quickly
brought to bear on the troops assembling with great effect so
that the attack when delivered was readily beaten back by the
troops of the Bn. right. At 9 P.M. the situation had become
normal and permitted of arrangements being made for the
withdrawal of the Battalion". O'Neill wrote, in his regimental
history, in regard to the 24th Battalion's role in the action on
23rd, "The conditions, in fine, were almost intolerable; but the
battalion went through the barrage cool, unhurried, unfaltering,
and, with the Highland Light Infantry, they reached and
consolidated the ridge west of Behagnies" (62). And in regard
their role on 25th, "Many young and untried troops took part in
this action. It was their first battle, but they behaved with all
the *sang froid* of veterans". Lieutenant H.W. Griffiths, on
secondment from the 7th Battalion, was awarded a Military
Cross for the "resourcefulness and leadership" he displayed in
the course of the action at Behagnies. According to the
"*Battalion War Diary*", the 24th Battalion was in Courcelles
between August 26th-31st, undergoing "Reorganization,
refitting and rest" (89). Corporal Felix Grugan, formerly of the
25th Battalion, the Northumberland Fusiliers, was drafted into
the 24th Battalion, the Royal Fusiliers on 30th (*Plate 59*; see
also Appendix 1).

The 24th Battalion's total casualties for August were 238
(89). This was the third highest monthly total of the war,
exceeded only during the Battles of the Somme in July and
November, 1916 (indeed, the battalion's average monthly total
for 1918 was almost identical to that for 1916). One of the
fatal casualties was Lance-Corporal George Seth Dack, who
was killed on August 23rd, almost certainly in the initial phase

115

of the attack on Behagnies (see also Appendix 1). Lance-Corporal Dack is buried in Gomiecourt South Cemetery. Another fatal casualty was Lance-Corporal John Arthur Boote, who was killed on August 25th, aged twenty, almost certainly in the final phase of the attack on Behagnies (*Plate 60*; see also Appendix 1). Lance-Corporal Boote is buried in Gommecourt Wood New Cemetery in Fonquevillers ("Funky Villas": 8). Further fatalities were Private Thomas William Evans, aged nineteen, who died of wounds on August 25th, and Private Arthur Bailey, also aged nineteen, who died of wounds on 26th (*Plate 61*; see also Appendix 1). Both men are buried in Bagneux British Cemetery near Gezaincourt, suggesting that they may have died at No. 3, No. 29 or No. 56 Casualty Clearing Station, all of which were located in Gezaincourt at the time of their deaths (59).

The 23rd Battalion was also in action at Ayette on August 23rd, capturing first "Aerodrome Trench" and then the village itself (30; 90; 98). It was then in action again at "Slag Avenue" on September 6th-7th, where it sustained 103 casualties.

On the German side, *Leutnant* (Second Lieutenant) Ernst Junger was wounded, for the seventh time, leading his men in an ultimately unsuccessful counter-attack on Sepagnies, on August 25th (45). In fact, on this occasion, as he put it, "I was hit at least fourteen times, these being five bullets, two shell splinters, one shrapnel ball, four hand-grenade splinters and two bullet splinters, which, with entry and exit wounds, left me an even twenty scars". He would later be awarded the *Pour le Merite*, the German equivalent of the Victoria Cross. He had earlier written that "The Great Battle [the German "Spring" Offensive] was a turning-point for me, ... because from then on I thought it possible that we might lose the war".

The Battles of the Hindenburg Line (September-October, 1918)

The Allies continued the Advance to the Hindenburg Line between September 2nd-11th, 1918 (49; 73). The Hindenburg

Line remained as formidable and seemingly impregnable as ever before. However, the Allies attacking it were emboldened now as never before, and the Germans defending it, if not intimated, certainly strained to breaking-point. Eventually, on September 29th, Fourth Army broke through the Hindenburg Line on the St Quentin Canal, in an action in which 46th (North Midland) Division distinguished itself by taking the bridge at Riqueval intact.

The Battle of Havrincourt

The 24th Battalion took part in the Advance to the Hindenburg Line between September 2nd-11th, 1918 (62; 89). It then took part in the first of the Battles of the Hindenburg Line, the Battle of Havrincourt, on September 12th, during which "the whole of the battn eventually went into action in support of 52nd L.I. [52nd Oxfordshire Regiment of Foot (Light Infantry)] and 2nd H.L.I. [Highland Light Infantry], and reached their objective" (89; see also *Map 8*). Byng later recounted to Charles a Court Repington, the war correspondent of *The Morning Post*, that he considered "his most important day with the 3rd Army to have been the capture of Havrincourt ... in September 1918. ... [T]he Boches threw two ... divisions of ... Brandenburgians and Hanoverians against him, with two more in reserve. They were well beaten, and the heart was out of the enemy afterwards".

The Battle of the Canal du Nord

After the Battle of Havrincourt, the Battalion went on to take part in some of the remaining Battles of the Hindenburg Line, including the Battle of the Canal du Nord, which began on September 27th (62; 89).

According to the *"Battalion War Diary"*, on September 27th, "24th R.F. moved to area east of CANAL DU NORD using the DEMICOURT-FLESQUIERES crossing" (89). And on 28th, "The 99th and 6th Bdes. continued their attack on CANTAIGN SUPPORT area + NINE WOOD. Bdes. exploited the area in front of their objectives. 57th [2nd West Lancashire]

Divn. attacked simultaneously with 2nd Divn. Zero 5.15 am. 6th + 99th Bdes. reached line of CANAL and were held up by M.G. [machine gun] fire on east bank. Units of 5th Bde. moved on receipt of order No. 336. 24th R.F. moved to trenches W of FLESQUIERES".

Subsequent Battles

Again according to the *"Battalion War Diary"*, between September 30th and October 3rd, the Battalion took part in a notable attack on Rumilly–en-Cambresis on the Brunhilde Line, east of the St Quentin Canal, and immediately south of Cambrai (89). On September 30th, "63rd [Royal Naval] Divn. on left and 67th [2nd Home Counties] Divn. on right were attacking these positions. ... . The Battn was ordered to support 63rd Divn. in its attack on RUMILLY. At 10 a.m. the situation was not clear and the coys of the 24th were ordered not to become involved in further fighting until situation on flanks was clearer". And according to shakily-written notes sent back to Battalion Headquarters by runner by the wounded officer in command of "C" Company, Lieutenant R.J. Pring, at 10.10, "Rumilly is strongly held by G.M.G. [machine guns] ... . I am knocked out for the time being hit in the back"; and at 2.30 p.m., "Still enfiladed + sniped like hell from ... Rumilly. Had eight casualties before I moved a few yards. ... . In my opinion it is sheer murder to attack till dusk". On October 1st, "The enemy were reported to be holding all of RUMILLY except Southern edge. At 5.45 p.m. 52nd [Lowland] Division were attacking the village. 5th Bde were ordered to support the attack by clearing the ground N.E. of RUMILLY + establishing a line E. of the CAMBRAI Railway. 2 Companies of 24th Royal Fusiliers were ordered to attack. To "B" Coy was allotted the attack proper and 1 Coy passed through to establish the new line. The attack, commenced at 6.30 p.m., was made with 4 Platoons in the line and the men, keeping close up to the [creeping] barrage, rushed the enemy posts consisting of two quarries honeycombed with dugouts + organised for a determined resistance. The garrison of these quarries was very large, but the attacking Coy soon overcame all resistance + so enabled the supporting Coy to push through + establish the new line E. of the CAMBRAI Railway. Altogether, over 200 Prisoners and 50 Machine Guns were captured by the leading Company, whose strength was only 3 Officers + 67 other ranks. Altogether the operation was a striking success, especially as the garrison of the quarries had defied previous attempts made to dislodge them". On 2nd, "Consolidation + reorganization of positions won. Dispositions improved + preparations made for continuing the advance". And on 3rd, "New posts established in advance of line gained on high ground. 5th Brigade relieved in line by 6th Infy Bde. 24th Royal Fusiliers relieved by 1st King's Regt. On relief Battn moved back to billets at NOYELLES". According to the summary of events given by O'Neill, in his regimental history, "two companies of the 24th Battalion were ordered to clear the ground north-east of the village [Rumilly] and establish a line east of the railway. ... [A]t 6.30 B Company ... advanced close up to the barrage and rushed the enemy positions. ... . B were only 3 officers and 67 men strong ... , but they captured over 200 prisoners and 50 machine guns, and the supporting company were able to pass through and establish the line east of the railway with ease. The position was consolidated after a very striking success" (62).

The 24th Battalion's total casualties for September were 170 (89). One of the fatal casualties was Private Laurence Edward Courtney, who was killed on September 11th, aged thirty-six, and who is commemorated on the Vis-en-Artois Memorial in Haucourt (see also Appendix 1). Others included Privates Frederick Child, John Alfred Mayes, aged nineteen, and Percy Charles Pereira, who were killed on 12th, and are commemorated on the Vis-en-Artois Memorial (see also Appendix 1). Also Private George Louis Parris, who was killed on 13th, and who is buried in Vaulx Hill British Cemetery (see also Appendix 1). And Private John Robert Warriner, who was also killed on 13th, aged thirty-eight, and who is buried in Lowrie Cemetery in Havrincourt (see below; see also Appendix 1). Incidentally, Privates Child, Mayes, Parris, Pereira and Warriner were almost certainly all killed in the same operation at Havrincourt in which my maternal grandfather Private Charles Reuben Clements was wounded (see also Appendix 2).

Yet another of the 24th Battalion's fatal casualties for September was Private Reginald George Medlock, who was killed on 28th, aged nineteen, and who is buried in Flesquieres Hill British Cemetery (see also Appendix 1). The Battalion's casualties for October are not known, there being no casualty list for that month in the *"Battalion War Diary"* (89). It is known, though, that Private Harry Brown, M.M. was killed on October 1st, and is buried in Anneux British Cemetery, and that Lance-Corporal John William Fitton, M.M. was killed on the same day, aged thirty-eight, and is buried in Flesquieres Hill British Cemetery (*Plate 62*; see also Appendix 1). Also that Private Albert Edward Ward was killed on October 2nd, and is buried in Grevillers Cemetery (see also Appendix 1). And that Private George Joseph Burge, M.M., died on October 3rd of wounds suffered on September 30th, and is buried in St Sever Cemetery Extension in Rouen (see also Appendix 1). It is likely that he died in one of the many war-hospitals known to have been in operation in Rouen at this time. Moreover, Private Bernard James Mahoney died in German captivity on October 17th, 1918, after having been captured in the attack on Guillemont on July 30th, 1916 (see also above).

The 23rd Battalion was also in action at Rumilly, although a little later, on October 7th/8th (30; 90; 98). On 8th, "During a counter-attack, the enemy used tanks against the Battalion in an endeavour to out it from positions secured, but without success. On one tank, indeed, getting close to our line an officer, Lieutenant Anderson, armed with a rifle, and accompanied by his batman, got out of the trench, went forward under heavy fire, reached the oncoming tank, hammered on its side with his rifle-butt, and called on it to surrender. The iron door opened, and out came the crew, to be escorted back in triumph, as prisoners" (98). The same day, "'C' Company came under fire from some of the enemy who had surrendered ... and then decided to fight again. These men were soon put out of action" (90).

The Final Advance in Picardy (October-November, 1918)

With the Hindenburg Line breached, the path to Allied victory was finally clear (49; 73). On September 30th, a British pilot flew over German lines to drop a note reading, "In five weeks you'll have peace, though you swine don't deserve it". And on October 2nd, the German Military Command acknowledged in a report to the Reichstag acknowledged that "there is no longer any prospect of forcing peace on the enemy". Regardless, the German Army fought on until the bitter end, at the eleventh hour of the eleventh day of the eleventh month of 1918. *Leutnant* (Second Lieutenant) Harold Woehl would write in his diary on October 9th, "Dante's description of Hell was too mild for this agony"; and Ernst Kielmayer in his, on November 1st, "We keep shooting at different targets: at batteries, bridges, street crossings. We are trying to do to him what he loves to do to us".

After the Battles of the Hindenburg Line, the 24th Battalion took part in the Final Advance in Picardy (62; 89). After receiving specialist training in fighting in villages in Rumilly on October 13th, they were moved to Carnieres, east of Cambrai, on October 19th, to St Vaast, south of Valenciennes, on 20th, to Vertain on 22nd, to St Python on 24th, and to Ruesnes on 30th. They were then moved back to St Python again on November 3rd, and to Villers, in the rear, between Arras and Lens, on 9th.

The Battle of the Selle

According to the *"Battalion War Diary"*, on October 23rd, during the Battle of the Selle, the Battalion was involved in an attack on Vertain (89). On 22nd, "Battn. relieved 1st Bn. Irish Guards + 2nd Grenadier Guards in positions W of VERTAIN. Orders received for 5th Bde to attack on morning of 23rd October. 24th Royal Fus. On right of Bde + assigned the capture of all of the village of VERTAIN, N of the main road to ESCARMAIN, + the open ground N. of the village". And on 23rd, "The dispositions for the attack were :- "D" Coy, 24th Roy. Fus. on the right + attacking the village of VERTAIN. "C" Coy on left whose object it was to push on + capture line of road E of VERTAIN. 2 Platoons of "B" Coy were assigned to mop up for attacking Coys. "A" Coy were in reserve. At 3.20 a.m. the attack was launched + the right Coy attacked the village. To conform with the barrage arrangements the left Coy did not attack until 4.20 a.m. From the outset the attack was a complete success. The men, splendidly led, and full of fight, soon beat down all opposition and by 5.15 a.m. the left Coy reported all objectives gained. Very soon after, the right Coy, whose task was a more severe one reported all their objectives gained. The mopping up party met with some resistance and trouble from Machine Guns in houses in VERTAIN but so thoroughly did they do their work that 'all clear' was reported in time to allow the 52nd L.I. [52nd Oxfordshire Regiment of Foot (Light Infantry)] to pass through the Battn. at 8.20 a.m. to carry on the tide of the advance. Over 250 prisoners, 50-60 Machine Guns, one 77 m.m. Field Gun, 4 Trench Mortars, + much other valuable booty were captured in this most successful operation by the Battalion. That night, after a hard day, the Battn. had the novel experience of being billeted in houses in the village of VERTAIN which they had so finely won in the morning". And on 24th, the 24th Battalion "moved back to billets in ST PYTHON" (89). According to the summary of events given by O'Neill, in his regimental history, "The 24th Royal Fusiliers took up positions west of Vertain on the night of October 22nd, and at 3.30 a.m. [on 23rd] D Company attacked the village, C advancing against the road running from it an hour later. Both objectives were gained by 5.10 a.m., though the task of reducing the village was by no means easy" (62).

As noted above, the 24th Battalion's total casualties for October are not known. It is known, though, that Lance-Corporal Reginald Hyland died of wounds on October 19th, aged nineteen, and Lance-Corporal A. Leonard Benn, M.M. on 20th, both men being buried in Abbeville Communal Cemetery Extension (see also Appendix 1). It is also known that Second Lieutenant Edward Albert Newland was killed on October 23rd, aged twenty-nine, and is buried in St Hilaire les Cambrai Cemetery, a little to the west of Vertain (*Plate 63*; see also Appendix 1).

The 23rd Battalion was also in action in the Battle of the Selle, and on October 24th attacked, cleared and consolidated the village of Ruesnes, and sent outposts forward (30; 62; 90; 98). Its casualties during this action were thirty-six killed or wounded, and five gassed. It was their last action of the war.

The Battle of Valenciennes

On November 1st, during the Battle of Valenciennes, the 24th Battalion was involved in its last action of the war, at Ruesnes, near Valenciennes, where it had "2 Coys in front line + 2 in support" (89). It sustained nineteen casualties that day, out of a total of twenty-one for November. The nine men who were killed that day were Corporal George Alvey, Private Frank Ambrose, Private Alfred Thomas Baker, Private Thomas John Batchelor, Private Alfred Edward Foskett, Private Arthur Samuel Gillard, aged nineteen, Corporal Herbert Jackson, Private Walter Redshaw, aged twenty, and Private Frederick Haywood Reeves (see also Appendix 1). Corporal Alvey, Private Ambrose, Private Baker, Private Batchelor, Private Gillard and Corporal Jackson are buried in Cross Roads Cemetery in Fontaine-au-Bois, a little to the south of Ruesnes; Private Foskett and Private Redshaw, in Vertain Communal Cemetery Extension; and Private Reeves, in Romeries Communal Cemetery Extension. Private Baker's service number was 930, indicating that he had signed up in November, 1914, and served for almost exactly four years. The last man from the Battalion to die in the Great War was Lance-Corporal William Albert Batrick, who died of wounds on November 7th, and who is buried in Etaples Military Cemetery (see also Appendix 1).

The last man from the 24th Battalion to be killed during the Great War was Private Ernest Jackson, aged thirty-two (2; see also Appendix 1). Private Jackson had been conscripted into the Army in July, 1916, and sent to the Western Front in the November of that year. He had later gone Absent Without Official Leave in 1917, for which he had been sentenced to two years imprisonment with hard labour. Upon his early release, he had gone A.W.O.L. again in September, 1918, near Flesquieres, and yet again in October, 1918, near Noyelles. On October 8th, 1918, he was court-martialled on the capital

123

charges of desertion and "shamefully casting away his arms, ammunition and equipment in the presence of the enemy" on the second of these occasions. He argued in his defence that he suffered from "mental disease caused by worries", and added that both his parents died in an asylum. But he was shown no mercy, and indeed not even given a psychiatric evaluation. Rather, he was summarily convicted, and sentenced to death, his own Commanding Officer insisting that "cowardly action of this kind should be made an example of". Private Ernest Jackson was duly shot at dawn on November 7th, 1918 - only four days before the end of the war. He is buried in Romeries Communal Cemetery Extension, with nothing on his headstone to indicate his fate. He is not mentioned either in the "*Battalion War Diary*" (89), or in the volume of "*Soldiers Died in the Great War* ... " pertaining to the Royal Fusiliers (95).

Incidentally, over the course of the Great War, 346 British and Empire soldiers - and others subject to the Army Act - were executed, following capital courts-martial that, in many cases, as in Private Jackson's, essentially ignored mitigating evidence offered on their behalf (2; 97). Nearly a century later, on November 7th, 2006, the British Government issued posthumous pardons to the 306 who had been executed for offences other than murder or mutiny, including the 284 who had been executed for desertion or cowardice. These men are also commemorated on the "Shot at Dawn" Memorial in the National Memorial Arboretum in Alrewas in Staffordshire (*Figure 19*).

Interestingly, only forty-eight German soldiers were executed over the course of the war, perhaps not least in part because they were allowed qualified legal representation in courts-martial.

Armistice (November 11th, 1918)

The 24th Battalion was at Villers, between Arras and Lens, on November 11th, 1918, when an Armistice was signed between the French and British on the one side, represented by *Generalissime* (Supreme General) Ferdinand Foch and First Sea Lord Admiral Rosslyn Wemyss, and the Germans on the other, represented by *Generalmajor* (Major-General) Detlof von Winterfeldt and *Kapitan zur See* (Captain) Ernst Vanselow (9). The killing machine had at last ground to a halt, in a railway siding in Compiegne. Reaction to the news was not as universally celebratory as might have been expected. Major Chapman of the 13th Battalion later wrote, "The news ... was accepted with a shrug. ... . On 11th November ... a blanket of fog covered the countryside. At eleven o'clock we slung on our packs and tramped on along the muddy *pave*. The band played but there was very little singing. ... . We were very old, very tired and now very wise" (16).

Based in the main on figures in the *"Battalion War Diary"*, the 24th Battalion's total casualties - that is, officers and other ranks killed, wounded or missing - between November, 1915 and November, 1918 were 1 869 (89). Of these, 1 was sustained in 1915, 790 in 1916, 367 in 1917, and 711 in 1918 (89). The Battalion's total fatalities – killed or assumed killed in action, died of wounds or died in enemy captivity - were 557 (62; 89; 94; 95). The British and Empire Armies' total casualties over the course of the Great War, most of which were sustained on the Western Front, were 3 190 235, and their fatalities were 908 371 (97). The French and Empire Armies' total casualties on the Western Front are not accurately known, but their fatalities were at least approximately 1 357 000 (97). The German Armies' total casualties on all fronts were 7 025 972, and their fatalities were 1 718 246 (97).

Certain elements of the 24th Battalion remained on the continent after the war, with elements from the 4th, 17th, 23rd and 26th Battalions, as part of the Army of Occupation, entering German territory for the first time on December 9th, 1918 (62; 89). Most were sent home after a farewell inspection and address by Major-General Cecil E. Pereira, the officer-in-command of 2nd Division, on March 13th, 1919, although some stayed on until at least March 31st, 1919. Then, on June 28th, 1919, the Treaty of Versailles was signed, between all the Allied and Associated Powers on the one side, and the Germans on the other, and the Great War was finally formally over. It had been five years to the day since the triggering assassination by Gavrilo Princip, a Serbian nationalist, of Archduke Franz Ferdinand, the heir-presumptive to the throne of the Austro-Hungarian Empire.

The British Empire and Army had survived to fight another day. The German Empire had fallen, as also, indeed, had the Austro-Hungarian and Ottoman Empires. Significantly, though, the German Army had not, as they came to imagine it, been decisively beaten on the field of battle. With uncanny prescience, Foch predicted after the end of the Great War, the supposed "War to end all Wars", that there would be another within twenty years. He was only sixty-five days out. The Second World War broke out on September 1st, 1939.

THE WESTERN FRONT BATTLEFIELDS TODAY

Time, nature and agriculture have reclaimed most of the Western Front battlefields now, although some still yield an annual "iron harvest" of unexploded ordnance as well as one of wheat (12; 22). Only in a few places are there extensive sections preserved, complete with Allied and German trench-lines separated by a No Man's Land cratered by shells and mines. Two such are the Memorial Parks at Beaumont-Hamel (*Figure 20*) and Vimy (*Figures 21-23*). These commemorate the many thousands of Newfoundlanders and other Canadians who fought and died in, respectively, the Battles of the Somme in 1916 and of Arras in 1917. It has been said, and not only by jingoistic British Imperialists, that Newfoundland and Canada, which at the time of the Great War were separate self-governing Dominions of the British Empire, were somehow forged into something stronger in the heat of these battles (Canada eventually became an essentially independent nation in 1931, and Newfoundland finally formally united with it in 1949). The same thing has been said of Australia and New Zealand, which were also Dominions of the British Empire, in regard to Gallipoli and the Somme. And also of the Union of South Africa, which had secured its measure of autonomy after the Boer War of 1899-1902, in regard to Delville Wood on the Somme.

There are cemeteries scattered throughout the area of the battlefields, immaculately maintained by the body nowadays known as the Commonwealth War Graves Commission (22; 41). Some are small and intimate, others vast and overwhelming; all, in their own ways, intensely moving.

On the Somme, just south of the South African National Memorial in Delville Wood are the Caterpillar Valley and Delville Wood Cemeteries, where are buried many men of the 24th Battalion who were killed in the unsuccessful attack on the German trenches east of Waterlot Farm on July 30th, 1916, in

127

the Second Phase of the "Somme" Offensive (*Figure 24*). Just north of the Newfoundland Memorial Park in Beaumont-Hamel are the Redan Ridge, Munich Trench, and Serre Road Cemeteries, where lie men of the 24th Battalion killed in the successful attack on Beaumont-Hamel on November 13th, 1916, in the Third Phase (*Figure 25*). And at the high point of Thiepval is Sir Edwin Lutyens's Thiepval Memorial, the harrowing Memorial to the Missing of the Somme, the 72 195 missing British and Empire soldiers who have no known grave (*Figure 26*; see also 28; 48). Among the "Missing" commemorated on the Thiepval Memorial is the previously mentioned Private Sidney Richard Worger of the 24th Battalion, who is commemorated on Pier/Face 8C (*Figure 27*). Also among them are 117 other men from the 24th Battalion, and a total of 2 484 from the Royal Fusiliers, who are commemorated on Pier/Faces 8C, 9A and 16A (48). Thiepval is the largest of the British memorials, bearing the largest number of names, and was the last to be completed, in 1932.

At Arras is Lutyen's Arras Memorial to the 34 808 soldiers who went missing in the Arras sector during the Great War, many of them during the Battles of Arras in April-May, 1917, some of them from the 24th Battalion (22; 41). Nearby are Bois-Carre Cemetery, near Thelus, and Orchard Dump Cemetery, near Arleux-en-Gohelle, where are buried more men of the 24th Battalion, killed in the unsuccessful attacks directed towards Oppy in April, 1917.

Lest we forget, also at Arras is a small memorial to the Chinese Labour Corps, 140 000 of whom were deployed in the service of the Allies not only during the Great War but also in its aftermath, when they were tasked with filling in the thousands of miles of trenches, and clearing the battlefields of dead bodies and debris, including dangerous unexploded ordnance (61). A total of 2 500 men from the Chinese Labour Corps died during the course of their deployment, alongside some 1 500 men from the Indian Labour Corps. Ten miles south of Arras is the Ayette Indian and Chinese Cemetery, where sixty-four men, mainly of the Indian and Chinese Labour Corps, are buried (22; 41).

At Louverval, midway between Bapaume and Cambrai, is Harold Charlton Bradshaw's Cambrai Memorial to the 7 120 who went missing during the Battle of Cambrai in November-December, 1917, among them men from the 23rd and 24th Battalions.

At Havrincourt, a small village south-west of Cambrai, is Lowrie Cemetery (*Figure 28*). This cemetery is located no more than a matter of yards from the spot where my maternal grandfather, Private Charles Reuben Clements (CRC), was wounded on September 12th, 1918, in the Battle of Havrincourt, the first of the Battles of the Hindenburg Line (see Appendix 2). Here is buried the previously mentioned Private John Robert Warriner of the 24th Battalion, who was killed on September 13th, 1918, almost certainly in the same operation at Havrincourt in which CRC had been wounded on the previous day (*Figure 29*; see also Appendix 1). The two men had served together for almost three years, and would have known one another well.

And at Bailleulval, south-west of Arras, is Bac du Sud Cemetery (*Figure 30*), on the site of No. 46 Casualty Clearing Station, where CRC was treated for his wounds on September 12th-13th, 1918 (59). Here lies Private Arthur Anelay of the 24th Battalion, aged only eighteen, who died on September 13th, 1918, of wounds sustained on 10th (*Figure 31;* see also Appendix 1). Also Private William Albert Jarrett of the 23rd Battalion, aged nineteen, who died on September 12th, 1918 (*Figure 32*).

We will remember them.

Figure 1 - The Tower of London from Tower Hill. Image: Author. This view has changed little since the seventeenth century.

Figure 2 - The Royal Fusiliers War Memorial, Holborn, City of London. Image: Author.

Figure 3 - The Church of St Sepulchre-without-Newgate (Holy Sepulchre London), City of London. Image: Author. The railings are painted in the regimental colours of blue, crimson and gold.

Figure 4 - The Royal Fusiliers Memorial Chapel in the Church of St Sepulchre-without-Newgate (Holy Sepulchre London), City of London. Image: Author. Note the Roll of Honour in the foreground, the colours in the middle ground, and the stained-glass window in the background.

Figure 5 - Detail of the stained-glass window in the Royal Fusiliers Memorial Chapel. Image: Author. Note the Royal Fusilier in full dress uniform in front of the Tower of London. Note also the ornamental border recording the Regiment's Great War battle honours, including the Somme, Arras, Cambrai, and the Hindenburg Line.

Figure 6 - King's Colours in the Royal Fusiliers Memorial Chapel. Image: Author. From left to right: 1st Battalion; 2nd Battalion; 23rd (1st Sportsmen's) Battalion; 8th Battalion; 19th (2nd Public Schools') Battalion; 25th (Frontiersmen's) Battalion; 34th (Labour) Battalion. The 24th (2nd Sportsmen's) Battalion's colours are kept in the Association Room in the Regimental Headquarters in the Tower of London, which is not open to the public.

Figure 7 - Mrs Emma Pauline Cunliffe-Owen, the founder of the Sportsmen's Battalions. Image: www.inspirationalwomenofww1.blogspot.com. Mrs Cunliffe-Owen had been an active sportswoman in her youth, but later in life came to suffer from rheumatoid arthritis, and often had to resort to travelling in a wheelchair. Also in this picture of her are, to her left, her husband, Mr Edward Cunliffe-Owen, and to her right, her son, Lt Alexander Robert Cunliffe-Owen, of the 24th Battalion.

The 2nd Sportsmen's Battalion marching across Trafalgar-square on their way to Liverpool-street to entrain for Harehall Camp near Romford.

Figure 8 - The 24ᵗʰ Battalion marching through Trafalgar Square on the way from Horse Guards' Parade in Whitehall to Liverpool Street Station on March 17ᵗʰ, 1915. Image: *Birmingham Gazette.*

Figure 9 - The memorial marking the site of the former Hare Hall Camp, Romford. Image: Author. The "Artists' Rifles" Officers' Training Corps was based at the camp from 1915-1919. The other faces of the memorial feature poems by Wilfred Owen and Edward Thomas, and a painting by John Nash, all of whom served with the "Artists' Rifles" (both Owen and Thomas were killed in action). The site of the camp is currently occupied by the Royal Liberty School.

Figure 10 - A squad of the 24ᵗʰ Battalion being instructed in musketry at Hare Hall Camp, near Romford, in 1915. Image: *The Illustrated War News*, issue dated August 4ᵗʰ, 1915. The men are awaiting the order, "Rapid fire".

Figure 11 - Regimental Serjeant-Major E.M.S. Morris instructing in musketry at Camp in 1915. Image: *The Illustrated War News*, issue dated August 4ᵗʰ, 1915.

Figure 12 - The Regimental Band at Camp in 1915. Image: *The Illustrated War News,* issue dated August 4th, 1915.

Figure 13 - A typical Camp hut in 1915. Image: *The Illustrated War News,* issue dated August 4th, 1915.

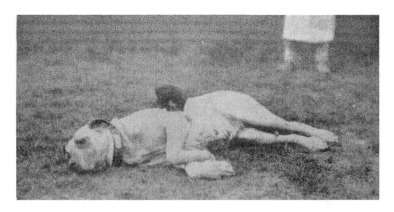

Figure 14 - Everyday life at Camp in 1915. Image: *The Illustrated War News,* issue dated August 4th, 1915. The large white dog was called "Sally", and the small black puppy, "Nell".

Figure 15 - The 24th Battalion's Officers in 1915. Image: *The Illustrated War News,* issue dated August 4th, 1915. Back row, left to right: 2nd Lt. Smith, 2nd Lt. Durand, 2nd Lt. Montgomery, Lt. Green, Lt. Perkins, Lt. Templeman, Lt. Enderby, Lt. Kay. Middle row, left to right: Capt. Franks, Capt. Browne, Major Enderby, Col. Paget, Major Elwell, Capt. McRedmond, Capt. Bagot. Front row: 2nd Lt. Blaauw, 2nd Lt. Edwards, Lt. Shaw, Lt. Cunliffe-Owen.

Figure 16 - The 24th Battalion's Non-Commissioned Officers in 1915. Image: *The Illustrated War News*, issue dated August 4th, 1915. Back row (standing), left to right: Sjts. Clair, Day, Remnant, Lce-Sjt. Barr-Hamilton, Sjts. Tottie, Burton, Dent, Ellis, Samuels, Little, Wellington. Second row from back (standing): Sjts. Artis, Whitfield, Punchard, Orderly-Room Sjt. Challenger, Sjts. Fairburn, Wakefield, Baines, Morris, Lce-Sjt. Mason, Sjts. Wilson, Harvey. Middle row (standing), left to right: Sjt. Essex, Co. Sjt.-Major Finch, Sjts. Evans, Hurst, Denton, Cox, Hadaway, Lce-Sjt. Bedbrooke, Sjts. Adams, Heaton. Second row from front (seated), left to right: Co. Q.M.S. Drew, Co. Q.M.S. Stuart, Co. Sjt.-Major Towler, Regt. Sjt.-Major Morris, Major Enderby, Regt. Q.M.S. Axten, Co. Sjt.-Major Harmer, Co. Q.M.S. Cronin, Co. Q.M.S. Scobell. Front row (seated), left to right: Co. Q.M.S. Busby, Sjt. Shields, Lce-Sjt. Brock, Sjt. May, Provost Sjt. Hayward, Pioneer Sjt. Watson. Sjt. Adams played football for Fulham; Sjt. Evans, for Exeter City.

Figure 17 - Reconstructed fire-step, Vimy Ridge. Image: Author. The cordon and red flag beyond the parapet indicate the still-present danger of unexploded past ordnance.

Figure 18 – Reconstructed trench, Vimy Ridge. Image: Author.

Private Ernest Jackson
Royal Fusiliers
7th November 1918
Aged 32

www.findagrave.com.

Figure 20 - Preserved section of battlefield, Newfoundland Memorial Park, Beaumont-Hamel, from the air. Image: www.newfoundlandonthesomme.com. The British front lines are to be seen to the left of the image (south), and the German front lines to the right (north), with a shell-cratered "No Man's Land" in between. The so-called "Danger Tree" in "No Man's Land" marks the approximate limit of the advance of the Newfoundland Regiment on the first day of the Battle of the Somme, July 1st, 1916. This particular unit was almost wiped out that day, suffering 684 casualties out of a force of 752 (a casualty rate of 91%). The Newfoundlanders are also commemorated on the "Caribou Memorial".

Figure 21 - Preserved section of battlefield, Vimy Memorial Park. Image: Author. At the top of the Ridge is the Canadian National Vimy Memorial, designed by W.S. Allward. Beyond lies the Plain of Flanders and the city of Lens, with its distinctive pyramidal heaps of coal slag.

Figure 22 - Preserved mine crater, Vimy Ridge. Image: Author. My shadow for scale.

Figure 23 - Preserved trench, Vimy Ridge. Image: Author.

Figure 24 - Delville Wood Cemetery, near Longueval. Image: www.cwgc.org.uk (reproduced with permission).

Figure 25 - Serre Road Cemetery No. 2, near Beaumont-Hamel.
Image: www.cwgc.org.uk (reproduced with permission).

Figure 26 - Thiepval Memorial. Image:
www.ww1cemeteries.com.

Figure 27 - Commemoration of Private Sidney Richard Worger, Pier/Face 8C, Thiepval Memorial. Image: www.essexandsuffolkinsurancecompanywarmemorial.wordpress.com.

Figure 28 - Lowrie Cemetery, Havrincourt. Image: Author. On the far side of the embankment lies the Canal du Nord, which effectively formed part of the Hindenburg Line.

Figure 29 - Grave of Private John Robert Warriner, 24th
Battalion, Lowrie Cemetery. Image: Author.

Figure 30 - Bac du Sud Cemetery, near Bailleulval. Image: Author.

Figure 31 - Grave of Private Arthur Anelay, 24th Battalion, Bac du Sud Cemetery. Image: Author.

Figure 32 - Grave of Private William Albert Jarrett, 23rd (1st Sportsmen's) Battalion, Bac du Sud Cemetery. Image: Author.

Figure 33 - 109 Yeldham Road. Image: Author. The adjoining large yard, which extends further round the side of the house than appears in this image, is where CRC's father is believed to have kept his horses and horse-drawn vehicles

Figure 34 - CRC with his mother ("Ma") and his sisters ("Jess" and "Lily"). Image: Author's private collection. Probably taken shortly after CRC's father died in 1913, and possibly on the day of his funeral. CRC is wearing his father's wedding ring on the middle finger of his left hand.

Figure 35 - CRC in army uniform at the beginning of his service. Image: Author's private collection. This photograph was likely taken in a photographer's studio around the time he enlisted on May 30th, 1915.

Figure 36 - CRC in army uniform toward the end of his service.
Image: Author's private collection. This photograph was taken
on August 17th, 1918, while the 24th Battalion was stationed
near Bapaume (around a month before CRC was wounded at
in the Battle of Havrincourt).   Note the three "Overseas
Service Chevrons" on CRC's lower right sleeve, one for each
year of overseas service; and the "Good Conduct Chevron" on
his lower left sleeve. Note also the customary cigarette!

Figure 37 - CRC in army uniform after the war (note the medal ribbons). Image: Author's private collection. CRC's left eye appears to be injured; his expression, haunted – or is that my imagination?

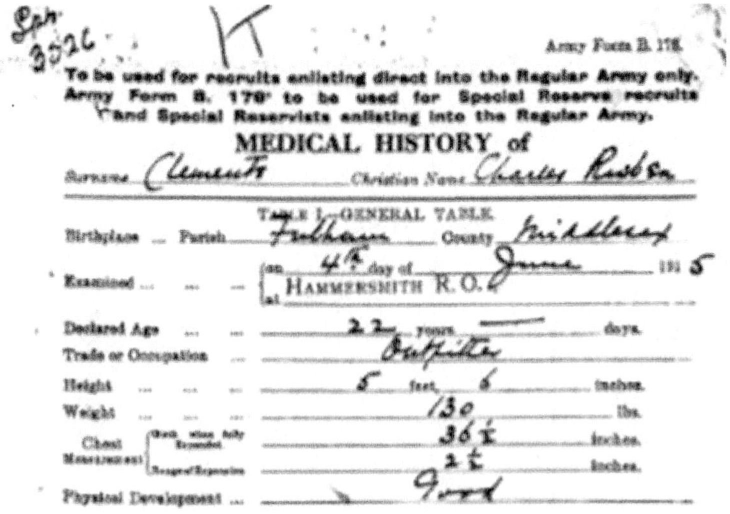

Army Form B. 178.

To be used for recruits enlisting direct into the Regular Army only. Army Form B. 178* to be used for Special Reserve recruits and Special Reservists enlisting into the Regular Army.

MEDICAL HISTORY of

Surname Clements Christian Name Charles Robson

TABLE I.—GENERAL TABLE.

Birthplace — Parish	Fulham County Middlesex
Examined	on 4th day of June 1915 at HAMMERSMITH R.O.
Declared Age	22 years — days.
Trade or Occupation	Outfitter
Height	5 feet 6 inches.
Weight	130 lbs.
Chest Measurement (Girth when fully Expanded)	36½ inches.
Chest Measurement (Range of Expansion)	2½ inches.
Physical Development	Good

Figure 38 - CRC's "Medical History" Form. Image: National Archives.

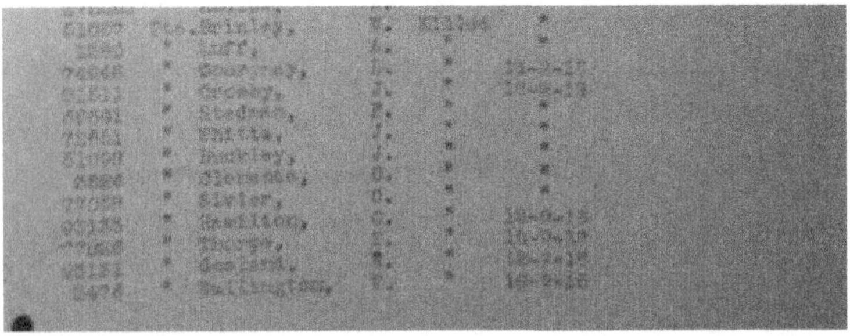

Figure 39 - The exaggerated report of CRC's death in the "Battalion War Diary".

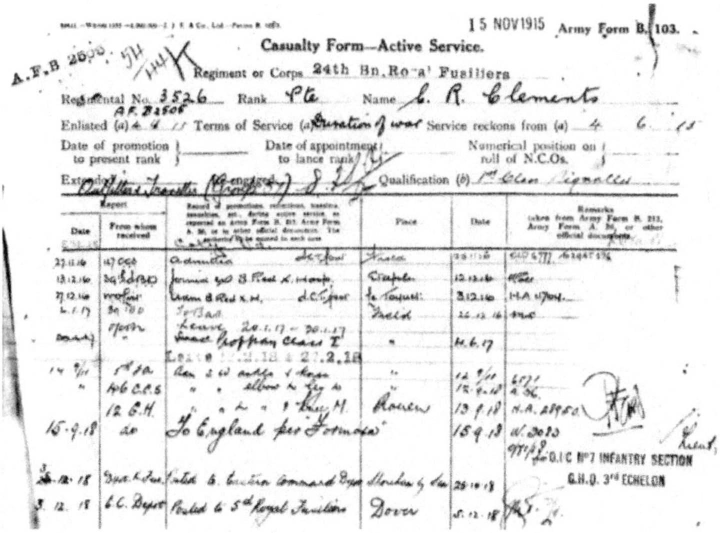

15 NOV 1915   Army Form B. 103.

Casualty Form—Active Service.

Regiment or Corps 24th Bn.Ro~a' Fusiliers

Regimental No. 3526   Rank Pte   Name C. R. Clements

Enlisted (a) 4   Terms of Service (a) Duration of war   Service reckons from (a) 4   6   15

Date of promotion to present rank | Date of appointment to lance rank | Numerical position on roll of N.C.Os. |

Qualification (b) 1st Class Signaller

Date	Report From whom received	Record of promotions, reductions, casualties, etc., during active service, as reported on Army Form B. 213, Army Form A. 36, or in other official documents.	Place	Date	Remarks (when from Army Form B. 213, Army Form A. 36, or other official documents
27.11.16	47 CCS	Admitted	Trieste	28.11.16	
13.12.16	34		Etaples	12.12.16	
7.12.16				3.12.16	
4.1.17	34	To Base	Field	26.12.16	
		Leave 20.1.17 – 30.1.17		14.6.17	
		Passed Class I			
14.9/11				12.9.11	
	46 CCS			12.9.18	
	12 GH		Rouen	13.9.18	
15.9.18	20	To England per Formosa		15.9.18	
26.12.18				26.10.18	O.I.C N°7 INFANTRY SECTION G.H.Q. 3rd ECHELON
3.12.18	6 C. Depot	Posted to 5th Royal Fusiliers	Dover	5.12.18	

Figure 40 - CRC's "Casualty Form – Active Service". Image: National Archives. From this, it is clear that CRC had been wounded on September 12th, and treated at No. 46 C.C.S. (Casualty Clearing Station) in Bac du Sud, near Bailleulval on 12th-13th, and at No. 12 G.H. (General Hospital) in Rouen, in Normandy on 13th, before being repatriated to the U.K. on 15th. Bac du Sud Cemetery stands on the site of No. 46 Casualty Clearing Station today.

Figure 41 - His Majesty's Hospital Ship "Formosa". Image: Postcard. The "Formosa" was a passenger-*cum*-cargo steamship built on Clydeside in 1906. She was converted for use as a 417-berth hospital ship in 1915, and remained in use as such until 1919. She was broken up in 1929.

Figure 42 - CRC's shop front at 180 South Ealing Road. Image: Author's private collection.

Figyre 43 - CRC in the back garden at 180 South Ealing Road.
Image: Author's private collection.

Figure 44 - Ealing Wednesday Football Club (1). Image:
Author's private collection. The occasion is clearly that of a
cup final. It is not known for certain which, although the cup –
in the centre - appears to be the same as that displayed on the
right of *Text-Figure 97*, which is either the Ealing Hospital Cup
or the Roose Francis Cup. The location is also unknown, but
could be Wimbledon's old ground at Plough Lane, featuring
the south stand acquired from Clapton Orient in 1923. CRC is
seated in the front row, fifth from the left. His friend Herbert
Peckham is seated next to him in the front row, middle; T.
Wallis in the front row, fifth from the right; E.J. Thrower in the
front row, third from the right; and Club President Mr G.
Turton, in the middle row, third from the right.

Figure 45 - Ealing Wednesday Football Club (2). Image: Author's private collection. Taken at the end of the 1923-24 season. Back row (standing), left to right: G.H. Goldsworthy (Trainer), G. Coster, E.J. Thrower, J.G. White. Middle row (standing), left to right: Mr G. Turton (President), S.J. Rayner, H. Ross, T. Wallis (Captain), Mr H. Lyon (Patron). Front row (seated), left to right: H. Evans, H.L. Peckham, L. Sinden, C.R. Clements, W.H. Lacey. Based on the legible parts of the inscriptions, the trophy on the left is the Kingston and District Wednesday Football League Cup; and the one second from the left, the Philanthropic Cup. The one in the centre is the Harrow Charity Shield. By a process of elimination, the two on the on the right must be the Ealing Hospital Cup and the Roose Francis Cup, but it is not known which is which.

Figure 46 - CRC and Gladys Mabel Millard on their wedding day in 1921. Image: Author's private collection. CRC's widowed mother Jessie Clements is standing to the right; his widowed mother-in-law Sarah Ann Millard, to the left. His best man Archie Bannister is seated to the right.

Figure 47 - CRC's mother-in-law Sarah Ann Millard in her Voluntary Aid Detachment nurse's uniform. Image: Author's private collection. The dog was called "Trixie".

Figure 48 - CRC's daughter Peggy Anne Clements and Emrys Wynn Jones's wedding day in 1954. Image: Author's private collection. EWJ is wearing his army dress uniform (he did his compulsory National Service in the Royal Engineers). His father Francis Wynn Jones is standing to the left, with his wife next to him. CRC is standing third from the right, with his wife "Mabs" next to him.

Figure 49 - Able-Bodied Seaman Francis Wynn Jones. Image:
Author's private collection. The insignia on the uniform he is
wearing are those of the Royal Marine Artillery. The picture
was likely taken in a photographer's studio around the time he
enlisted.

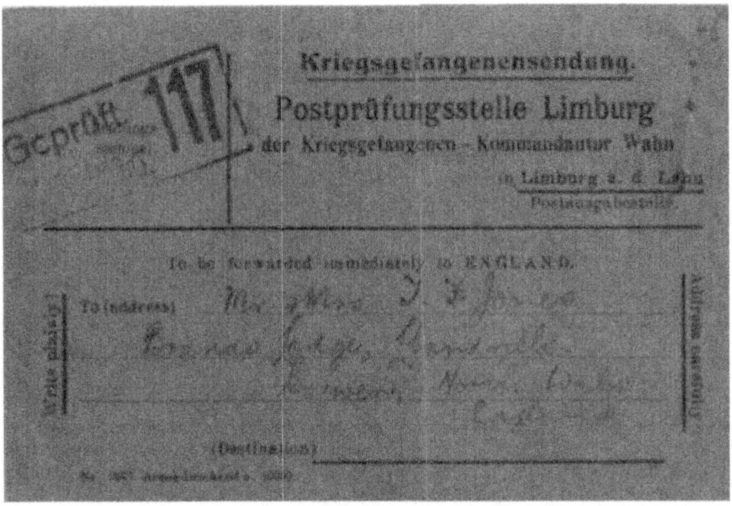

Geprüft 117

Kriegsgefangenensendung.

Postprüfungsstelle Limburg

der Kriegsgefangenen-Kommandantur Wahn

in Limburg a. d. Lahn

Postausgabestelle

To be forwarded immediately to ENGLAND.

Write plainly

To (address)

(Destination)

Address carefully

Figure 50 - Front of postcard from FWJ to his parents informing them that he was a Prisoner-of-War. Image: Author's private collection.

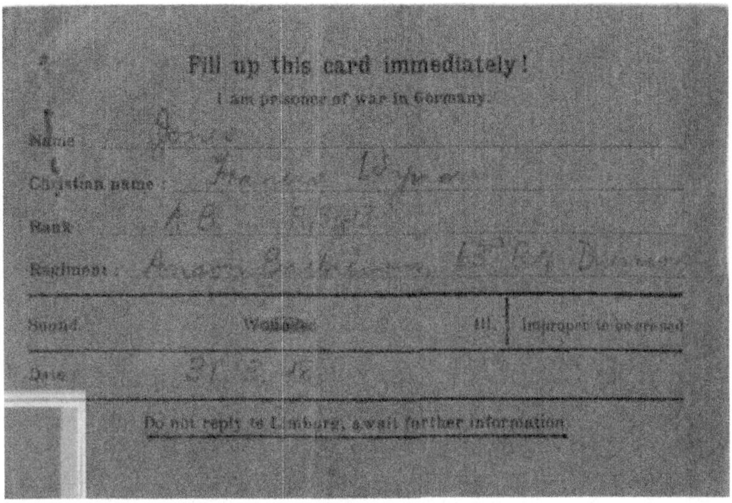

Fill up this card immediately!

I am prisoner of war in Germany.

Name:

Christian name:

Rank:

Regiment:

Sound | Wounded | Ill. | Improper to be erased

Date:

Do not reply to Limburg, await further information.

Figure 51 - Back of postcard. Image: Author's private collection.

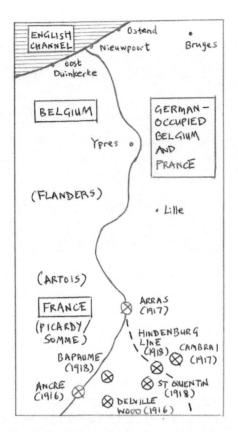

Map 1 - The British Sector of the Western Front. Solid line indicates approximate position of front line before Allied "Somme" Offensive of 1916. Dashed line indicates approximate position of front line after German withdrawal to Hindenburg Line in 1917. Subsequent movements associated with Allied Offensives of 1917, German "Spring" Offensive of spring-early summer, 1918, and Allied "Hundred Days" Offensive of late summer and autumn, 1918, omitted for clarity. Crossed swords indicate approximate sites of significant battles involving the 24th Battalion, the Royal Fusiliers. The length of this part of the front was approximately one hundred miles.

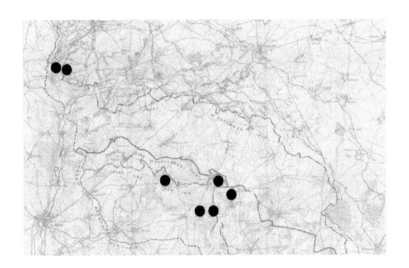

Map 2 - 24th Battalion Positions and Movements, July 1st-November 18th (Battles of the Somme). Base map reproduced with the permission of the National Library of Scotland. Showing successive battle-fronts as at July 1st (beginning of First Phase), July 17th (end of First Phase), September 17th (end of Second Phase), and November 30th (end of Third Phase). British trenches to the left; German ones to the right. Lower row of dots indicates 24th Battalion positions during Second Phase (see also *Maps 3-4*); upper row, those held during Third Phase (see also *Maps 5-6*). The maximum advance between July 1st and November 18th was approximately seven miles.

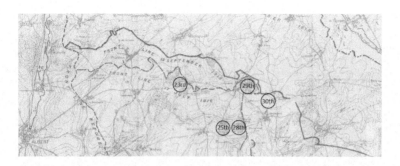

Map 3 - 24th Battalion Positions and Movements, July 23rd-31st, 1916 (Battle of Delville Wood). Base map reproduced with the permission of the National Library of Scotland. Showing battle fronts as at July 17th (and September 13th). British trenches to the left; German ones to the right. On July 23rd-24th, the 24th Battalion was in Happy Valley; on 25th-27th in Bernafay Wood; on 28th in Trones Wood; and on 29th-31st in action in and around Delville Wood (see also *Map 4*).

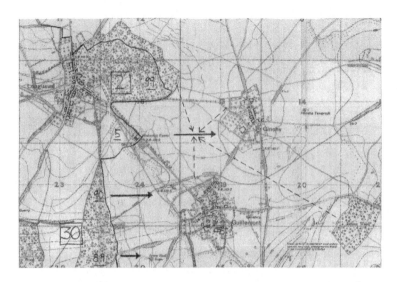

Map 4 - 24th Battalion Positions and Movements, July 30th, 1916 (Attack on Guillemont). Based on a detailed trench map of the time. British trenches to the left; German ones to the right. Arrows indicate direction of British attack (**2** = 2nd Division; <u>5</u> = 5th Brigade). The 24th Battalion's primary objective was the German trench system east of Waterlot Farm. Dashes indicate selected lines of fire from German defensive positions. The side of each numbered square measures one thousand yards.

Map 5 - 24th Battalion Positions and Movements, November 13th-18th, 1916 (Battle of the Ancre). Base map reproduced with the permission of the National Library of Scotland. Showing battle fronts as at November 30th. British trenches to the left; German ones to the right. On November 13th, the 24th Battalion was in action in the Redan sector, between Beaumont-Hamel and Serre (see also *Map 6*).

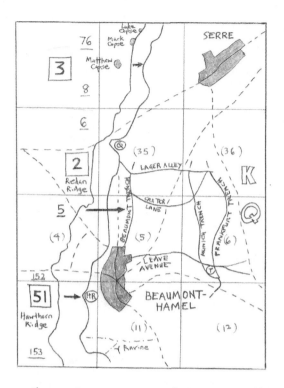

Map 6 - 24th Battalion Positions and Movements, November 13th, 1916 (Attack on Redan Ridge). Simplified from a detailed trench map of the time. British trenches to the left; German ones to the right. Arrows indicate direction of British attack (**2** = 2nd Division; <u>5</u> = 5th Brigade). The 24th Battalion's primary objective was Beaumont Trench. Munich and Frankfurt Trenches were secondary objectives. HR = Hawthorn Redoubt; Q = The Quadrilateral; T = The Triangle. The side of each numbered square measures one thousand yards.

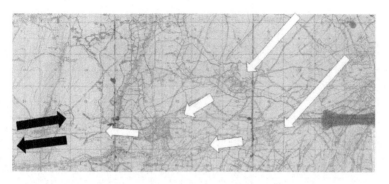

Map 7 - 24th Battalion Positions and Movements, March 21st-23rd, 1918 (First Battles of the Somme, 1918). Base map reproduced with the permission of the National Library of Scotland. Showing battle fronts as at January 3rd. British trenches to the left; German ones to the right. White arrows indicate direction of German attack; black arrows British counter-attack. On March 23rd, the 24th Battalion advanced to Hermies, before being forced to retreat to Bertincourt. The side of each numbered square measures one thousand yards.

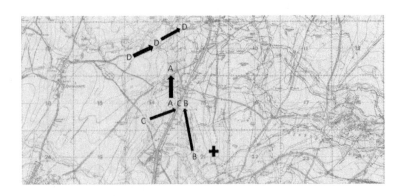

Map 8 - 24th Battalion Positions and Movements, September 11th/12th, 1918 (Battle of Havrincourt). Base map reproduced with the permission of the National Library of Scotland. Showing battle fronts as at September 21st. British trenches to the left; German ones to the right. Arrows indicate directions of attack of A, B, C and D Companies of the 24th Battalion. (+) indicates position of Havrincourt (Lowrie) Cemetery. The side of each numbered square measures one thousand yards.

Plate 1 - Albert Edward Dunn. Image: Flyer from 1906 election campaign.

Plate 3 – Serjeant Arthur Nicholas Evans. Image: www.grecianarchive.exeter.ac.uk.

Plate 5 - Private C.P. McGahey. Image: Cover of *Cheerful Charlie – A Biography of C.P. McGahey.* Note the Essex County Cricket Club cap.

Plate 6 - Frederick Courteney Selous. Image: Cover of *The Lion in South Africa.*

Plate 2 - Corporal Lewis Richard Lewis (left) and Serjeant Adams (right). Image: *Aberdeen Weekly Journal.*

Plate 4 - Private Henry George Purver. Image: www.isleworthww1.co.uk.

Plate 7 - Reginald Alexander John Warneford. Image:
www.ww1playingthegame.org.uk.

Plate 9 - Herbert Henry Raphael. Image: www.ukphotoarchive.org.uk.

Plate 8 - Rev. Frank Edwards. Image: *Hull Daily Mail.*

Plate 10 - Charles Edward Montague. Image: Cover of *A Hind Let Loose.*

Plate 11 - Captain Guy Threlkeld Edwards. Image: www.ww1photos.com.

Plate 15 - Lieutenant David Radcliffe. Image: www.ukphotoarchive.org.uk.

Plate 12 - Serjeant William John Punchard. Image: www.wartimememoriesproject.com.

Plate 16 - Private Denis Stuart Mitchell. Image: www.ukphotoarchive.org.uk.

Plate 17 - Private Edwin Wilfred Wrayford May. Image: www.lustleigh-society.org.uk.

Plate 13 - Second Lieutenant Charles William Stanley Spencer M.C. Image: Cover of published diary. Stanley Spencer, formerly a Private of the 24th Battalion of the Royal Fusiliers, is pictured here in the uniform of a Second Lieutenant of the 3rd Battalion of the West Yorkshire Regiment (he was originally from Sheffield).

Plate 14 - Siegfried Wedgwood Herford (left) with George Herbert Leigh Mallory (right) at Pen-y-Pass, December, 1913. Image: www.ukclimbing.com. Mallory survived the Great War, during which he served in the Royal Garrison Artillery. His brother Trafford served in the Royal Flying Corps in the First World War, and in the Royal Air Force in the Second.

Plate 18 - Second Lieutenant Francis Stanley Mott. Image: www.reigategrammar.org.

Plate 19 - Private Cecil Dobie Murray White. Image: www.mugs61.co.uk.

Plate 20 - Private Frederick Noel Bond. Image: www.ww1photos.com.

Plate 21 Private George Harrap Fish. Image: www.culturepics.org.

Plate 22 - Private David Bruce McKechnie. Image: www.heritage.saintandrews.org.au.

Plate 23 - Private Randolph Spencer Loibl. Image: www.ww1cemeteries.com.

Plate 24 - Corporal Robert Stuart Hawcridge. Image: www.legaciesofwar.leeds.ac.uk.

Plate 25 - Captain Cecil Stanley Meares. Image: *Shropshire Star.*

Plate 26 - Private Arthur Alexander Stokes. Image: BBC.

Plate 27 - Second Lieutenant Francis John Eathorne. Image: University of Reading Special Collections.

Plate 28 - Lance-Corporal William Austin McCready. Image: www.northernbankwarmemorials. blogspot.com.

Plate 29 - Hylton Reginald Cleaver (in his Second World War uniform) Image: www.heartheboatsing.com

Plate 30 - Private Louis Lawrent D'Abadie. Image: www.brentfordfc.com.

Plate 31 - David Louis Clemetson. Image: www.trinitycollegelibrarycambridge.wordpress.com. This photograph shows Clemetson in his rowing gear at the "Lent Bumps" in Cambridge in February, 1914, at which he rowed in Trinity College's "Rugger Boat". He went on to enlist in the 23rd (2nd Sportsmen's) Battalion later that same year.

Plate 32 - *Private Oswald Baron.*
Image: www.ww1photos.com.

Plate 33- Private Bernard Warth. Image:
www.ukphotoarchive.org.uk.

Plate 34 - Private Eric Montagu.
Image: *Daily Mirror.*

Plate 35 - Second Lieutenant Andrew William Burnham. Image: *Buckinghamshire Herald.*

Plate 36 - Private Horace George Dunham. Image: www.worldwar1.luton.com.

Plate 37 - Private Joseph Edmund Alexander Anderson. Image: www.ww1photos.com.

Plate 38 - Private William John Bell. Image: www.ww1cemeteries.com.

Plate 39 - Private Charles Frederick Brinklow. Image: Imperial War Museum (reproduced with permission).

Plate 40 - Private Francis Robert Clayton. Image: www.cornwallfhs.com.

Plate 41 - Private Edward Minty Miller. Image: Imperial War Museum (reproduced with permission)

Plate 42 - Private Yorke Smith
Image: www.oldbarrovians.org.

Plate 43 - Private Laurence John Francis Rhydding Ridding.
Image: www.ww1photos.com.

Plate 44 - Second Lieutenant Harry Daft. Image:
www.nottinghamshire.gov.uk.

Plate 45 - Private John Basil Taylor. Image:
www.ukphotoarchive.org.uk.

Plate 48 - Private Arthur Thomas Collins. Image: www.wartimememoriesproject.com.

Plate 46 - Second Lieutenant Cyril Francis Stafford. Image: www.ww1photos.com.

Plate 50 - Private Frank Allan Urry. Image: www.ukphotoarchive.org.uk.

Plate 49 - Private James George Simco. Image: www.ukphotoarchive.org.uk.

Plate 47 - Lance-Corporal John Henry Bright Millar. Image: www.padstowmuseum.co.uk.

Plate 51 - Second Lieutenant Douglas Maurice Jacques Ullman. Image: www.ww1photos.com.

Plate 52 - Private Malcolm Cedric Alston. Image: www.findagrave.com.

Plate 54 – Stanley Ferns Jeffcoat. Image: www.britishempire.co.uk.

Plate 53 - Private Robert Wishart Barrowman. Image: www.ww1photos.com.

Plate 55 - Henry John Hayes. Image:
www.nottinghamshire.gov.uk.

Plate 56 - Private William John Black. Image: www.newmp.org.uk.

Plate 57 - Private Charles Sidney Ralph. Image: www.ww1photos.com.

Plate 58 - Private Richard Haynes Nelson Mintorn. Image: www.harrowschool-ww1.co.uk.

Plate 59 - Corporal Felix Grugan. Image: www.durhamatwar.org.uk.

Plate 60 – Lance-Corporal John Arthur Boote. Image: www.ww1photos.com.

Plate 61 - Private Arthur Bailey. Image: www.cpgw.org.uk.

Plate 62 - Lance-Corporal William John Fitton. Image: www.nlwmemorial.tripod.com.

Plate 63 - Second Lieutenant Edward Albert Newland. Image: www.masonicgreatwarproject.org.uk.

APPENDIX 1 –
BIOGRAPHICAL SKETCHES
OF MEN FROM THE 24th
BATTALION, THE ROYAL
FUSILIERS

Serjeant Adams played professional football for Southend United and Fulham before enlisting in the 24th Battalion. He featured in a photograph captioned "Well-Known Footballers in the Sportsman's Battalion" in the *Aberdeen Weekly Journal* in March, 1915. Alongside him in the photograph was Corporal Lewis Richard Lewis (see below).

Private Malcolm Cedric Alston was born in San Fernando in Trinidad, the son of J.W. Alston, Esq., and his wife. He later emigrated to Canada, and on the outbreak of the Great War returned to the "Mother Country" to enlist in the Army, at Chislehurst in Kent.

Corporal George Alvey was born in Blackwell in Worcestershire, and enlisted in Mansfield in Nottinghamshire.

Private Frank Ambrose was born in Castle Hedingham in Essex, the son of Mr & Mrs C. Ambrose. He enlisted in Warley Green, also in Essex.

Private Joseph Edmund Alexander Anderson was born in Lerwick in Shetland, the son of John Bannatyne and his wife Minnie Jane, *nee* Boyd. He was educated at the University of Edinburgh, where he read Law, and went on to be employed as a Law Agent. He enlisted in Edinburgh.

Private Arthur Anelay was born in 1899 in Kingston-upon-Hull in the East Riding of Yorkshire, the son of Arthur Anelay, Senior, and his wife Ann Elizabeth, *nee* Robinson. He also enlisted in Hull.

Serjeant James Matthew Armstrong was born in Anwoth near Gatehouse of Fleet in Kirkcudbrightshire in Scotland in

1875, the fourth son of Andrew Armstrong and his wife Margaret, *nee* Wilson. He was educated at Kirkcudbright Academy. After leaving school, he joined the Army, and served in the Boer War of 1899-1902. At the outbreak of the Great War, he was living in Argentina, and working as a farmer. He enlisted in the 24th Battalion in April, 1915. He stood 6' tall, weighed 12st, and had a dark complexion, with brown hair and grey eyes.

Company Serjeant-Major Alfred Edgar Arrowsmith was born in Crouch End in Middlesex, the son of William Arrowsmith, a wood engraver, and his Emma Jane, *nee* Godden. Before the Great War, he had been educated at Stroud Green Grammar School, and gone on to be employed by a firm of motor manufacturers. He had enlisted in London on January 18th, 1915, and served in France from November 15th of that year. After his death, a comrade wrote, "We, the few pals who are left, shall always reverence him [*sic*]. He was a soldier every inch, and ... never flinched at facing death or any hardships. Before going into action he was always cheery and encouraging, and we who were under him would never considers anything too big to do for him". His obituary recorded that he had received a "Certificate of Merit", signed by Major-General Cecil E. Pereira, the officer-in-command of 2nd Division, for his "conspicuous bravery in the field" on April 13th-14th, 1917, during the Battles of Arras. And that he had been a brilliant footballer in his youth.

Arthur Bailey was born in Skipton in Yorkshire, the son of Thomas Bailey and his wife Sarah Ann, *nee* Myers. At the outbreak of the war, he enlisted in the South Lancashire Regiment, and later transferred to the London Regiment, and in turn to the 24th Battalion, the Royal Fusiliers.

Private James Geddes Baird-Smith was born in Glasgow, the son of John Baird-Smith and his wife. At the outbreak of the Great War, he was living in Glasgow, and working as a Chartered Accountant. He enlisted in the 24th Battalion in London.

Private Alfred Thomas Baker was born in Putney in Surrey, the son of Mr & Mrs S.E. Baker. He enlisted in Fulham in Middlesex.

Captain William Herbert Bambridge was the only son of William Samuel and Louisa Maria Bambridge of Marlborough in Wiltshire. Before the war, he had been educated at Marlborough College (a public school), and had then briefly emigrated to British Columbia in Canada to work as a farmer. In 1910, he had returned to England to study at the Royal Academy of Music in London. It seems that he had been a fine baritone, and had performed in musical comedies as part of George Edwardes's theatrical company at the Adelphi. He had also been a "fairly good bat", and had played cricket for Marlborough College and Wiltshire, and been a member of the M.C.C. He is commemorated on the Great War Honours Board at Lord's cricket ground, the home of the M.C.C.

Harold Victor Barnes was born in Plymouth in Devon. He enlisted as a Private soldier in the 24th Battalion also in Plymouth. His Army Service Number, 2027, indicates that he did so sometime between November 26th-December 3rd, 1914.

Second Lieutenant Vincent Kendall Barnes was the eldest son of Mr & Mrs H. Kendall Barnes of Orpington in Kent. He had been gazetted on September 14th, 1915.

Private Oswald Baron was born in the Norwich in Norfolk, the son of Isidore and Emelie Baron. He enlisted in Manchester.

Private Robert Wishart Barrowman was born in Shawlands in Glasgow, the son of David and Christina Barrowman. He enlisted in Glasgow.

Private Thomas John Batchelor was born in Sittingbourne in Kent, and enlisted in Hounslow in Middlesex.

Private Frederick William Bates was born in Marylebone in the County of London, and enlisted in Paddington.

Lance-Corporal William Albert Batrick was born in the Metropolitan Borough of Camberwell in London, the son of Mr & Mrs William Batrick. He enlisted in London.

Lance-Corporal Beard was born in Devizes in Wiltshire. At the outbreak of the Great War, he was living in Hanwell in Middlesex. He enlisted in London.

Private William Stewart Becher was born in Skibbereen in Co. Cork in Ireland, the son of Michael and Mary. At the outbreak of the war, he was living with his wife Annie Becher in Randalstown in Co. Antrim, and working as a Civil Engineer. He enlisted in Aberdare in South Wales.

Serjeant Duncan Harry Bedbrook was born in Wimbledon in Surrey, the son of Mr & Mrs Rose C. Bedbrook. At the outbreak of the war, he was living in Richmond. He enlisted in London.

Private William John Bell was born in Kingswear in Devon, the son of John Amos and Sarah Elizabeth Bell. At the outbreak of the war, he was living in Dartmouth. He enlisted in Exeter.

William's younger brother, Cyril Bell, was also in the 24th Battalion, and their consecutive service numbers - 3129 and 3130 – indicate that they enlisted together, sometime between February 10th and March 6th, 1915. Cyril survived the war.

Lance-Corporal A. Leonard Benn was born in Retford in Nottinghamshire. At the outbreak of the war, he was living in Worksop, also in Nottinghamshire, with his wife Mrs Benn, *nee* Stringfellow. The couple had two children together. A well-known footballer in local circles, Leonard enlisted in the 2nd Sportsmen's Battalion in Nottingham. He was awarded a Military Medal in 1918 for crawling across No Man's Land, under fire, to rescue a wounded officer.

William Bentley was originally from Rossendale in rural Lancashire. At the outbreak of the Great War, he enlisted in one or other of the Universities and Public Schools Battalions, the Royal Fusiliers, as a Private soldier (these were 18th, 19th, 20th and 21st Battalions, of which the 18th, 19th and 21st were disbanded in April, 1916). Later, he joined the 24th (2nd Sportsmen's) Battalion as a Lance-Corporal, and a specialist Tunneller, in which role the small stature that earned him the nickname "Wee Willie" was a great advantage. He was awarded a Military Medal on March 23rd, 1918, and either on this or on a separate occasion, reputedly saved the life of my maternal grandfather, Private Charles Reuben Clements, also of the 24th Battalion (see section on "The First Battles of the Somme, 1918 ... " above; see also Appendix 2 below). Both men survived the war, and remained the best of friends ever afterwards. Having studied for his accountancy examinations while in the trenches, Bentley eventually went on to become the Borough Treasurer for Shoreditch. I still remember him as "Uncle Billy", a tiny, kindly old man who, with his wife, "Auntie Alice", would send me 13/4d and my sister 6/8d for Christmas.

Private Percival Biddlecombe was born in Southampton in Hampshire, the son of Mr & Mrs Gertrude Biddlecombe. At the outbreak of the war, he was living in Gravesend in Kent, where he also enlisted.

Private Percy Bishop was born in Torquay in Devon. Upon the outbreak of the Great War, he enlisted in Exeter.

Second Lieutenant Henry Thomas Gillman Blaauw was born in Newick in Sussex in 1875, the son of Thomas St Leger Blaauw and his wife Fanny Alice, *nee* Bigge. Before the war, he was educated at Christ Church, Oxford; and in 1912 married Mary Verner Anderson, the couple going on to have a daughter, Margaret Esme. He survived the war, despite losing his right leg below the knee. He died in Lewes in Sussex in 1949.

William John Black was born in Tweedmouth in Berwickshire in 1880, the fifth son of George and Margaret Black. He received his primary and secondary education at Berwick School and Berwick Academy. He then went on to study at the Edinburgh School of Pharmacy, and to enter employment as a pharmacist. He was a member of Berwick Rowing Club and Berwick Golf Club. Upon the outbreak of the Great War, he enlisted as a Private soldier in the 24th (2nd Sportsmen's) Battalion in Berwick in April, 1915. At the time of his death in November, 1917, he was serving with the 9th Battalion.

Frederick Noel Bond was born in Swadlincote in Derbyshire in 1897, the second son of the Rev. Kenneth Herbert Bond and his wife Emma Louisa, *nee* Baker. He received his secondary education at Chesterfield Grammar School, where, according to the school magazine, he was "perhaps the most popular boy throughout the whole school" and "one of the most thorough sportsmen", excelling at cricket and football. He enlisted as a Private soldier in the 2nd Sportsmen's Battalion in Chesterfield on March 15th, 1915, which was his eighteenth birthday. He was killed in the Battle of Delville Wood on July 28th, 1916. According to his obituary in the *Derbyshire Courier*, he had been expecting a commission at the time of his death, "the necessary documents having been sent to the proper quarters". His parents received the news of his death in the form of a letter from Captain W.C. Green, and which read in part as follows, "I regret to inform you that your son ... is missing. A shell burst in the midst of our company well behind our lines, and when the roll was called your son was among those who did not answer, and I feel there is little or no hope of his being found alive".

Lance-Corporal John Arthur Boote was born in Hornsey in Middlesex, the son of John Henry and Edith May Boote. He enlisted in Mill Hill.

Lance-Corporal John Allen Bowen, whose real name was John William Wheeler, was born in Eltham in Kent, the son of John and Agusta Wheeler. At the outbreak of the war, he had been living with his wife Ellen Wheeler in the Royal Albert Docks. He had enlisted in London.

Edward Bowes was born in Gleaston in the Furness Peninsula in what was Lancashire and is now Cumbria. At the outbreak of the war, he enlisted as a Private soldier in the 24th Battalion in Ulverston.

Lieutenant Frederick Sidney Bracey was the husband of Kate Bracey of Colchester in Essex.

Private Cyril Christopher David Bradberry was born in Longton, the son of the Rev. Thomas Christopher and Edith Alice Bradberry. At the outbreak of the war, he was living in Castle Carrock, and enlisted in Brampton. According to his obituary, "he died bravely fighting for King, Home and Country".

Charles Frederick Ghost was born in Hemel Hempstead in 1890, the illegitimate son of Emily Ghost. He came to be known as Brinklow when his mother married Frederick Brinklow in 1893. At the outbreak of the war, Charles was living in Hemel Hempstead, and working as a labourer. He enlisted as a Private soldier in the 24th Battalion in Watford in April, 1915, and married Mary Ann Horne in the July of the same year.

Private Harry Brown was born in Holmfirth near Huddersfield in Yorkshire, the son of Frederick and Ruth

Brown. He went to school in Holmfirth and Woodhouse. He was a porter in a paper warehouse before he joined the Army. He enlisted in the Northumberland Fusiliers in 1917, before transferring to the 24th Battalion, the Royal Fusiliers in April, 1918. He was awarded a Military Medal for "bravery and resourcefulness during an attack on an enemy defensive system" on October 1st, 1918. Sadly, he was killed during the attack.

Private George Joseph Burge was born in Stonehouse in Devon, the son of Mr G.A. & Mrs G. Burge. He had enlisted in the 24th Battalion in Plymouth sometime between January 6th and February 10th, 1915.

Andrew William Burnham was born in Aston Clinton in Buckinghamshire in 1887, the fourth and youngest son of James Burnham and his wife Emma, *nee* White. At the outbreak of the war, he had been working as a farmer. He had then enlisted as a Private soldier in the Coldstream Guards. He had been made a Second Lieutenant in the 15th (Reserve) Battalion, the Royal Fusiliers in August, 1916, and at the time of his death in the Battle of the Ancre on November 13th of that year had been on secondment to the 24th Battalion. His parents received the news of his death from Lieutenant Hagan, which read in part as follows, "I am deeply grieved to have to convey to you the sad news of your son's death. He was killed in action about six o'clock on the morning of the attack [on Beaumont Trench]. He was struck by a large piece of shrapnel in the right breast and killed instantly. He was buried on the field of battle where he lay, and a service was read over him ... [the grave was later lost]. He had ... showed great promise as an officer. Being always considerate and extremely popular with his men, who had every confidence on him. I saw him on my way across [No Man's Land], leading his platoon and cheering them on. ... [Y]our son died the most gallant death a soldier desires".

Private Charles William Gammicott Burston was born in Langport in Somerset, the son of William and Clara Burston. At the outbreak of the war, he was living in St Ives in Cornwall. He enlisted in Hayle.

Private George Ernest Burston was born in the Metropolitan Borough of Southwark in London in 1894, the son of Henry Charles Burston and his wife Elizabeth, *nee* Turle. In 1911, according to the census of that year, he was living with his uncle William Isaac Burston and his family in Taunton in Somerset, and working as a clerk in a shirt collar factory. At the outbreak of the war, he was living in Ludlow in Shropshire, and he also enlisted there.

Private Richard James Carpenter was born in Alphington in Devon, the son of Mr. W. and Mrs. Louisa Carpenter. He enlisted in Exeter.

John Alford Cheston was born in Chelsea in 1889, the son of Horace Cheston and his wife. Before the Great War, he was an architect, like his father before him. He was made a Captain in the 24th Battalion in 1917. After the war, he became the Surveyor to the Bridewell and Bethlehem Royal Hospital. He also dedicated a considerable amount of his time to the welfare of his former comrades-in-arms in the 24th Battalion, and was instrumental in organising a number of reunions for them.

Private Frederick Child was born in Canning Town in the East End of London. At the outbreak of the war, he was living in Forest Hill, a little to the south-east. He enlisted in the 24th Battalion in Lewisham.

Lance-Corporal Alfred Frederick Clare was born in Bedford, the son of Alfred Howard and Ann Clare. Before the war, he had been educated at Bedford Modern School. He had also been a member of St Paul's Methodist Church, and was commemorated on a memorial there (the church has since been demolished). He enlisted in Bedford.

Private Sidney Bertram Clarke was born in Plymouth in Devon, and also enlisted there.

Private Francis Robert Clayton was born in Westminster in 1882, the first child and only son of Robert Carr Clayton, a baker, and his wife Rachel, *nee* Sharpe. After leaving school, he was employed as a gardener on a succession of estates in the West Country. At the outbreak of the war, he was working on the Earl of St Germans's estate in Cornwall, and living in St German's with his wife, Eva Elizabeth Mary, *nee* Goodman, who he had married in 1912, one daughter, born in 1913, and another on the way. A keen cricketer, he enlisted in the 24th (2nd Sportsmen's) Battalion in Plymouth in Devon, alongside a number of other estate workers. His Army Service Number, 2926, indicates that he did so sometime between January 6th and February 10th, 1915. He went on to be wounded during the Battle of Delville Wood on July 28th, 1916. He was then reported as "missing" during the Battle of the Ancre on November 13th, 1916. He was later found dead by a soldier from another regiment, who wrote to his widow of his death, and buried him. His grave was then lost.

Hylton Reginald Cleaver was born in Putney in Surrey in 1891. Before the Great War, he was educated at St Paul's, a private school in Hammersmith, and went on to be self employed as a writer of short stories (in the *Ladies' Gazette*, and later in the *Boys' Own Paper*, the *Captain Magazine*, and the *Strand Magazine*). Upon the outbreak of the Great War, he enlisted in the 24th Battalion, the Royal Fusiliers, although he also continued to write even when he was in the trenches. In May, 1917, Corporal Cleaver was made a Second Lieutenant in the Machine Gun Corps. Later, in September, 1918, he was awarded the Military Cross "for conspicuous gallantry and devotion to duty" in holding up a German advance in French Flanders. After the war, he returned to writing, becoming a sports journalist on the *Evening Standard*, and publishing a number of non-fiction books on sporting topics, including *Knights of the Knuckles*, *A History of Rowing*, and *On Horsemanship*, as well as adventure fiction. He also served as a Lieutenant in the Second World War. Hylton Cleaver died in Wandsworth in 1961, leaving a widow, Bettie, *nee* Parsons, a son and a daughter.

Second Lieutenant Gilbert Colin Clifford was born in Brockley in the Metropolitan Borough of Lewisham in London in 1891, and was still living there in 1911, according to the census of that year.

David Allen Cole was born in Twickenham in Middlesex. At the outbreak of the war, he was living in Eltham in Kent. He enlisted as a Private soldier in the 24th Battalion in London.

Private Charles Richard Collier was born in York, and enlisted in Bolsover in Derbyshire.

Private Arthur Thomas Collins was born in Trumpington in Cambridgeshire, and had enlisted in Cambridge, having previously been in the East Kent Regiment.

Second Lieutenant Charles Richard Stewart Coppack was the son of Mr & Mrs F. Stewart Coppack of Catford in the County of London. Before the war, he had been educated at Colfe's School in Lee, and had gone on to be employed at the London County & Westminster Bank.

Charles's brothers Arthur Henry and Frank Victor Coppack were also killed in the war.

Second Lieutenant William John Coppard was the son of George Coppard of Brighton. Before the war, he was a legal clerk.

Private Thomas Cordwell was born in Manchester, the son of Henry Rawson and Amelia Cordwell. Before the war, he had been employed as a clerk in the Manchester & District Banking Company. He had enlisted in Manchester in October, 1915.

Private William John – Willie – Coulson was born in Ardara in Co. Donegal in Ireland, the son of the Rev. John and Jeanie A. Coulson. The family later moved to Bangor in Co. Down. He had enlisted in Dublin.

Private Laurence Edward Courtney was born in Chelmsford in Essex in 1882, the son of Stanley T. and Gertrude Courtney. Before the Great War, he had been living in Beckenham in Kent, and working in the Stock Exchange in London. Upon its outbreak, he had enlisted in the 10th (Stockbrokers') Battalion, the Royal Fusiliers, and later transferred to the 24th (2nd Sportsmen's) Battalion.

Second Lieutenant Ronald Orme Crookes was the son of James and E.J. Crookes of Burton-on-Trent in Staffordshire.

Private Ernest William Cross was born in Sudbury in Suffolk in 1890, one of the nine children of William Cross and his wife Sarah. Before the Great War, he was living in Sudbury, and working as a bricklayer's labourer. He enlisted in the 24th Battalion in Bury St Edmunds. After his death, his Captain wrote to his widow, Harriet "Nellie", *nee* Clarke,

"Throughout the whole day's fighting your husband fought as fearlessly as any man could fight and he died bravely and like a soldier". And his Serjeant, "Ernest was well in front of the advance and was doing splendid work when the first wave took a German trench. As the lads were going up this particular trench a German officer came up from a dugout and shot your husband. He was a good soldier, ever willing and ever cheerful, even in adverse circumstances".

His brother George Cross, of the Suffolk Regiment, was captured by the Germans during the war. He died on December 17th, 1918, a month after the armistice was signed.

Lance-Serjeant Frederick Cross was born in Teignmouth in Devon, and also enlisted there.

Bertram Edward Crosse was born in Greenwich in Kent in 1897, the son of Edward Crosse and his wife Emily, *nee* Hopkins. He married Isabel Lilian Hilditch in Greenwich in 1905. At the outbreak of the Great War, he was living with his wife and their servant in Old Charlton, and working as a clerk in the Stock Exchange. He enlisted in the London Rifle Brigade, part of the London Regiment, as a Private soldier in November, 1914, and saw service with them at Ypres in 1915, on the Somme in 1916, and at Arras in 1917. He later joined the 24th Battalion, the Royal Fusiliers as a Temporary Quarter-Master and Honorary Lieutenant in February, 1918, and went on to serve with them - some of the time as part of the Army of Occupation in Germany - until he was demobilised in April, 1919. He later rejoined the London Rifle Brigade in 1924, and retired in 1935. Shortly after the outbreak of the Second World War, he joined the Local Defence Volunteers – later renamed the Home Guard - in Norwood, in June, 1940. He died in Norwood in 1955.

Alexander Robert Cunliffe-Owen was born in Sonning in Berkshire in August, 1898, the younger of two sons and youngest of four children of Edward Cunliffe-Owen, a barrister, and his wife Emma Pauline Cunliffe-Owen, the founder of the two Sportsmen's Battalions of the Royal Fusiliers - not to mention the godson of the future Queen Alexandra. He made a Temporary Lieutenant in the 24th Battalion in October, 1914, aged sixteen, and later a Second

Lieutenant in the Welsh Guards in March, 1916, aged seventeen. He survived the war, despite being gassed, and died in 1937.

Louis Lawrent D'Abadie was born in Trinidad in 1877, the third son of Sainte-Luce and Ida Francoise. Before the war, he had been educated at St Augustine's Roman Catholic School in Ramsgate in Kent, where he had been a diligent student and a brilliant debater, and had had an aspiration to go on to study the law. He had also been a keen cricketer, and had played football for Brentford Reserves. He had enlisted as a Private soldier in the 2nd Sportsmen's Battalion in London, his Army Service Number, 2276, indicating that he had done so sometime between December 3rd, 1914 and January 6th, 1915. He had gone on to be killed in the Battle of Delville Wood on July 31st, 1916. He had evidently been a devout Catholic, and had attended a Mass and taken Holy Communion in the field on the previous day, which had been a Sunday. A comrade later wrote of him, "Darby (as we always called him) was beloved by all, and every one of us will, deep in our hearts, treasure his memory as one of the finest men and truest comrades we ever had the good fortune to meet".

Lance-Corporal George Seth Dack was born in Repps-with-Bastwick near Martham in Norfolk, the son of Robert George Dack and his wife Anna. At the outbreak of the war, he was living in with his wife Agnes Mary in Hickling, also in Norfolk. The couple had two children together. George enlisted in the 24th Battalion in Norwich.

Harry Daft was born in Nottingham in 1894, the youngest of the five children of John Daft and his wife Elizabeth, *nee* Anderson. He was educated at Nottingham High School, and later at University College, Nottingham, where he was a member of the Officers' Training Corps (like John Henry Hayes, although probably not at the same time). Upon the outbreak of the war, he had enlisted in the 7th Nottinghamshire and Derbyshire Regiment (the Sherwood Foresters) as a Private soldier. He had later been made a Second Lieutenant in the 17th London Regiment, and at the time of his death had been on attachment to the 24th Royal Fusiliers.

Private Albartus Degens was born in Arnhem in the Netherlands in 1883, the son of Albartus Degens Senior and his wife Catharine Maria. At the outbreak of the Great War, he was living in Isleworth in Middlesex, with his wife Helen, *nee* Gray, and their three young children, and working from home as a barber. He enlisted in the 24th Battalion in Hounslow in Middlesex.

Private Frederick William Dey was born in Exmouth in Devon, and upon the outbreak of the war had enlisted in Paignton.

Arthur Gilbert Decimus Dorman was born in Eastbourne in Sussex in 1896, the seventh son and, as his unusual middle name suggests, the tenth child of John Joseph Dorman and his wife Emily Keziah, *nee* Matthews. He was killed in the Battle of the Ancre on November 13th, 1916. At the outbreak of the Great War, he had been living in Heathfield in Sussex. He had enlisted as a Private soldier in the Cameronians (Scottish Rifles) in August, 1915 before transferring to the 24th Battalion, the Royal Fusiliers. He had been a member of a Lewis Gun team.

Coincidentally, Arthur's brother, Acting Captain Anthony Godfrey Dorman, M.C., aged thirty, of the 13th Battalion of the East Yorkshire Regiment, was killed on the same day as he was. Like Arthur, he is commemorated on the Thiepval Memorial.

Private Horace George Dunham was born in Luton in Bedfordshire in 1892, the third son of Alfred Dunham, a baker and confectioner, and his wife Mary. He was killed in the Battle of the Ancre on November 13th, 1916. Before the Great War, he had worked for the family bakery business. He had also been a fast bowler for Luton Town Cricket Club. He had enlisted in the 2nd Sportsmen's Battalion in Luton, his Army Service Number, 2783, indicating that he had done so sometime between January 6th and February 10th, 1915. He had been a machine-gunner.

Albert Edward Dunn was born in Exeter in Devon 1864, the son of William Henry Dunn and his wife. Before the war, he had been educated at Hallam Hall College in Clevedon in Somerset, and had subsequently embarked on a career as a lawyer. He had also been active in politics, and had served as Mayor of Exeter in 1900-01 and 1901-02, and as the Liberal Member of Parliament for Camborne in Cornwall in 1906-10 and 1910-14. Upon the outbreak of the war, he was made a Captain in the 24th Battalion. He survived the war, and afterwards returned to the law and politics, unsuccessfully standing as the Labour candidate for the seat of St Ives in the 1918 and 1923 elections. He died in 1937.

Ralph Anthony Durand was born in Earley in Berkshire in 1876, the son of the Rev. Haviland Durand and his wife Mary, *nee* Hawtrey. When his father died in 1884, his mother moved with the rest of his family to Guernsey, and he was sent to Christ's Hospital, a boarding school in the City of London. He left school in 1892, aged sixteen, and travelled to Australia, where an aunt found temporary work for him on a cattle station, and later in a bank. He then worked in a series of itinerant jobs, as a cook to a party of cattle drovers, as a sheep-shearer, as a labourer on a sugar plantation, as a general labourer, and as a tin-miner, before finding more settled employment as a tutor to two small boys. This gave him a certain amount of free time, which he devoted to writing poetry, short stories, and various articles, one of which was published in the *Sydney Herald*. In 1897, he came into an inheritance, and used the money to enter into business with his brother as a cattle-trader in Salisbury (now Harare in Zimbabwe). He then fought with Thornycrofts' Mounted Light Infantry in the Boer War of 1899-1902, after which he went back to teaching, in Kwa-Zulu Natal. Eventually, he returned to England to concentrate on his writing, publishing the first of his many works of non-fiction in 1909, the first of his many works of fiction in 1911, and *A Handbook to the Poetry of Rudyard Kipling* in 1914. At the outbreak of the Great War, Ralph Anthony Durand enlisted in the Queen's Own West Kent Yeomanry as a Private soldier, and later joined the 24th Battalion, the Royal Fusiliers, as a Second Lieutenant. He was deployed with the battalion to France in November, 1915, and sent home suffering from gallstones a year later. He then transferred to the Royal Guernsey Light Infantry, and returned to France with them, only to be sent home with gallstones for a second time. This time he was not allowed by the Army Medical Board to return to active service, and instead was assigned to a desk job working for Military Intelligence   in Italy, where he saw out the war. He was finally demobilised in September, 1919, whereupon he   returned to writing. In 1929, he became the Librarian at the Priaulx Library in Guernsey. And in 1933, he and his wife Violet Picton-Warlow, who had married in 1904 but had had no children of their own, adopted   Violet's brother's grand-daughter Rosemary Edmondes, who was disabled. In the Second World War, during which Guernsey suffered under Nazi occupation for five years, he was a member of the Guernsey Underground News Service (GUNS), which secretly distributed transcripts of BBC news broadcasts around the island. Ralph Anthony Durand died a matter of months after the end of the war, in December, 1945, still in a malnourished state. Perhaps his most famous work, *Guernsey under German Rule*, was published in 1946.

Private Alfred Baverstock Dykes was born in Chelsea, the son of Alfred Dykes Senior and his wife Harriett. He was educated at the Church School in Headcorn in Kent. At the outbreak of the Great War, he was living in Limpsfield in Surrey with his wife Rhoda, *nee* Webb, who he had married in 1904, and working as a shop assistant. He enlisted in the 24th Battalion in Faversham in Kent.

Francis John Eathorne was   born in Utah in the United States of America in 1892, the son of James Eathorne and his wife Jane Davey, *nee* Uren. It is possible that his father,   who was originally a tin-miner from Cornwall, had emigrated to America during one of the gold rushes of the late nineteenth century. The family had later returned to Cornwall, and Francis had received his primary and secondary education in schools there. He had then gone on to study Primary Education in the University of Reading in Berkshire, where he had also been the Deputy Captain of the Football Club, and an active   member of the Officers'   Training Corps, the Students' Union,   the Students'   Christian Union, and the Debating Society. Immediately before the Great War, he had been employed at Redruth County School in Cornwall. After its outbreak, he had been made a Second Lieutenant in the Royal Fusiliers in May,

1915, and, like Captain Meares (see below), had served with the 19th (2nd Universities and Public Schools) Battalion until that unit was disbanded in April, 1916, whereupon he had transferred to the 24th (2nd Sportsmen's) Battalion. He was officially reported missing, assumed killed, on July 31st, 1916 – the day after the disastrous attack on Guillemont. One of his men, Private Paul Vaughan, wrote of him, in a letter published in *The Cornishman*, "He was beloved and respected by his men – just the man for C Company, to which he belonged. A Cornishman himself, knowing the traits of his men ... . Eathorne was so unselfish, his motto was 'My men first' ..., and I know of many things he did for them at his own expense ... . He was a rare example of how an officer could be pals with his men, still maintain discipline, and hold their respect".

Frank Edwards was born in South Wales. He served as a chaplain with the South Wales Borderers in the "South African War", during the course of which he was promoted to the rank of Captain for his bravery in the field, by no less a personage than the Commander-in-Chief of the Forces, Frederick Sleigh Roberts (Lord Roberts of Kandahar). He later served as an ordained minister in the Brunswick Wesleyan Chapel in Hull. Upon the outbreak of the war, he enlisted in the 24th Battalion as a Private soldier, and was later promoted to Lance-Corporal, Corporal and Serjeant.

Guy Threlkeld Edwards was born in Hampstead in Middlesex in 1891, the fourth and youngest son of Dacre George Edwards and his wife Laura Emily, *nee* Dickinson. He was educated at Marlborough College (a public school), and at Kings College, Cambridge, and while at Cambridge rowed for his College, and was the Secretary of his College Boat Club. At the outbreak of the Great War, he was living in Yarmouth on the Isle of Wight with his wife Olivia, *nee* Stutchbury, who he had married in Victoria in British Columbia in Canada in 1912, and their two children Fonda, who had been born in 1913, and Joyce, born in 1914. He was made a Second Lieutenant in the 2nd Sportsmen's Battalion, the Royal Fusiliers in late 1914 or early 1915, and later promoted to Captain. He was killed on July 31st, 1916, in the aftermath of the attack on Guillemont. His Colonel wrote to his widow, "Your husband was killed while gallantry directing the withdrawal of his men, who had been relieved, from a trench. There was no more popular officer in the regiment, and we all feel his death very much". A cross inscribed with Captain Edwards's name was discovered by a Labour Company near Longueval in 1920, but there was no body associated with it. The cross was relocated to the Memorial Plot in Delville Wood Cemetery,

Lieutenant Arthur Aaron Enderby was one of the seven children of Major Harold Henry Enderby and his wife Emma Jane, *nee* Cole (see also below). He was born in Canterbury in Kent, and educated at King Edward Grammar School in Retford in Nottinghamshire. Before the war, he had been a gifted linguist, speaking French, German, Italian, Russian, Spanish and Welsh, and a fine pianist, and had once made a break of 250 at billiards.

Major Harold Henry Enderby was born in Lincolnshire in or around 1864. He was a crack shot, and, in addition to regularly competing at Bisley, had once hit twenty-five successive bulls at five hundred yards at Retford. At the outbreak of the war, he was the proprietor of the Liverpool Arms Hotel in Beaumaris on the Isle of Anglesey in North Wales.

Serjeant Arthur Nicholas Evans was born in Horwich in Lancashire in 1887, the second son of George Evans and his wife Margaret, *nee* Gallaway. He grew up to be, by the standards of the age, a fine physical specimen, standing 5'10½" tall, and weighing 11st10lb. Before the Great War, he had played football for Manchester City, Blackpool and Exeter City, as a half-back and stand-in forward. At the outbreak of the war, he was living in Exeter, and working as a professional footballer, and a part-time cricket coach at West Buckland School. He enlisted in the 2nd Sportsmen's Battalion in Exeter in November, 1914. He was officially reported missing, assumed killed, on July 31st, 1916 – the day after the disastrous attack on Guillemont. A former comrade, Corporal Frederick Pearce Hancock, was later able to shed some light on what actually happened to him, in a letter written to the Mayoress of Exeter, forwarded by her to Evans's parents in Bolton, and finally published in *The Western Times*. It seems that, while in a Prisoner-of-War Camp, from which he had been released in 1917, Corporal Hancock had met another comrade of Serjeant Evans's, who had "found him lying in a shell-hole very severely wounded. He bandaged him and made him as comfortable as he possibly could, but later on had to leave him. He said ... he felt that ... Evans must have died shortly after, as his wounds were so serious".

Private Thomas William Evans was born in Cardiff in South Wales in 1899, the son of Henry and Jennie Evans. Before he joined the Army, he had been employed in a tin-plate works in Melingriffith.

Private W.S. Ferrie was the son of the Burgess of Coxdale in Dumbartonshire in Scotland. Before the war, he had been educated at Glasgow University, and had gone on to become a Minister in the United Free Church in Hamilton in South Lanarkshire. At the outbreak of the war, after an unsuccessful attempt to join the Officers' Training Corps in the Inns of Court in London, he enlisted in the 24th Battalion as a Private soldier. He was eventually able to secure a commission with the Argyll and Sutherland Highlanders in August, 1915, with his father's assistance. Ferrie's wartime letters still survive in the Imperial War Museum, and include detailed descriptions of his time in the 24th Battalion. It seems that he was more than a little disapproving of the behaviour of some of the men from the battalion towards some of the townswomen of Romford.

Corporal Ernest Albert Firstbrook was born in Lelant in Cornwall in 1996, the son of John and Elizabeth Firstbrook. Before the war, he had been a caddy and then the resident professional golfer at the West Cornwall Golf Club. He had also been a keen cricketer. His local cricket club's records show that he had resigned to go to South Africa in 1906, and returned in 1909. Ernest Firstbrook had married Gladys Bartle in Lelant in 1912, and the couple had had two children, a son, John Charles, born in 1913, and a daughter, Kathleen Maud, born in 1913. In January, 1915, shortly after the outbreak of the war, Ernest had enlisted in Hayle in Cornwall. He had gone on to be awarded the Military Medal for his conspicuous bravery in the field on July 30th, 1916 (during the Battle of Delville Wood).

George Harrop Fish was born in Snaith in Yorkshire, the son of Earnshaw and Jane Fish. At the outbreak of the war, he was still living in Snaith. He enlisted as a Private soldier in the 24th Battalion in London. His Army Service Number, 3736, indicates that he did so between July 5th-August 5th, 1915.

Lance-Corporal John William Fitton was born in Runcorn in Cheshire in 1880. He had fought in the Boer War of 1899-1902. At the outbreak of the Great War, he had been living with his wife and three small children in Newton-le-Willows in Lancashire. He had enlisted in the 24th Battalion in Shepherd's Bush in London in September, 1914. And he had gone on to win a Military Medal in the Battle of Delville Wood in July, 1916. He is believed to have been a Signaller.

Lance-Corporal Charles Ford was the son of Mr & Mrs J. Ford of Exeter in Devon. He enlisted in Exeter.

Private William Henry Fortnam was born in Willenhall in Staffordshire, the son of George and Eliza Fortnam. At the outbreak of the war, he was living in Liverpool. He enlisted n London.

Private Alfred Edward Foskett was born in the Metropolitan Borough of Wandsworth in London, and enlisted in Southwark.

Private Francis Caleb Fowler was born in Wealdstone in Middlesex in 1890, the son of William Fowler and his wife Ellen Elizabeth Martha, *nee* Cable. At the outbreak of the war, he was working as a printer. He enlisted in the Middlesex Regiment, and later transferred to the 24th Battalion, the Royal Fusiliers. His death in 1916 left a widow, Florence Ethel, *nee* Simper, who he had married in 1915.

Private Arnold Russell Garcia was born in Sunderland in Co. Durham in 1895. Upon the outbreak of the war, he had enlisted in the 24th Battalion in London. He had later transferred to the 23rd Battalion.

Private Frederick John Geary was born in Berkhamstead in Hertfordshire, the son of William Owen and Sarah Arm Geary. At the outbreak of the war, he was living in St John's Wood in London with his wife Francis Louisa Geary. He enlisted in London.

Private Arthur Samuel Gillard was born in Plaistow in Essex, the son of Mr & Mrs Edward J. Gillard. He enlisted in Stratford.

Private Ernest Arthur Godfrey was born in Luton in Bedfordshire, the son of Arthur Frederick and Kitty Godfrey. At the outbreak of the war, he had been living in Luton with his wife, Daisy Emily, *nee* Going, who he had married in 1906, and his two children, Leslie Gilbert, who had been born in 1906, and Daphne Phyllis, born in 1908. He had enlisted in the Royal Field Artillery before transferring to the 24th Battalion, the Royal Fusiliers.

Second Lieutenant Charles Layton Green was born in Norwood in 1893, the son of Dr Edward Green and his wife. Before the war, he was educated at Swanage in Dorset, at St Bees in Cumberland, and at the University of Edinburgh, where he read Medicine, and where he was a member of the Officers' Training Corps. Upon the outbreak of the war, he joined the Essex Regiment, before transferring to the 24th Battalion, the Royal Fusiliers, and later transferring again the Royal Flying Corps.

Private Francis Idris Greenwood was born in Hebden Bridge in Yorkshire, the son of Mr & Mrs W.H. Greenwood. He enlisted in York.

Second Lieutenant Stanley Harris Gregory was the son of Joseph and Ernestine Gregory of Hillingdon in Middlesex. At the time of his death he had been on secondment from the 15th (Reserve) Battalion.

Lieutenant Leon David Griffiths was the son of Llewellyn and Elizabeth Griffiths of Harrow in Middlesex.

Corporal Felix Grugan was born in Ebchester in Co. Durham in 1897, the third of the five sons and eight children of William and Mary Grugan. At the outbreak of the war, he was working in Ebchester Main Colliery as a "colliery labourer on bank" (that is to say, at the pit bank or pit head, above ground). He enlisted in the 25th Battalion, the Northumberland Fusiliers – the famed "Tyneside Irish" - in November, 1914, and was drafted into the 24th Battalion, the Royal Fusiliers in August, 1918. He survived the war, and died in 1969.

One of his older brothers, Joseph Grugan, also of the "Tyneside Irish", was killed on the first day of the Battle of the Somme, on July 1st, 1916. The other, Owen, of the Durham Light Infantry, was killed on October 1st, 1916.

Private Frederick Grundy was born in Manchester, the son of Frederick and Annie Elizabeth Grundy. He also enlisted in Manchester.

Frederick Pearce Hancock enlisted as a Private in the 24th Battalion, the Royal Fusiliers in 1915, his Army Service Number, 3303, indicating that he did so sometime between February 10th and March 6th. He was later promoted to Corporal. He was wounded in the leg, and subsequently captured, in the attack on Guillemont on July 30th, 1916. According to the historical archives of the International Committee of the Red Cross, he was then held captive in two Prisoner-of-War camps in Germany, one at "Cassel" - possibly Niederzwehren- in Hesse, and the other at Ohrdruf in Thuringia, before eventually being released in 1917 to Switzerland, as unfit to work.

Lance-Corporal George Hague Hatfield was born in Rotherham in Yorkshire, the son of George Carr and Clara Hatfield. He enlisted in London.

Robert Stuart Hawcridge was born in Barrow-in-Furness in what was Lancashire and is now Cumbria in 1887, the second son of Thomas Arthur and Emma Hawcridge. He is known to have received some of his secondary education at Manchester Grammar School between 1901-05, finishing the year before Siegfried Wedgwood Herford (see below) started, and he went on to read Classics at St John's College, Cambridge, between 1905-08. He then began work as a schoolmaster at Manchester Preparatory School in 1908, moving to Batley Grammar in 1913, and while he was at Batley he also gave lectures on industrial history to the working men of the town. He enlisted as a Private soldier in Dewsbury in January, 1915, and was later promoted to Corporal. Even while serving in the trenches, he was in the habit of writing letters to his school, which were published in its magazine. He was killed in the Battle of Delville Wood on July 28th, 1916.

221

Harry Hayes was born in Horwich in Lancashire in 1897, the son of John William and Ellen Hayes. At the outbreak of the war, he was living in Levenshulme. He enlisted in the 24th Battalion in Manchester.

John Henry – also known as "Harry" – Hayes was born in Leicestershire, the son of Walter Palmer and Elizabeth Allen Hayes. He was educated at West Bridgford High School on the outskirts of Nottingham, and at University College, Nottingham, where he enrolled in the Officers' Training Corps (like Harry Daft, although probably not at the same time). And he went on to be employed as a teacher of Arts and Humanities at the Acourt Street Technical Centre in Nottingham. Upon the outbreak of the Great War, he enlisted in the 24th Battalion, the Royal Fusiliers on March 1st, 1915 - and his father Walter became a munitions contractor. Later, after further officer training, Harry joined the 17th Battalion, the Royal Welch Fusiliers as a Second Lieutenant in December, 1916. He went on to be killed on the first day of the Battle of Ypres, 1917, on July 31st, 1917. His death left a widow, Mabel.

Corporal William Henley was born in the village of Eaton Bray near Dunstable in Bedfordshire in 1886, the son of John Henley and his wife Sarah Jane, *nee* Boarder. After he left school, he went into work as a duck-breeder's help and farm-hand. He married Mary Nichols in 1911. He enlisted in the Middlesex Regiment at the outbreak of the Great War, and later transferred to the 24th Battalion, the Royal Fusiliers. Corporal Henley went on to receive multiple awards and commendations for his bravery, including the Distinguished Conduct Medal and the Military Medal. He survived the war, and afterwards returned to village life. He died, aged forty-eight, in 1935.

Siegfried Wedgwood Herford was born in Aberystwyth in mid-Wales in 1891, the son of Charles Harold Herford, a professor of English, and his wife Marie Catherina, *nee* Betge, who was of German extraction. He appears to have been home-schooled in Aberystwyth between 1896-99. He then went to school at Lady Barn House in Manchester, an institution founded on Unitarian principles by his great uncle, William Henry Herford, between 1899-1903; at Boxgrove House in Guildford in Surrey, between 1903-06; at Manchester

Grammar School between 1906-08, starting the year after Robert Stuart Hawcridge (see above) finished; and at the Herman Leitz-Schule in Schloss Bieberstein in Hesse in Germany, between 1908-09. He went on to read Engineering at the University of Manchester, between 1909-12, graduating with first-class honours, and afterwards entered employment, as a research aeronautical engineer at the Royal Aircraft Factory in Farnborough in Hampshire, in 1912. At the outbreak of the war, he had applied for a commission, but had been rejected, seemingly on account of his various connections to Germany, and in February, 1915, had enlisted as a Private soldier in the 24th Battalion, the Royal Fusiliers in London (after a short spell as an assistant to a war correspondent in Belgium, and another as a driver for the Red Cross). After his death, a comrade wrote of him to his parents, "Among us all he was not only very popular, but respected too, and we all feel his loss sorely. On the march he never tired, and on innumerable occasions ... was to be seen cheerfully striding along carrying another man's rifle in addition to his own. On our first visit to the trenches I sprained my ankle rather badly, and though we were in the open and under fire, it was your splendid son who ... gave me a shoulder to the field dressing station". Many obituaries were written about him. One read, in part, "His genius was not, like his father's, literary, but mechanical". Another, that Herford Junior had been "A man of beautiful character and great promise". He had also been "a magnificent climber", "the greatest ... England has yet produced", and had climbed peaks in the Peak and Lake Districts in England, often partnering up with Stanley Ferns Jeffcoat (see below), in Snowdonia in north Wales, in the Cuillins on Skye in Scotland, in the Dolomites in Italy, and in the Alps in Germany and Switzerland. C.E. Montague (see below), a fellow climber and close friend, wrote, "I remember him as he stood at the top of Kern Knotts Crack [a stage in the ascent of Great Gable in the Lakeland Fells], which he had just climbed for the first time, holding the rope for the second man and ... never for a moment ... off his guard. All English rock climbers who knew him would say that he was the best of them all".

Lance-Corporal Charles Alfred Hicks was born in London, the son of George Thomas and Harriet Mercy Hicks. At the outbreak od the war, he had been a carter's boy and market gardener, living in Colnbrook in Buckinghamshire. He had enlisted in London.

Serjeant Joe Leslie Hicks was born in Banbury in Oxfordshire, the son of Harry John and Gertrude Hicks. He enlisted in Huntingdon.

Corporal Sidney George Hindom was born in Newton Abbot in Devon in 1886. At one time, he was the south coast high-diving champion, and regularly dived off the 85' high Thatcher Rock off Torquay. During the Great War, he was wounded and captured in the attack on Guillemont on July 30th, 1916. He was then sent to a Prisoner-of-War camp at Hammelburg in Bavaria in German, and later repatriated as unfit to work. After the war, he went on to marry and have three children. He died in 1939.

Private Frederic Thomas Horne was born in Harrow in Middlesex, the son of Frederic and Mary Ann Nicholson Horne. Before the war, he had been the Liberal Agent for West Gloucestershire, living in Moreton-in-Marsh. He had enlisted in Stow-on-the-Wold.

Private Fred Howarth was born in Manchester, the son of Fred and Jane Ann Howarth. He had also enlisted in Manchester.

Private W.A. Hoyle wrote an account of the British retreat in the face of the German "Spring" Offensive of March, 1918, in which he was wounded (see section on "The First Battles of the Somme, 1918 ... " above).

Serjeant Geoffrey Leonard Hughes was born in Stourbridge in Worcestershire, the son of Mr William Henry & Mrs Edith Hughes. Before the war, he had been a legal clerk in Coventry. At the outbreak of the war, he joined the Royal Warwickshire Regiment, and later transferred to the Royal Sussex Regiment, and then to the Royal Fusiliers.

Private and later Warrant-Officer Second-Class Joseph Henry Hughes " ... was one of just six men of the original ... Battalion ... remaining at the end of the war. He was a specialist in grenades, explosives and bombing raid training and leadership from 1916-18 ... . He had refused the offer of a commission because it would have meant leaving the battalion, and he was determined to see the war through with his friends and comrades. Apart from being awarded the MM [Military Medal] for his part in taking a heavily defended quarry at Rumilly, Cambrai, in [September-October] 1918, his other distinction was that he was probably the first man to fire a Bangalore Torpedo ... . He was an enthusiastic member of the regimental association ..., and kept a fascinating collection of documents, photographs and artefacts, which are now with the Museum of the Royal Fusiliers in the Tower of London. He also left a fascinating collection of stories ... about life in the battalion, through training in England – when the men went on strike over the quantity and quality of their food, and were threatened with cavalry and machine guns before returning to duty – and the three years on the western front that followed ... ".

Private Eric Gordon Hutchins was born in Streatham in the County of London, the son of Mr & Mrs Margaret Hutchins. At the outbreak of the war, he was still living in Streatham. He enlisted in the 24th Battalion in London.

Lance-Corporal Reginald Hyland was born in Pudsey in Yorkshire, the son of Thomas Edward and Nancy Hyland. He went to school in Pudsey, and at the outbreak of the Great War was still there. He enlisted in the 24th Battalion in Leeds.

Lance-Corporal Walter Tichbourne Irons was the born in Ealing in Middlesex, the son of William Irons, a labourer, and his wife Jane Elizabeth, a laundress. He had enlisted in Hounslow.

Corporal Thomas Edward Isaac was born in Wickham Skeith in Suffolk in around 1896. Upon the outbreak of the Great War, he enlisted in the 24th Battalion, his Army Service Number, 2970, indicating that he did so between January 6th-February 10th, 1915. He went on be awarded a Military Medal for the bravery he showed during a trench raid on the night of October 2nd/3rd, 1917. He was wounded on March 25th, 1918, but survived the war. He died in Wickham Skeith in 1975.

Private Balfour Jackson was born in Ballymacarrett in Co. Down, the son of William and Jane Jackson. The family later moved to Belfast. He enlisted there.

Private Ernest Jackson was born in Covent Garden in central London in 1886, the son of Edward William Jackson and his wife Mary Anne, *nee* Hill. He was 5'7" tall, with brown hair and green eyes. Before the war, he had been employed as an errand-boy. He had also spent two years in H.M. Prison Wandsworth for larceny.

Private Herbert Jackson was born in Leeds in Yorkshire, and also enlisted there.

Stanley Ferns Jeffcoat, who was originally from Stretford in Manchester, enlisted in the 24th Battalion as a Private soldier upon the outbreak of the war, and later joined the 22nd Battalion as a Second Lieutenant. He was the son of John Joseph Jeffcoat, a salesman, and his wife, Alice; the husband of Ada Jeffcoat, *nee* Burton, who he married in 1915; and the father of Stanley Junior, who was born in 1916. Before the war, he had been an estate agent, and in his spare time a keen climber, often partnering up with Siegfried Wedgwood Herford (see above). Jeffcoat's Ledge, on the route up England's highest mountain, Scafell Pike, is named after him.

Private James Lambert Jenkin was born in Redruth in Cornwall, the son of Samuel and Mary S. Jenkin. He enlisted in Cambourne.

Corporal Norris Ridley Johnson was born in Wark-on-Tyne in Northumberland, the son of John and Isabella Johnson. He enlisted in London.

Private Percy Johnson was born in Northwich in Cheshire, and enlisted in Manchester.

Private Sydney Herbert Kirby was born in Hoxne in Suffolk in 1893, the son of John William Kirby and his wife Anna Maria, *nee* Rash. Before the Great War, he had been educated at Eye Grammar School in Cambridgeshire, and had gone on to be employed as a clerk in a bank. At its outbreak, he had enlisted in the 7th Battalion, the Bedfordshire Regiment before transferring to the 24th Battalion, the Royal Fusiliers. His brother, Private John Russell Kirby of the London Regiment, died of wounds suffered at Neuve Chapelle in 1915.

Private Walter G. Knight was born in Wells in Somerset, and had enlisted at Clapham Common in London.

Cyril Alexander Knust, who, judging from his name, may actually have been of Germanic ancestry, was made a Second Lieutenant in the 24th Battalion, the Royal Fusiliers in September, 1915. Later, as Captain, he was wounded at Arras in April, 1917, and made acting second-in-command of the Battalion in April, 1918. And as Major, he was made officer-in-command in October, 1918.

Corporal Lewis Richard Lewis was born in Machynlleth in mid-Wales in 1890. In his youth, he was a gifted inside-right, described by one newspaper as a "a fine strapping fellow with a good shot". Even after enlisting in the 24th (2nd Sportsmen's) Battalion at the outbreak of the Great War, he had a trial with Southampton. Sometime probably in 1916, he was injured in the ankle in a shell explosion, and repatriated to the Eastern Command Depot in Shoreham to recuperate. He played occasional football for Queen's Park Rangers and Southampton in 1916-1917, before being forced to retire on account of his injury. He died in Pontypridd in South Wales in 1959.

Bernard Henry Limpus was born in 1876 in Twickenham in Middlesex, the son of Henry Francis Limpus and his wife Agnes Maria, nee Layard. Before the Great War, he had been educated at Keble College Oxford, and had gone on to be employed as an actor. Upon the outbreak of the war, he had enlisted as a Private soldier in the 24th Battalion, his Army Service Number, 2030, indicating that he had done so between November 26th-December 3rd, 1914. His death on March 1th, 1917 left a widow, Lucy May, nee Faunce, who he had married in 1902.

Private Arthur Linsdell was born in Stonehouse in Devon, the son of William Henry and Louisa Linsdell. He enlisted in Plymouth.

Serjeant Arthur Joseph Little was the son of Mr & Mrs M.E. Little of Rochester in Kent. At the outbreak of the war, he had been living with his wife Florence Little in Rochester, and working as a teacher. He had enlisted in Chatham.

Arthur's brother James Charles Henry Little had been a Conscientious Objector in 1916, but had eventually enlisted in the Army, and died on active service with the Lincolnshire Regiment in India in 1919.

Private Willis Rees Lloyd was born in Penygraig in the Rhondda Valley in South Wales, the son of Rhys and Jane Snowden Lloyd. He enlisted in Cardiff.

Private Randolph Spencer Loibl was born in 1895 in well-to-do Maida Vale in the County of London, the son of Emil Loibl, who was from what is now Austria, and his second wife Emma, *nee* Tannenbaum, from New York. He was educated at Cranleigh School in Surrey, where he was a contemporary of Francis Stanley Mott (see below). And he had gone on to be employed as a farm-hand in Canada. At the outbreak of the Great War, he had returned to the "Old Country", and had enlisted in the 24th Battalion, the Royal Fusiliers in Chichester in Sussex.

Second Lieutenant Angus Mackay was the son of Simon Mackay, a tailor, and his wife Jessie, a schoolmistress, of Holyhead on Anglesey (both of whom were actually originally from the Highlands of Scotland).

Angus's brother, Alexander William Mackay, a Captain in the 26th (Bankers') Battalion, the Royal Fusiliers, was killed at the Battle of Ypres, 1917.

Private Bernard James Mahoney was the born in Saltash in Devon, the son of Lieutenant-Commander John Mahoney R.N. and his wife. He enlisted in Plymouth.

Private Thomas Robert Marchant was born in West Ham, the son of Robert and Selina Marchant. At the outbreak of the war, he was living in Pevensey in Sussex. He enlisted in Eastbourne.

Private Hubert Henry Marrable was born in Cranham in Essex, the eldest of the five sons of Hubert and Alice Marrable. At the outbreak of the war, he was still living in Cranham. He enlisted in the 24th Battalion in nearby Romford.

Private Herbert George Marshall was the son of George James and Elizabeth Marshall of St Albans in Hertfordshire. He also enlisted in St Albans.

Private Ernest John Martin was born in Ramsey in Huntingdonshire, the son of Mr J.M. & Mrs. Ellen Martin. He enlisted in March in Cambridgeshire.

Private Edwin Wilfred Wrayford May was born in Lustleigh in Devon in 1891, the son of Edwin May, a farmer, and his wife. Before the war, he had excelled at country and other sports, and it was said that "it took a good man to beat him with gun, rod, bat or racket". His had evidently been a gentle soul, and a friend had told him "it will not do for you to fight". He had enlisted in the 24th Battalion, the Royal Fusiliers anyway, at Exeter. When he was killed, a fellow soldier wrote to his father, as follows, "It is with deepest regret that I write to you, to condole with you on the loss of your son. Fred and I stood side by side when we took the oath of service to our King. In training, we were always together. In France, we slept next to each other, and in the trenches we stood shoulder to shoulder. The night you lost a son, I [lost] an incomparable comrade in arms. A mine exploded, and Fred was among the first to jump the parapet and take up a position on top of the crater. In the willing discharge of his duty, he was hit by pieces of a grandee and was mortally wounded, dying in my arms". His captain wrote that he had been a "splendid soldier ... admired and respected by his officers, beloved by his comrades". It seems that he had twice been offered a commission, and had twice declined, preferring to continue to serve in the ranks, alongside his comrades. May's obituary recorded that his personality had "endeared him to the whole countryside, and made him a favourite in the village".

Serjeant Oliver Bertram May was born in Sundridge in Kent, and had enlisted in the 24th Battalion, the Royal Fusiliers in Mill Hill in Middlesex, having previously been in the Middlesex Regiment.

Private John Alfred Mayes was born in Bayswater in what is now West London, the son of James Alfred and Ellen Mayes. At the outbreak of the war, he was living in Kilburn, a little to the north-west. He enlisted in the 24th Battalion in Willesden.

Lance-Corporal William Austin McCready was born near Canterbury in New Zealand in 1883. Between 1900-1914, he worked for the Northern Bank at various locations in the north of Ireland. He enlisted in the 24th Battalion shortly after the outbreak of the war in 1914. He survived the war, despite spending over two years as a prisoner after having been captured in July, 1916. After his demobilisation from the Army in 1919, he went back to work for the Northern Bank in the north of Ireland, eventually becoming the manager of the Ballynahinch branch in Co. Down. He died in 1939.

Private Charles Percy McGahey was born into a working-class family in Bethnal Green in the East End of London on February 11th, 1871, the third and youngest son, and fifth and last child, of John McGahey, a railway clerk, and his wife Elizabeth, *nee* Walker. Before the war, he played county cricket for Essex, as "a tall, right-handed, hard-hitting, front-foot batsman, a useful slow leg-break bowler, and a good field", making his debut in 1894. And he was part of the Essex XI that famously beat Australia by 126 runs at the County Ground in Leyton in 1899. He also played international cricket for England against Australia, on the "Ashes" tour of 1901-02. Even during the war, he continued to play cricket, on a pitch at Etaples. McGahey survived the war, and afterwards briefly returned to county cricket, before finally retiring in 1921, after scoring over twenty thousand runs at an average of just over thirty, and taking over three hundred wickets, at an average of just over thirty. He died of septicaemia in Whipps Cross Hospital in Leytonstone in the Municipal Borough of Leyton on January 10th, 1935, aged sixty-three, a few days after injuring a finger in a fall on a wet pavement on Christmas Eve, 1934.

Private David Bruce McKechnie was born in Wedderburg in Victoria in Australia in 1888, the fourth child and second son of William McKechnie and his wife Charlotte, *nee* Guthrie. In 1905, he left the family farm to go to Melbourne in Victoria to work as a clerk in the Patents Office, and, at the same time, to study Engineering Drawing, Applied Mechanics, Theoretical Chemistry and Electricity in evening classes in the Working Men's College. Then, in 1907, he became a Junior Assistant Engineer in the Postmaster-General's Department in Melbourne; and in 1913, an Assistant Engineer in the Postmaster-General's Department in Brisbane in Queensland. At the outbreak of the Great War, he sailed to the United Kingdom to enlist in the Army, eventually joining the 24th Battalion, the Royal Fusiliers in London on August 8th, 1915.

His uncle, Trooper Alexander Richard Guthrie of the 10th Australian Light Horse, died during the Gallipoli Campaign in 1915, and is commemorated on the Lone Pine Memorial. Two of his half-brothers also served in the Australian Imperial Force in the Great War, in the Middle East theatre. And his sister served as a nurse on a hospital ship.

Captain Cecil Stanley Meares was the son of Thomas Meares, a tea-plantation owner, and his late wife Agnes Meares, of Clive in Shropshire. Before the war, he had been privately educated at Bilton Grange and Uppingham Schools, and had gone on to train as a chartered accountant, and to establish his own accountancy company, Meares & Co., in the City of London. He had been a keen ornithologist, and indeed had even been able to keep up his interest in birds while at the front, watching kestrels hunting in the few surviving scraps of cover around the trenches for small mammals. Meares had also been a "most energetic" sportsman, who had particularly excelled as a horseman and marksman, and who had once narrowly missed out on winning the prestigious Spencer Cup for marksmanship at the National Shooting Centre at Bisley. At the time of his death, he had only been in the 24th (2nd Sportsmen's) Battalion a matter of weeks. Like Second-Lieutenant Eathorne (see above), Captain Meares had previously served in the 19th (2nd Universities and Public Schools) Battalion, which had been disbanded in April, 1916. Captain Meares had apparently been affectionately known by the men under his command as "Daddy", as he had taken "a great personal interest ... in their welfare and comfort".

Second Lieutenant Walter Barrington Medlicott was born in 1872, a second son to Walter Edward Medlicott, a curate, and his wife Edith Louisa, *nee* Sumner, of Swanmore in Hampshire. Before the war, he had been educated at Winchester College (a public school), and employed as an architect. He had married Hilda Fothergill Robinson in 1900, by which time he was living in London, and the couple had had a daughter, Eleanor Betty – Bet – Medlicott, in 1901. In 1915, he joined the 18th Battalion, the Royal Fusiliers as a Serjeant, despite being over-age, and in 1916, he transferred to the 24th Battalion as a Second Lieutenant. He was then seriously wounded at the

Battle of the Ancre in 1916, on the eve of which he had written a letter to his wife, which still survives (see section on "The Battles of the Somme ... " above). After recovering from his wounds, he transferred again, to the newly-formed Tank Corps, in 1917. He survived the war, and afterwards emigrated to Asia Minor, in 1919. He died of fever in Cilicia in Asia Minor on September 18th, 1920, while being held captive by Turkish nationalists under Mustafa Kemal (Kemal Ataturk). A memorial service was held for him in St John's church in Red Lion Square in Bloomsbury in London on March 8th, 1921.

Private Reginald George Medlock was born in Great Gransden in Huntingdonshire, the son of Mr & Mrs E. Medlock. At the outbreak of the war, he had enlisted in the 24th Battalion in Huntingdon.

Lance-Corporal James Henry Bright Millar was born in Trevone near Padstow in Cornwall in April, 1898, the son of James Henry Millar and his wife Mabel, nee Key. At the outbreak of the war, he was still living there. He enlisted in the 24th Battalion in Wadebridge in Cornwall in March, 1915, aged only sixteen. He survived the ill-fated attack on Guillemont on July 30th, 1916, only to be killed at Arras on April 28th, 1917.

Private Edward Minty Miller was born in Colombo in Ceylon (Sri Lanka) in 1881, one of the sons of the Venerable Archdeacon Edward Francis Miller and his wife Caroline Louisa, nee Ford. Before the Great War, he had been educated in St Faith's School, Cambridge, and Marlborough College (a public school), and had been a keen sportsman. At the outbreak of the war, he had been living in Royston in Cambridgeshire. He had enlisted in the 2nd Sportsmen's Battalion in London in November, 1915. After his death in the Battle of the Ancre a year later, on November 13th, 1916, his Captain wrote to his parents, then living in Parkstone in Dorset, "I cannot tell you how sorry I am to lose him, as I had such great hopes for him".

Richard Haynes Nelson Mintorn was born in Harrow in Middlesex in 1864, the third son of John Haynes Mintorn and his wife Elizabeth, nee Mogridge. He attended Harrow School between 1877-82, and went on to be employed as a Mining Engineer in Australia and West Africa. Upon the outbreak of the Great War, he enlisted as a Private soldier in the 24th Battalion in January, 1915, although he apparently later transferred to the 20th Battalion. He was wounded an active service in February, 1917, and spent some months recovering in hospitals in France and in England. He never returned to active service.

Private Walter Misson was born in Kennington in London. At the outbreak of the war, he had been living in Par in Cornwall, and working as an accountant. He had enlisted in St Austell in Cornwall.

Private Denis Stuart Mitchell was the son of Brick Mitchell, a Lance-Corporal in the Australian Imperial Force, and his wife Marion Alice Mitchell, of St Leonard's in Sussex. Before the war, he had been educated at the University School in Hastings, and had gone on to be employed by a firm of architects in Bexhill in Surrey. He had also been a keen footballer, cricketer and golfer, and a chess player.

Private Eric Montagu was born in Shepherd's Bush in Middlesex in 1896, the son of Arthur and Marjorie Montagu. Shortly before the outbreak of the war, in 1911, he was living in Ealing with his mother, his elder sister Irene, and his two younger brothers Graham and Beresford. He survived the war, despite having been forced to cut off his own right arm in an incident on October 25th, 1916, during the Battle of the Ancre (see section on "The Battles of the Somme ... " above). Major-General Cecil E. Pereira, the officer-in-command of 2nd Division, wrote in a letter to Private Montagu, "I should like you to know that your gallant action is recognised, and how greatly it is appreciated". And Captain Cecil Palmer Harvey of the 24th Battalion wrote in a letter to Private Montagu's mother, "He is a great loss to me, and his place will be difficult to fill. I am sure it will be a pleasure to you when I tell you that he was one of the bravest and coolest men I have ever met. He displayed the most remarkable courage and endurance during the time that he was wedged in by the debris of the dug-out, and I really thank God that we managed to extricate him alive."

One of Eric's two younger brothers, Rifleman Graham Montagu, of the King's Royal Rifle Corps, was killed at Guillemont on August 28th, 1916. The other, Lance-

Bombardier Beresford Montagu, of the Royal Field Artillery, was the only one of the three to survive the war unscathed - and with a Distinguished Conduct Medal to boot.

Charles Edward Montague was born in Ealing in Middlesex in 1867, the son of Francis Montague, an Irish Roman Catholic priest who had given up his vocation in order to marry and have children, and his wife Rosa. Before the war, he had been educated at the City of London School and at Balliol College, Oxford, and while at Oxford had saved the life of a man drowning in the Isis, for which he had been awarded the Bronze Medal of the Royal Humane Society. And he had been employed as a newspaper reporter with *The Manchester Guardian*. He had married his editor's daughter, Madeleine Scott, in 1898, and the couple had gone on to have seven children (one of whom, Evelyn, had in turn gone on to be a noted athlete, and to finish sixth in the final of the Steeplechase in the Olympic Games in Paris in 1924). And in his spare time, he had enjoyed mountain-climbing both in Britain and on the continent, and had scaled Mont Blanc and the Eiger. Upon the outbreak of the war, he joined the 24th Battalion, the Royal Fusiliers as a Private soldier, despite being over-age, at forty-seven - it is said that he dyed his prematurely white hair black in order to pass muster! Later, as a Serjeant, he suffered a serious injury while demonstrating the use of the Mills bomb during training, which left him hospitalised for a month. And then, in France, he suffered a serious bout of trench fever. At this point, his doctors advised him that he was no longer fit for front-line service, so he transferred to the Intelligence Corps as a staff-officer (Second Lieutenant, and later Captain). However, even in his new role, he managed to return to the front a number of times, under the pretext of guiding V.I.Ps. One of his charges, George Bernard Shaw, wrote, "The standard joke about Montague was his craze for being under fire, and his tendency to lead distinguished visitors, who did not necessarily share this taste ... into warm corners". Montague survived the war, and afterwards returned to writing newspaper articles, and also books, of which perhaps his most famous was *Disenchantment* (see sections on "Training for the Great War", "Life on the Western Front" and "The Battles of the Somme ... " above). He retired in 1925, and died in Manchester in 1928.

Walter Thomas Harold Montgomery was born in 1887, the son of William John Montgomery and his wife Henrietta Rebecca, *nee* Theobald. Before the war, like Charles Layton Green (see above), he had studied Medicine at the University of Edinburgh. Upon the outbreak of the war, he was made a Second Lieutenant in the 24th Battalion, and later was promoted to Captain. He survived the war, and died in 1955.

Corporal Charles George Moon was born in Ilkeston in Derbyshire in 1895, the son of Arthur Henry Moon and his wife Mary Tamar, *nee* Gregory. At the outbreak of the war, he had been living in Gunthorpe on the outskirts of Nottingham, and working as a lace embroidery draughtsman. He had enlisted in the 24th Battalion in Nottingham.

Private Henry John Morrell was born in Fulham in Middlesex. He also enlisted in Fulham.

Company Serjeant-Major Ernest John Morris was born in Colchester in Essex, the son of Captain Ernest William and Lucy Marion Morris.

Ernest John's younger brother Private Frederick Morris of the 9th Battalion, the Royal Fusiliers was also killed in the Great War, on July 9th, 1916, probably at Ovillers, also on the Somme.

Regimental Serjeant-Major E.M.S. Morris was already a veteran of nearly forty years service in the Army by the time of the outbreak of the Great War.

Second Lieutenant Francis Stanley Mott was born in Brixton in 1895, the son of Frank and Alice Mott. Before the war, he had been educated at Cranleigh School and Reigate Grammar School in Surrey, and gone on to be employed as an engineer, and to spend a year studying steelworks in Germany. At the outbreak of the war, he enlisted in the Royal Army Medical Corps, where his ability to speak German enabled him to assist in the treatment of wounded enemy soldiers. Shortly afterwards, he requested to be transferred to a fighting unit. The 24th (2nd Sportsmen's) Battalion, the Royal Fusiliers was an appropriate choice for him, as he was a fine cricketer and swimmer, and a crack shot. He joined as a Private soldier, but was quickly promoted from the ranks to Second Lieutenant. He wrote in a letter to his parents in April, 1916, when the Battalion was stationed somewhat to the west of Lens, "I hope they will let us go over the top and give the Huns "What Ho" and then let the war be at an end. I am sure it would be a blessing if we could get into open fighting again as when we started. I am now sitting on the veranda behind the firing line writing this letter and enjoying glorious sunshine". Within weeks, he was mortally wounded in the nearby front-line trenches. In a press release issued after his death, the *Surrey Mirror* described him as possessed of "a noble spirit", and "imbued with lofty ideals".

Lance-Corporal Edgar Murdock was born in Tunbridge Wells in Kent in 1879. At the outbreak of the Great War, he was living in Hampstead in Middlesex. He enlisted in the 24th Battalion in London. He went on to be killed in the Battle of Cambrai on December 1st, 1917. He is commemorated on a war memorial in the chapel in Bedford Schooll, suggesting that he had been a student there before the war.

Second Lieutenant William Neate was the son of Mrs P.A. Crane of Regents Park in London.

Second Lieutenant Edward Albert Newland was the son of James Edward Newland and his wife Ada Louise, *nee* Breeze, of Hampstead in Middlesex. He was also the husband of Amy Florence Newland of Romford in Essex, and the father of three small children, Amy Dorothy Newland, born in 1912, Winifred Newland, born in 1914, and Kenneth Edward Newland, born in 1916. He was an actuary.

Second Lieutenant Dudley Richard Nyren was the son of Richard and Louise Nyren of Caterham in Surrey. Before the war, he had been educated at Whitgift Grammar School in Croydon and at Trinity College, Cambridge, and at its outbreak had been a rubber planter in the Malay States.

Patrick Mangan, known as Patrick O'Kavanagh, was born in Whitwell in Derbyshire in 1896, the only son of John Mangan, an Irishman, and his wife Margaret Ann, *nee* Eadson. Before the war, he had worked as a journalist on the *Worksop Guardian*. He had enlisted as a Private soldier in the 24th Battalion in London in December, 1915. He stood over 6' tall.

Harry Packer was born in Chipping Norton in Oxfordshire in 1870. Before the war, he was educated at Devon County School, and had gone on to be employed as a wholesale merchant in Newport in South Wales. He also played rugby at club level for Newport, and internationally for Wales, as a prop forward – standing 5'11" tall, and weighing 13st, he was a big man for his time. Upon the outbreak of the war, he enlisted in the 24th Battalion, and served with them for the duration. After the war, he returned to his former occupation in wholesale. He also became active in sports administration, and was the manager of the British Lions tour to South Africa in 1924. He died in 1946.

Colonel A. de B.V. Paget was a career soldier, who had served in the Durham Light Infantry for twenty-eight years, including in the Tirah Campaign in India in 1897-8. He also belonged to His Majesty's Honourable Corps of Gentlemen-at-Arms.

Private Francis Austin Elliott Paget was born in Sturminster Newton in Dorset in 1890, the eldest of the seven sons of Cecil Gregory Paget and his wife Innes Elizabeth. He was educated at Dunford School in Langton Matravers in Dorset, and at Charterhouse School in Godalming in Surrey. He then went on to read Classics and Divinity at Hertford College, Oxford, and Theology at Durham University. At the outbreak of the Great War, he enlisted in the 24th Battalion in Dorchester in Dorset.

Two of his brothers were also killed in the war, John Christopher Paget, a Captain in the Royal Garrison Artillery, at Arras in April, 1917, and Richard Theodore Paget, a Second Lieutenant in the Lancashire Fusiliers, at Sanctuary Wood in August, 1917.

Private George Louis Parris was born in Offham in Kent. At the outbreak of the war, he had been living in Platt, also in Kent, and had enlisted in Maidstone.

Second Lieutenant William Henry Liddon Parry was the only son of the Rev. Arthur L. Parry, the chaplain of Colney Hatch Lunatic Asylum in Friern Barnet in Middlesex, and his wife Margaret.

Private William George Miller Parsons was born in Brighton in Sussex, the son of Mr. J.M. and Mrs. Amelia Parsons. He enlisted in London.

Corporal Frank Leonard Patching was born in Brighton in Sussex, the son of Frank and Sarah Ann Patching. He enlisted in London.

Private William Hadwen Peake was born in Atherton in Lancashire, the son of Richard Manley and Emma Dorothy Peake. Before the war, he had been a travelling salesman based in Thundersley in Essex. Upon the outbreak of the war, he enlisted in Southend. After he was killed in action, his commanding officer wrote of him that he was "a most valuable man and reported by myself for most excellent work done under terrific shell fire that morning".

Private James Peduzzi was born in Manchester, the son of James Peduzzi senior and his wife. At the outbreak of the war, he had been living in Harpurhey in Manchester with his wife, Mary Peduzzi, who was from North Attleborough in Massachusetts in the United States of America. He had enlisted in Manchester.

Private Percy Charles Pereira was born in Kensington in London. At the outbreak of the war, he was still living there. He enlisted in the 24th Battalion in London.

Private George William Pereira born in Tottenham in Middlesex. At the outbreak of the war, he had been living in Tottenham with his wife Amy Gertrude Pereira. He had joined the Middlesex Regiment before transferring to the 24th Battalion, the Royal Fusiliers.

Lance-Corporal John Cecil Pickering was born in Co. Cork in Ireland, the only son of John Pickering and his wife Cecilia, *nee* Lennie. The family later moved to Ballymena in Co. Antrim. He enlisted in Belfast.

Lieutenant-Colonel Robert Henry Pipon was a career soldier, who had served in the campaign in Somaliland in 1908-10. Over the course of the Great War he was awarded a Military Cross and a Distinguished Service Order with clasp, and was also mentioned in despatches three times.

Private Thomas Ladas Powers was the son of Thomas Powers Senior of Torquay in Devon.

John Prior was born in Leamington in Warwickshire. He enlisted as a Private soldier in the 24th Battalion also in Leamington.

William John Punchard was born in Dartmouth in Devon in 1886, the son of John Edward Punchard and his wife Elizabeth Jane, *nee* Bonner. He married Gertrude Mary Burnell in 1912, and the couple went on to have three sons, William, Edwin George and Robert Punchard, born in born in 1914, 1916, and 1920, respectively. Upon the outbreak of the Great War, he enlisted in the 24th Battalion, the Royal Fusiliers, as a Serjeant, and later, in 1917, transferred to the Suffolk Regiment, providing training in the use of gas-masks. He survived the war, and died in Totnes in Devon in 1939.

William's wife Gertrude's three brothers, George, William Robert and Edwin Burnell, were all killed in the war.

Henry George Purver was born in Isleworth in Middlesex in 1891, the third son of William Richard Thomas Purver and his wife Honora, *nee* Mahoney. At the outbreak of the Great War, he was living in Isleworth, and working as a newspaper reporter, some of the time with *The Times*. He was also playing football for Brentford, alongside Elias Henry – "Patsy" – Hendren (see below). Purver enlisted as a Private soldier in the 2nd Sportsmen's Battalion in London in July, 1915. He then married Margaret, *nee* Wilford, in October, 1915, and, probably on account of his newly married status, was deployed to France some time later than the rest of his battalion, in April, 1916 rather than in November, 1915. He was killed in the Battle of Delville Wood on July 31st, 1916. His obituary in the *Middlesex Chronicle* read, in part, "The game of football has lost an ardent and clever devotee, and Isleworth a most popular and charming fellow", adding that he had "latterly gained ... prominence particularly as a prolific goal getter in the centre forward position in the Brentford Football Team".

"Patsy" Hendren was born in Turnham Green in Middlesex in 1889. Before the Great War, he played football for Brentford, as a wing-forward, and cricket for Middlesex, as a right-handed batsman (and occasional off-break bowler). He enlisted as a Private soldier in the 1st Sportsmen's Battalion in

September, 1914. And he played in the Sportsmen's Battalion cricket team that beat the Honourable Artillery Company in a match at Lord's on June 12th, 1915. He survived the war, although one of his brothers, Lance-Corporal John Michael – "Jack" - Hendren, who was also in the 1st Sportsmen's Battalion, was killed at the Battle of Delville Wood on July 27th, 1916. After the war, Hendren returned to his sporting pursuits. He played both football and cricket for England in friendly "Victory" international matches in 1919. Although he never played international football again, he eventually made 432 club appearances for Brentford, and scored seventy-four goals, before retiring from football in 1927, to concentrate on his cricket. By that time, he had already been voted one of Wisden's "Cricketers of the Year", in 1920, and had made his cricketing debut for England, against Australia, on the "Ashes" tour of 1920-21. By the time he finally retired from cricket in 1937, he had played fifty-one test-matches for England, and scored 3 525 runs, at an average of 47.63. And altogether he had played 833 first-class matches, and scored 57 611 runs, a total only exceeded by Jack Hobbs and Frank Woolley, at an average of 50.80. He had also scored 170 first-class centuries, a total only exceeded by Hobbs. His last was for Middlesex against Surrey in his last game at Lord's, and was greeted by a spontaneous rendition of "For he's a jolly good fellow" by the seventeen-thousand- strong crowd, holding up play for a full five minutes. After his retirement, Hendren coached cricket at Harrow School, and later at Sussex County Cricket Club. He also kept score at Lord's. He died, aged seventy-three, in 1962.

Lieutenant and Acting Captain David Radcliffe was the son of Sir Frederick Morton and Margaret Radcliffe of Mossley Hall, Liverpool, Lancashire. Before the war, he had been educated at Winchester College (a public school), and at Corpus Christi College, Oxford, and had rowed for his College VIII at Oxford. In spite of ill health, at the outbreak of war, he had joined the South Lancashire Regiment, and had later transferred to the Royal Fusiliers.

Serjeant Harry Rainford was born in St Helen's in Lancashire, the son of Alfred and Margaret Rainford. Before the war, he had been a joiner's apprentice. He had enlisted in St Helens.

Private Charles Sidney Ralph was born in Stoke Dowell in Devon, the son of Alonzo Horatio Ralph and his wife Louisa Elizabeth, *nee* Kearns. At the outbreak of the war, he had been living in Saltash with his wife Matilda Ralph, *nee* Wakeham, and had been the proprietor of the Railway Hotel in Saltash. He had enlisted in Plymouth. His obituary records that an officer wrote of him, "He was one of the best men I ever met, and was liked by all who met him. He was a very brave man, always jolly and always the same under all conditions ... . I had ... recommended him just before he was hit, but within the next few days I had to do the same for all the men under me".

Sir Herbert Henry Raphael was born into a wealthy family in the County of Middlesex in 1859, the second son of Henry Louis Raphael, of Raphael's Bank, and his wife Henrietta. He was educated in Germany, in Switzerland, and at Trinity Hall in Cambridge, where he studied law. He went on to a career in the legal profession, as a barrister, in 1883; and, in 1884, married Rosalie Coster. And in 1897, while living in Havering-atte-Bower in Essex, he acquired the nearby Gidea Park estate, which he later transformed into the garden suburb of Romford. Having turned his attention from the law to politics in 1889, he eventually became the Liberal Member of Parliament for South Derbyshire in 1906, a seat he was still holding in 1914. Upon the outbreak of the war, he enlisted in the 24th Battalion, the Royal Fusiliers, as a Private soldier, having previously held a commission in the 1st Volunteer Battalion, The Essex Regiment. He was soon promoted to Lance-Corporal. Then, in June, 1915, he was made a Major in the King's Royal Rifle Corps, going on to raise two new battalions in that regiment, the 18th (Service) and the 23rd (Reserve), and acting as second-in-command of both. The 18th Battalion was also known as the "Arts & Crafts", as Raphael had an active interest in, and indeed was also a noted patron of, the arts. The battalion went on to serve in France and Flanders on the Western Front, and also briefly in Italy on the Southern Front, between May, 1916-November, 1918. Raphael survived the war. He died of a heart attack while out shooting on his estate in 1924, aged sixty-four. His title of Baronet of Cavendish Square in the Metropolitan Borough of St Marylebone died with him, as he had no heirs. His name lives on in Raphael Park in Romford – and, by association, in "Raphael's" kebab-shop!

Company Serjeant-Major Frederick Herbert Read was born in Poplar in East London in around 1883. At the outbreak of the war, he had been living in East Ham. He had enlisted in Hounslow.

Private Walter Redshaw was born in Scarborough in Yorkshire, the son of Mr Richard B. and Mrs Rachael Eleanor Redshaw. He also enlisted in Scarborough.

Private Frederick Haywood Reeves was born in Hammersmith in Middlesex, and enlisted in Shepherd's Bush.

Second Lieutenant Wallace Remington was the son of William and Mary Remington of Birmingham; and the husband of Mary Gertrude Remington of Easton on the Isle of Portland in Dorset.

Private Sidney Charles Richards was born in Stoke Damerel in Devon in 1890. At the outbreak of the war, he had been living in Devonport. He had enlisted in Plymouth.

Private Laurence John Francis Rhydding Ridding was born in Slimbridge in Gloucestershire. At the outbreak of the war, he was living in Shanklin on the Isle of Wight. He joined the 10th (Stockbrokers') Battalion, the Royal Fusiliers, before transferring to the 24th Battalion.

Corporal Alexander Robertson was born in Logierait in Perthshire, the son of John and Margaret Robertson. He enlisted in Aberdeen.

Private Arthur Stanley Robinson was born in Holloway in Middlesex, the son of George Alfred and Elizabeth Mary Robinson. At the outbreak of the war, he was living in Walthamstow. He enlisted in London.

Private Robert Massingberd Rogers was born in Doncaster in Yorkshire, the son of Robert Massingberd Rogers Senior and his wife Minnie Jemima Charlotte. He also enlisted in Doncaster.

Lance-Corporal Herbert Sargant was born in Horley in Surrey, the son of Mr Henry and Mrs Eva Ann Sargant. At the outbreak of the war, he was living with his wife Margaret M. Sargant in Redhill. He enlisted in Redhill.

Frederick Courteney Selous was born into an aristocratic family in Regent's Park in London in 1851, the second of the five children and the first of the two sons of Frederick Lokes Slous (*sic*), the Chairman of the Stock Exchange, and his wife Ann Holgate, *nee* Sherborne, a published poetess. Before the Great War, he had travelled through South Africa to Matabeleland, where he had made a name for himself as a big-game hunter. And also as an explorer, notably of the then little-known area north of the Transvaal and south of the Congo Basin, for which he was awarded the Royal Geographical Society's Founder's Medal. He had then joined the British South Africa Company, at the request of its founder, Cecil Rhodes, and acted as a guide on its pioneering expedition to Mashonaland, later concluding arrangements to bring Manica under British control. In 1893-4, he had taken part in the First Matabele War, and been wounded at Bulawayo. And in 1896-7, he had taken part in the Second Matabele War, as part of the Bulawayo Field Force, and fought alongside Robert Baden Powell, who went on to found the Scout movement. He enlisted in the 24th Battalion, the Royal Fusiliers as a Private soldier in November, 1914. Shortly afterwards, though, he joined the 25th (Frontiersmen's) Battalion, in April, 1915, and arrived with them in the East African theatre in May, 1915, becoming a Captain in August, 1915, and being awarded a Distinguished Service Order in 1916. He was killed in action on January 4th, 1917, aged sixty-five, at Behobeho in what was then German East Africa, and is buried under a tamarind tree on the banks of the Rufiji River in what is now the Selous Game Reserve in Tanzania. His death moved even his adversary in the field, the legendary German General Paul von Lettow-Vorbeck, "*Der Lowe von Afrika*" ("The Lion of Africa"), to write a letter to the British expressing his condolences. The former President of the United States, Theodore Roosevelt, who was a close personal friend, wrote, "He led a singularly adventurous and fascinating life, with just the right alternations between the wilderness and civilization. He helped spread the borders of his people's lands. He added much to the sum of human knowledge. He closed his life exactly as such a life should be closed, by dying in battle for his country while rendering her valiant and effective service".

Selous was survived by his wife, Marie Catherine Gladys, *nee* Maddy, who he had married in 1893, and two sons, Frederick Hatherley Bruce, who had been born in 1898, and Harold Sherborn, born in 1899. Captain Frederick Hatherley Bruce Selous of the Royal Flying Corps was killed a year to the day after his father, on January 4th, 1918.

Private Harold Southwell Shearing was born in Brockley in the Metropolitan Borough of Lewisham in London, the son of Samuel Charles Shearing, an insurance clerk, and his wife Ada, *nee* Butler. He was educated at Colfe Grammar School in Lewisham, and went on to be employed by the Prudential Insurance Company. At the outbreak of the war, he was living in Eltham. He had joined the Queen's Own West Kent Yeomanry, which was part of the - Reserve - Territorial Force, on July 25th, 1916, and had transferred to the Royal Fusiliers on October 5th, 1917, he because he had decided he wanted to fight in France.

Private James George Simco was born in Clerkenwell in London, the son of Charles William and Elizabeth Simco. At the outbreak of the war, he was living in Tottenham. He enlisted in Mill Hill.

Lance-Corporal Edgar James Smith was born in 1892. During the Great War, he was wounded and captured on the attack on Guillemont on July 30th, 1916. He was later repatriated as unfit to work, having lost his right arm. Surviving records in the National Archives show that he was discharged from the Army on medical grounds on April 4th, 1917, and granted a pension. It is not known whether he was also able to return to his pre-war trade as a watch-maker.

Yorke Smith was born in Filey in Yorkshire in 1888, the fourth son of the Rev. J. Jeremy Smith and his wife Mary, *nee* Sherwin. He was killed in the Battle of the Ancre on November 13th, 1916. Before the Great War, he had been educated at Kingswood School in Somerset, and then at Hatfield College of Durham, and had gone on to be employed as a schoolmaster in Sittingbourne in Kent, and then in Barrow-in-Furness in Lancashire. At the outbreak of the war, he had been living in Barrow-in-Furness. He had, though, enlisted as a Private soldier in the 24th Battalion in London, his Army Service Number, 2261, indicating that he had done so sometime between December 3rd, 1914 and January 6th, 1915. He had been a Signaller.

Private Frank Edward Southgate was born in Hunstanton in Norfolk, the son of Samuel and Mary Southgate. Before the Great War, he had studied art at Bideford Art School and at the Cambridge School of Art, and had gone on to exhibit both at the Royal Academy and at the Royal Society of British Artists, and to make something of a name for himself as a "clever artist". Also a "keen sportsman", he had enlisted in the 2nd Sportsmen's Battalion, the Royal Fusiliers in Wells in Norfolk in January or early February, 1915. He left a wife, Ethel Southgate, *nee* Winlove.

Private Sidney Southgate was born in Chelmsford in Essex, one of the six sons of John Southgate, a florist, and his wife Elizabeth, *nee* Harrington. At the outbreak of the Great War, he had been living with his wife Emma Caroline, *nee* Ketley, and their two young sons, Wilfred and Cecil, in Dullingham in Cambridgeshire, and working as a market gardener. He had joined the Middlesex Regiment before transferring to the 24th Battalion, the Royal Fusiliers in June, 1916. After the war, his widow and two fatherless sons emigrated to Canada to begin a new life.

Charles William Stanley Spencer was born in Sheffield in Yorkshire in 1890, the only son of Louis Spencer, a local bank manager, and his wife. Before the war, he had been employed in the Sheffield branch of the London City and Midland Bank. In 1915, he enlisted in the 24th Battalion, the Royal Fusiliers as a Private soldier, and in 1918 he transferred to the West Yorkshire Regiment as a Second Lieutenant. Throughout over three years of active service he kept a diary describing his experiences. He was wounded three times, and awarded a Military Cross in August, 1918. He survived the war, though, and afterwards returned to Sheffield, and married Molly Breakey in 1924. Sadly, he was then taken ill, and forced to retire to Bournemouth, where he lived out the rest of his days, eventually dying in 1943, aged fifty-three. His son Tony Spencer later came across his diary, and saw to it that it was published.

Private William Arthur Spittels was born in Stoke Munden in Buckinghamshire. At the outbreak of the war, he had been living with his wife Flossie Spittels in Willesden in Middlesex, and their two small children. William had joined the Middlesex Regiment before transferring to the 24th Battalion, the Royal Fusiliers.

Second Lieutenant Cyril Francis Stafford was the son of Francis Bernardine Stafford and his Bessie Bourne, *nee* Langdon, of West Ham in Essex. Before the war, he had been a civil servant, and at the outbreak of war had joined the 1/15th Battalion, the London Regiment, popularly known as the "Civil Service Rifles". He had then transferred to the 6th (Reserve) Battalion, the Royal Fusiliers in November, 1916, and to the 24th Battalion in January, 1917. He had been made the Signals Officer of the 24th Battalion in February, 1917.

Private William Stephenson was born in Nottingham. At the outbreak of the war, he had been living in Newark with his wife May, and working as a professional golfer and club-maker. He had enlisted in Nottingham. As noted above, he had been writing a letter to his wife when he was killed (see section on "The Battles of the Somme ... "). He never got to see the youngest of his four children, Yvonne.

Arthur Alexander Stokes was born in Wolborough in Devon in 1894, the second son of James Stokes and his wife Mary Louise, *nee* White. Before the Great War, he had been living in Bovey Tracey in Devon, and working as a legal clerk. Upon the outbreak of the war, he had enlisted as a in the 24th Battalion in Bovey Tracey in Devon in January, 1915. He was killed in the Battle of Delville Wood on July 30th, 1916. A letter he wrote to his sister Marjorie just days before he was killed still survives (see section on "The Battles of the Somme ... " above).

Private Bertram Charles Stone was born in Abbotsbury in Dorset in 1895, the son of Charles Stone and his wife Emily Elizabeth, *nee* Harding. He died in Bristol in 1992.

Company Serjeant-Major Horace Oliver Stratford was born in St John's in Margate in Kent. At the time of the outbreak of the war, he was living in Kensington in London. He enlisted in London.

Private Charles Sutherland was born in Edinburgh in Scotland, and also enlisted there.

Private John Basil Taylor born in Sunderland in Co. Durham, the son of Frederic and Eliza Taylor. He enlisted in Bournemouth.

Lance-Serjeant Walter Prince Taylor was born in Dunedin in New Zealand. At the outbreak of the war, he had been living in Battersea in the County of London. He had enlisted in the 24th Battalion London.

Private James Benjamin Thomson was born in the Metropolitan Borough of Wandsworth in London, the son of Mr & Mrs Kate Buckland. At the outbreak of the war, he was living in Clapham. He enlisted in London.

Lance-Corporal Arthur Tipton was born in Penzance in Cornwall, the son of John and Elizabeth Tipton. He enlisted in Plymouth in Devon.

Private Albert Edward Turner was born in Exeter in Devon, and also enlisted there.

Second Lieutenant Douglas Maurice Jacques Ullman was born in London in 1891, the son of Julius Leopold Ullman and his wife Miriam, *nee* Phillips. Before the war, he had been educated in part in Dusseldorf and Geneva, and subsequently employed, as a managing director, by Soane & Smith, a firm of antique dealers, in London.

Private Frank Allan Urry born in Margate in Kent, the son of Walter B. Urry and his wife Elizabeth Frances. At the outbreak of the war, he was living in Catford in London. He enlisted in Lewisham.

Private George Charles Vickery was born in Bethnal Green in the East End of London. At the outbreak of the war, he was living in Enfield in Middlesex. He enlisted in London.

Private Jack Harry Vincent was born in Worcester in 1894, the son of Walter Vincent and his wife Elizabeth. At the outbreak of the Great War, he was living in Manchester. He enlisted in the 24th Battalion in Brierley Hill in the Black Country.

Lieutenant-Colonel Henry Ernest Walshe was a career soldier, who had served in the Boer War in 1899-1902.

Private Albert Edward Ward was born in Bethnal Green in the East End of London, and also enlisted there.

Reginald Alexander John Warneford was born in Cooch Behar near Darjeeling in India in 1891, the son of Reginald William Henry Warneford, a railway engineer and former soldier, and his wife Alexandra, *nee* Campbell. He received little formal education in his early childhood in India, instead riding the railways with his father, exploring the jungles, learning to read the sky by day and night, and developing a free – perhaps even wild – spirit. But in 1902, after his parents had separated, his father had died and his mother had remarried, he was sent to England to live with his grandfather, the Rev. Thomas Lewis Warneford, and in turn, as a boarder and choral scholar, to King Edward VI School in Stratford-upon-Avon – "Shakespeare's School". Here, he excelled in scientific and practical subjects, although he was "not at all keen on ... football ... played on wet cold fields on winter afternoons". In 1905, when he was still only thirteen, he left school to join the Merchant Navy, and at the outbreak of the Great War in 1914, he applied to join the Royal Navy, but was rejected. He then enlisted in the 24th Battalion, the Royal Fusiliers as a Private soldier on January 8th, 1915, but transferred to the Royal Naval Air Service as a Flight Sub-Lieutenant on February 10th, qualifying as a pilot after only fifteen days training on 25th. Flight Sub-Lieutenant Warneford went on to bring down Zeppelin LZ37 over Ghent in German-occupied Belgium on June 7th, 1915, for which he was awarded not only a Victoria Cross but also a Knight's Cross of the Legion of Honour (*Legion d'Honneur*). He was fatally injured in a flying accident at Buc aerodrome near Paris in France ten days later, on June 17th, 1915. It is said that he had had a premonition of his death at a reception held in his honour in Paris the previous day, where he had told a well-wisher that her gift of flowers would be for his grave, "for ... I will not live to see England again". He is buried in Brompton Cemetery in London, near his beloved grandfather. A poetic tribute to him read, "Hush! For his heart, that knew not any fear|Is stilled for ever, and our praises fall|Upon deaf ears. He is no longer there|To spend himself, a splendid prodigal,|As the two crosses that the Nations gave|Will shine, not on his breast, but on his grave".

Private John Robert Warriner was born in Ulverston on the Furness Peninsula in what was Lancashire and is now Cumbria. At the outbreak of the war, he was living with his wife Mrs M.E. Warriner in Kirkby-in-Furness. He enlisted in Ulverston. His service number, 4594, indicates that he did so in November, 1915.

Private Bernard Warth was born in London in 1887, the son of John Warth, a farmer, and his wife Louise Cawthorn, *nee* Brooks. Before the war, he had gone to school in Chatteris in Cambridgeshire, and in 1911 had emigrated to what was then Selukwe in Southern Rhodesia, and is now Shurugwi in Zimbabwe, to become a farmer. At the outbreak of the war, he had returned to his mother country to volunteer for active service in the army, enlisting in the 24th Battalion, the Royal Fusiliers in Ipswich in Suffolk on December, 1914. In 1915, he had married Elsie Mary Collins of Norwich in Norfolk. On hearing that he had been wounded, his wife travelled to Boulogne to visit him in hospital, but sadly he died before she got there.

Bernard's brother Thomas Warth was also killed in the Great War, fighting for the King's African Rifles in what was at the time part of British East Africa and is now Kenya.

William Waymark was born in Hastings in Sussex in 1896 or 1897 (sources differ), the son of Henry and Sarah Waymark. His Army Service Number, 21051, indicates that he enlisted as a Private soldier in the 24th Battalion in around mid-July, 1916. According to the Red Cross's database of Great War Prisoners of War, Private Waymark was taken prisoner by the Germans on November 28th, 1917 – during the Battle of Cambrai. He survived the war.

Second Lieutenant George Tudor Webb was the second son of Dr William H. Webb of Kingsbridge in Devon. Before the war, he had received his primary and secondary education at Sherborne School in Dorset and Kingsbridge Grammar School in Devon, respectively, and had then gone on to study medicine at Durham University. At the outbreak of the war, he had been in the Malay States.

Private Edwyn Cyril Wellicome was born in Marlow in Buckinghamshire, the son of Richard and Emily Wellicome. He enlisted in Epsom in Surrey.

Cyril's older brother, Serjeant William Cecil Wellicome of the Seaforth Highlanders, was also killed in the Great War, in the Battle of the Ancre on November, 13th, 1916, and is buried in Mailly Wood Cemetery in Maiily-Maillet.

Private Charles William Edward Wells was born in Shoreham in Sussex, and enlisted in Hove.

Private James Francis Wells was born in Barnham in Suffolk 1881, the son of James Wells and his wife Alice, *nee* Cawley. He was educated at Elvedon Voluntary-Aided Primary School, also in Suffolk. At the outbreak of the Great War, he was living in Elveden, and working as a garden labourer. He enlisted in the Suffolk Regiment before transferring to the 24th Battalion, the Royal Fusiliers.

His brother, John James Francis Wells of the Suffolk Regiment, died in France on November 28th, 1918, seventeen days after the end of the war.

Lance-Corporal Frederick Harold Wescott was born in and educated in Torquay in Devon, and enlisted in Exeter. At the time of his death, his mother, Mrs A. Nowell-Usticke, formerly Wescott, was still living in Torquay.

Private Alfred John Westlake was born in Dartmouth in Devon, the son of John H. and Selina Westlake. At the outbreak of the war, he was living in Ipswich in Suffolk with his wife, who was from there. He enlisted in the 24th Battalion, the Royal Fusiliers before going on to transfer to the Suffolk Regiment. In late 1915, he wrote a vivid account of the 24th Battalion's "first taste of the trenches" (see section on "Deployment to the Western Front" above).

Two of Alfred's brothers also died during the war: one, William James Westlake, a Royal Marine, at the Battle of Coronel in November, 1914; and the other, Wilfred Grey Westlake, a Boy 2nd Class, also in the Navy, in a naval hospital in Plymouth in February, 1916. Wilfred was aged only 15¾.

Private Richard Frederick Arthur Westphal was born in Jamaica in 1896, the son of Bishop Augustus Westphal and his wife Georgine. Before the war, he had been educated at Fulneck School near Leeds, and in 1914 had enrolled onto an Arts course in the University of Manchester. On reaching the age of nineteen in 1915, he had enlisted in the 24th Battalion, the Royal Fusiliers in Fairfield in Manchester.

Richard's older brother Benjamin Augustus Westphal, who was a Second Lieutenant in the 18th Battalion, the Manchester Regiment, was killed at Arras, and is commemorated on the Arras Memorial and in Fairfield Church.

Cecil Dobie Murray White was born in Wigan in Lancashire in 1896, the third and youngest child and only son of Arthur Pretyman White and his wife Lucy Murray, *nee* McKenzie. He was educated at home by a private tutor, and at schools in Upholland in Lancashire, and in Giggleswick in Yorkshire. And he went on to be employed as a trainee locomotive engineer in the works in Crewe (his father also worked on the railways). At the outbreak of the Great War, he was living in Hale in Cheshire. He enlisted as a Private soldier in the 24th Battalion in Epsom in Surrey.

Serjeant William Albert Whitfield was born in Clement's Town in Cornwall. At the outbreak of the war, he was living in St Annes. He enlisted in Camborne.

John Wilcock was born in Wennington in Lancashire, the son of William Wilcock and his wife Jane, *nee* Carter. At the outbreak of the war, he was still living in Wennington, and working as a grocer's assistant and travelling salesman. He enlisted as a Private soldier in the 24th Battalion in Lancaster.

Private Tom Wood was born in Doddiscombsleigh in Devon. He enlisted in Exeter.

Sidney Richard Worger was born in Pimlico in Middlesex in 1875, the first son of the Richard Worger, a coach-maker, and his wife Anna Maria, *nee* Fulton. Before the war, he had been employed as an apprentice coach-maker, and then as an insurance clerk, initially in Westminster, and subsequently in the Essex and Suffolk Fire Office in Colchester. He had also been a part-time actor, with the stage name Richard S. Fulton. And he had married the divorcee Gertrude Mary

Mortimer Bardmann, *nee* Evans, an actress, in Westminster in 1904. Upon the outbreak of the war, he had enlisted in the 24th Battalion, the Royal Fusiliers in Colchester in Essex in March, 1915. During the war, Private Worger wrote a series of letters to his wife, that still survive, in the Imperial War Museum in Kennington (see section on "Deployment to the Western Front" above). Sadly, he was killed, in the Battle of Delville Wood, on July 31st July, 1916 (see section on "The Battles of the Somme ... " above). An obituary to him was published in the theatrical trade newspaper, *The Era*, commonly known as *"The Actor's Bible"*, on August 23rd, 1916. It read, *"Another actor hero*. I regret to have to announce the death of Richard Fulton (Sidney Richard Worger), who will be remembered as acting under the management of Mr W. Maclaren, Messrs Hill and Ayrton, Mr J.A. Campbell and others. Attached to the ... 24th Royal Fusiliers since the outbreak of the war, Richard Fulton has been at the front for the past nine months, and met his death while doing stretcher bearing work. The sympathy of our readers will be extended to his widow (Gertrude Evans), who is nursing at the Military Hospital, Colchester, and also to his mother and sisters (Olive and Mary [May] Fulton) and his brother (Geoffrey Fulton), who is shortly leaving for the front with the King's Royal Rifles". Worger is also commemorated – as Fulton – in *"The Stage" Year Book* for 1918; and on the Roll of Honour in the vestibule of the Theatre Royal, Drury Lane, as one of 250 "Actors, Musicians, Writers and Workers for the Stage who have given their lives for their country".

Sidney's brother and fellow-actor Richard Fulton Worger, who went by the stage-name of Geoffrey Fulton, survived the war, having served as a Private soldier in the King's Royal Rifle Corps, and, as from April 26th, 1917, as a Second Lieutenant in the Royal Fusiliers.

Private Henry William Wyatt was born in Hammersmith in Middlesex, the son of Mr & Mrs Henry Wyatt. At the outbreak of the war, he had been living in Uxbridge with his wife, Mary Marriott Wyatt. He had enlisted in Exeter in Devon.

APPENDIX 2 – PRIVATE CHARLES REUBEN CLEMENTS

Before the Great War

My maternal grandfather, Charles Reuben – "Charlie" - Clements (CRC), was born at home in Hammersmith in Middlesex on January 12th, 1896, the son of Charles Ernest Clements, a carman and contractor, and his wife Jessie, *nee* Percy, a part-time music teacher. Home was 109 Yeldham Road, a small end-of-terrace Victorian house at the end of a quiet *cul-de-sac* off Fulham Palace Road (*Figure 33*). CRC received his education at Latymer School in Hammersmith. However, he was forced to leave school early, aged seventeen, in 1913, after his father died suddenly, aged only forty-two, in order to enter the workplace – as an assistant in a gentlemen's outfitter's shop – to help provide an income for his family. At this time, his family consisted of him; his widowed mother, familiarly known to him as "Ma"; and his two younger sisters, Jessie Winifred ("Jess"), who had been born in 1901, and Lilian Edith ("Lily"), born in 1904 (*Figure 34*). His elder brother John Edwin, who had been born in 1893, had died in 1894; and his younger brother, John Percy, who had been born in 1900, in 1901.

CRC was evidently a conscientious man, with a strong work-ethic. He never gambled, although he did "do the Pools", which he considered to be a game of skill rather than chance. And, after an unfortunate early experience at a friend's coming-of-age party, he never drank. He had a dry sense of humour. When my mother wrote to inform him of my – premature – birth in 1958, he wrote back that he was "delighted of course to hear that Robert Wynn is progressing so well" and "flattered at first to hear he resembled myself but on reading ...

that he was short of ... hair and putting on weight am rather in doubt". In his free time, he enjoyed a range of sporting pursuits.

The Great War

CRC voluntarily enlisted in the 24th (2nd Sportsmen's) Battalion, the Royal Fusiliers on May 30th, 1915, and was given the regimental number 3526 (*Figures 35-37*). It is evident from his surviving "Medical History" (Army Form B178), in the National Archives, dated June 4th, 1915, that he lied about his age when he volunteered, claiming to be twenty-two when he was actually only nineteen - possibly because he looked about sixteen (*Figure 38*). Also, that he stood only 5'6" tall, and weighed only 9st4lbs.

After enlistment, CRC was sent to Hare Hall Camp in Romford in Essex, where the 24th Battalion had just set up its base, for training. He emerged from training as a Private soldier and 1st Class Signaller. As a Signaller as well as a Private soldier, one of his responsibilities on the battle-front would be to relay communications. In the Great War, this was generally done by using field telephone networks, rather than by the hitherto conventional means of signalling with flags (using Semaphore), or with lamps or mirrors, or with a Heliograph (using Morse Code). It would involve the laying and constant repairing of miles of telephone cable in and around front-line trenches, often under fire. And it would be dangerous work. In April, 1917, the then Signals Officer for the 24th Battalion, Second Lieutenant Cyril Francis Stafford, would suffer a mortal wound while supervising the laying of telephone cables near Vimy Ridge while under heavy shell-fire (see also the section on "The Battles of Arras ... " and Appendix 1 above). Private Richards of the Royal Welch Fusiliers wrote, "Signallers who went into attacks with their companies had to muck in with the scrapping until the objective was taken and then if they were still on their feet were generally converted into runners [tasked with delivering messages by hand]. A runner's job was very dangerous: he might have to travel over ground from where the enemy had just been driven and which now was being heavily shelled. In shell holes here and there might be some of the enemy who had been missed by the mopping-up party or who had been shamming dead; they would pop up and start sniping at him. I remember one show we were in ... where extra runners had been detailed off for the day, losing fifteen out of twenty" (75).

CRC went on to serve with the 24th Battalion on the Western Front for three years, fighting in the Battles of the Somme in, 1916; in the Battles of Arras and Cambrai in 1917; and in the First and Battles of the Somme, and the Battle of Havrincourt, the first of the Battles of the Hindenburg Line, in 1918. At one point during the First Battles of the Somme, 1918, specifically on March 23rd, 1918, he was very close to where his future brother-in-law, my paternal grandfather, Able-Bodied Seaman Francis Wynn Jones of the Anson Battalion of 63rd (Royal Naval) Division, was captured by the advancing Germans, on the Flesquieres-Havrincourt Salient (see Appendix 3).

According to his "Casualty Form – Active Service", CRC was twice treated for "d. C.T. [?disease of Connective Tissue] Foot" – which I take to be "Trench Foot" - in the Winter of 1916/17. The first time was in the field, at No. 47 C.C.S. (Casualty Clearing Station), in Beauval, somewhat to the west of Beaumont-Hamel, on November 27th, 1916 (59). The second time was to the rear, at No. 8 Red X.H. (Red Cross Hospital), in Paris-Plage (Le Touquet), on the coast, near Etaples Camp, on December 27th (59). CRC was granted two ten-day periods of home leave over the three-year course of his service, the first between January 20th-30th, 1917, when his battalion was in the rear, and the second between February 12th-22nd, 1918, when it was on the front, near Courcelette.

CRC was reported in the "Nominal roll of casualties sustained during month of SEPTEMBER 1918" in the "*Battalion War Diary*" (89) as having been killed on September 10th (*Figure 39*)! In fact, according to his "Casualty Record – Active Service" (Army Form B103), he had been seriously wounded by shrapnel – or possibly shell fragments – in the left arm (elbow) and leg (thigh, knee and ankle) on September 12th (*Figure 40*). He was carried from the field to the 5th F.A. or

Field Ambulance, and from there he was taken – either by an actual ambulance or a horse-drawn cart - to No. 46 C.C.S or Casualty Clearing Station at Bac du Sud, near Bailleulval, just south-west of Arras (51; 56; 59; 78). F.As., including Dressing Stations, were staffed by Medical Officers of the Royal Army Medical Corps, supported by orderlies and teams of stretcher-bearers, and were, alongside Regimental Aid Posts, the first links in the "chain of evacuation" to mobile C.C.Ss. and stationary General Hospitals. C.C.Ss. were essentially field emergency hospitals, operating out of tents or wooden huts, but staffed by fully qualified medical doctors and nurses, supported by orderlies. They were also staffed by chaplains - religion, it seems, was a tenet central to the lives of soldiers on both sides. Both F.As. and C.C.Ss. saved a great many soldiers' lives. Soldiers whose lives were beyond saving often ended up in the so-called "Moribund Wards" at the C.C.Ss., and eventually in the cemeteries that sprang up adjacent to them. From No. 46 C.C.S. at Bac du Sud, CRC was transferred to No. 12 G.H. or General Hospital in Rouen on September 13th. And from there he was repatriated to the U.K., on board His Majesty's Hospital Ship "Formosa", on 15th (*Figure 41*). He spent the remaining two months of the war receiving treatment in hospitals in Keighley and Shoreham, and some time after the war convalescing in the Star and Garter Home in Richmond in Surrey. On September 20th, 1918, while he was at Shoreham, an X-Ray was taken of his wounded arm, and, according to his medical records, "a piece of shrapnel was found, localised and measured", but "the surgeon thought an operation inadvisable + it was left in situ". A later "Statement As To Disability" noted "metal fragments still in arm", and occasional "shooting pains", on account of which he was entitled to a Disability Pension of "5/- Dept Allowance + 3/6d allot weekly". He had "copped a Blighty one" (8). His only visible scar was the size and shape of a teardrop, under his eye.

CRC was almost certainly wounded in an operation in the Battle of Havrincourt, the first of the Battles of the Hindenburg Line, which took place on September 12th, 1918. The "*Battalion War Diary*" (89) contains a "NARRATIVE of part taken in operations 11/12th. SEPT. 1918", written by Lieutenant-Colonel Pipon, which reads in part as follows:

"As the BATTALION was resolved into it's component Companies for the fighting ... on both sides of the CANAL du NORD [which effectively formed part of the Hindenburg Line] on September 11th. and 12th. ... I ... give a brief account of what each COMPANY did.

... 'A' COMPANY (Capt. L.A. EKINS, M.C.) ... was not called upon for any particular task until the afternoon of the 12th. Then they were ordered to clear up the situation in FAGAN SUPPORT on the West side of the Canal, where pockets of Germans were still established and giving a good deal of trouble. At 4 o'clock Captain EKINS set out to do this and succeeded without suffering very heavy casualties. He then sent two platoons to bomb up (that is, northwards) HUNT AVENUE to the point where the trench was already clear and our posts established. The Platoons made good progress and unearthed a good many Germans as they went. It was necessarily a slow business, and, darkness falling, the enemy, whom Captain EKINS estimates at 30, were able to slip eastwards and escape. This was just south of COOPER TRENCH, where it had been hoped to corner the Germans ... , and force a surrender. This company got out of the line at 6-30 A.M. on the 13th ... .

... 'D' COMPANY (Capt. J.A. CHESTON [see also Appendix 1]) ... were under orders to form a defensive flank on the north in protection of the left of the 52nd. [HIGHLAND] LIGHT INFANTRY who were to be the assaulting Battalion. This was successfully accomplished, the Company following the line of KELLET TRENCH, occupying the northern section of ALBAN AVENUE which was the Brigade's objective and ADAM and EVE POST on the north [on the 11th]. Further the Company attacked and occupied German positions to the N.E. which threatened to be a menace to the new front line. During the evening a very heavy barrage was put down on the northern end of our new position and Captain CHESTON posted his men in shell-holes well in advance of the trench line and saved a good many casualties by doing so as the trenches were very badly knocked about indeed [Cheston was later awarded a

Military Cross for this piece of quick thinking and action]. At 3 A.M. on the 12th, this Company was relieved by the GRENADIER GUARDS ... .

... 'C' COMPANY (2/Lieut. C.M. CURTIS, M.C.) ... was ordered to carry out a bombing attack down FAGAN TRENCH and SUPPORT on the east side of the Canal [on the 12th]. On the way however they tumbled up against quite unexpected German opposition in the portion of FAGAN SUPPORT ... west of the Canal with several machine guns firing from shell-hole positions in the triangle to the south between it and the Canal. 2/Lieut. CURTIS at once embarked on an attack to clear the area, but, though three machine guns were taken and casualties were inflicted, the 1½ platoons of which the Company consisted at the time were not sufficient to drive the enemy out, and a line of posts was finally formed which kept the Germans thoroughly occupied until ... 'A COMPANY arrived to help clear up the position. The platoons of this ['C'] Company were very late in getting relieved from the line and the last did not reach ... HERMIES until 2 P.M. on the 13th.

... 'B' COMPANY (Capt. C.H. RUSSELL) ... were sent to clear the enemy out of LONDON TRENCH and LONDON SUPPORT, northward of the point where these trenches were held by posts of the 2nd. H.L.I. ... [on the 12th]. This company had the hardest fighting of any to do. The Germans were strong and stubborn and the platoons working parallel up these two trenches had to fight for every yard of the 700 of trench to be cleared. They did so in a way that speaks for itself of the spirit of the Company and its leaders. All that evening gradual progress was being made, [and] posts established to cover the new front and Eastward bound trenches. At dusk Lewis Guns dealt with what might have proved to be a counter bombing attack on LONDON TRENCH ... . It was not until the early hours of the 13th. when parties of the 2nd. S. STAFFORDS. were met coming across the Canal from SLAG AVENUE ... that the whole front could confidently be reported clear of the enemy. Twelve Machine Guns (heavy and light) were ... taken by the Company, probably many others were over-ran and overlooked. This Company eventually returned to ... HERMIES on the afternoon of the 13th.

CASUALTIES during these operation were KILLED 8 [+]
WOUNDED 49 [+] MISSING 1 [=] 58".

After the Great War

After the war, in 1919, CRC returned to work, in Harrods, a
luxury department store in Knightsbridge in the fashionable
West End of London, which at the time provided employment
for large numbers of ex-Servicemen. In 1921, he came   to
own and manage his own gentlemen's outfitter's shop at 180
South Ealing Road in Ealing in Middlesex, and to live in the
modest rooms above (*Figures 42-43*). As   befitting for
someone in that line of work, he was always very smartly
turned out. In 1933, he bought his first car, a "Baby Austin",
and thereafter spent a certain amount of time   each year
travelling round the south of England selling his wares.
Besides his retail business, he also dabbled in property.

CRC also returned to his sporting pursuits. He played
football for the amateur   side Ealing Wednesday, so-called
because most of the players were independent shopkeepers, and
they preferred to play on early closing day, which was
Wednesday, rather than on Saturday, so as not to lose their best
trading day's takings. The team had a particularly successful
season in 1923-24, ending up as winners of the Ealing Hospital
Cup, the Harrow Charity Shield, the Kingston and District
Wednesday League, the Philanthropic Cup, and the Roose
Francis Cup, and as runners-up in the Hounslow League and the
Middlesex Mid-Week Cup (*Figures 44-45*). They also won the
London Mid-Week Cup in 1930-31. CRC reportedly also
played on an *ad hoc* basis for the professional side Fulham,
who were in the Second Division of the English League, in the
early 1920s. However, he always supported, and would have
liked to play for, his local team, Brentford. Notwithstanding
this, he never really seriously   thought about becoming a
professional footballer, because the pay was poor – difficult to
believe as that is today. He did, though, represent the Thames
Valley Harriers at long-distance running, and Middlesex at
bowls, both, again, on an amateur basis. He also played tennis
to a high standard, including at the prestigious Queen's Club in

West Kensington in London, which, incidentally his father had helped to build in 1886. Here, he played with Fred Perry, who went on to win three Wimbledon Men's Singles titles, in 1934, 1935 and 1936.

On October 21st, 1921, CRC married Gladys Mabel Millard, familiarly known to him as "Mabs" (*Figure 46*). "Mabs's" mother, Sarah Ann Millard (*Figures 46-47*), incidentally, had served as a Voluntary Aid Detachment or V.A.D. nurse on the Home Front during the Great War (see also 7). In 1934, "Mabs" had a baby daughter, Peggy Anne, my mother. The family would come to enjoy taking in not only sporting events but also sundry other entertainments such as comedy shows or musicals at the Chiswick Empire or the "Q" Theatre (in Kew), or, on special occasions, in the West End. During the Second World War of 1939-45, CRC joined the Middlesex Home Guard (of "*Dad's Army*" fame), one of whose duties was to help to man a heavy anti-aircraft gun battery in Gunnersbury Park. According to one family story, which may or may not be entirely true, at the beginning of the *Vergeltungswaffen* or Vengeance-Weapon campaign directed against London, in June, 1944, he and his comrades, while attempting to shoot down a low-flying V-1 flying bomb or "Doodlebug", instead inadvertently shot up part of a nearby building! After the Second World War, in 1954, his daughter Peggy Anne married Emrys Wynn Jones (*Figure 48*). Then, in 1956, his wife "Mabs" died; and, in 1957, he married his second wife, a divorcee, Alice Elizabeth Ashton, *nee* Gooding.

CRC remained close throughout his later life to a number of his comrades from the Great War, especially to William "Billy" Bentley, who he regarded as once having saved his life, and who was his best friend (see Appendix 1 above); and to Archibald "Archie" Bannister, who was his best man (*Figure 46*). The old soldiers would all meet up in London every November, on the Friday closest to Remembrance Sunday, and would then all go together to the Cenotaph in Whitehall to attend the National Service of Remembrance. Like so many of his generation, CRC scarcely ever spoke, at least outside this closed circle, of his wartime experiences. However, he did once allude to the suffering of the horses on the Western Front (he had grown up around horses). He never committed to paper any of the thoughts or feelings he might have had about the war. These he took with him to his grave.

CRC died, after a sudden unexplained illness, on April 27th, 1958, aged sixty-two, and was cremated in Mortlake Cemetery on May 2nd. I was only three months old when he died, and, sadly, have nothing to remember him by bar these bare facts about his life, some faded photographs, and replacements for his lost 1914-15 Star, British War and Victory medals ("Pip, Squeak and Wilfred"). I am strangely comforted, though, by the knowledge that he would have had memories of me. My mother told me that she took me with her to see him when he was in what turned out to be his final days, and that he regained consciousness long enough to recognise me, and to lay his hand on my head, before drifting away again, for the final time.

APPENDIX 3 – ABLE-BODIED SEAMAN FRANCIS WYNN JONES

My paternal grandfather ("Taid"), Francis Wynn - known as "Wynn" - Jones (FWJ), enlisted in the 2/1ˢᵗ Pembroke Yeomanry, part of the Territorial Force, on January 18ᵗʰ, 1916, just after his eighteenth birthday on 15ᵗʰ, and just before conscription was introduced on 21ˢᵗ (*Figure 49*). At this time, the Pembroke Yeomanry was based in Suffolk, and formed part of the 1ˢᵗ Mounted Division, which later became the 1ˢᵗ Cyclist Division (part of the "Pneumatic Cavalry": 8). The Regiment was in Southwold during the German naval bombardment of nearby Lowestoft and Great Yarmouth on April 24ᵗʰ, 1916. On July 11ᵗʰ, 1917, FWJ was taken on by the 4ᵗʰ Reserve Battalion of the Royal Naval Volunteer Reserve, becoming an Able-Bodied Seaman. Then, on August 6ᵗʰ, 1917, he was drafted into the 5ᵗʰ (Nelson) Battalion of 2ⁿᵈ Brigade of 63ʳᵈ (Royal Naval) Division, based in Blandford in Dorset (the former Royal Naval Division had been incorporated into the 63ʳᵈ Division of the Land Army in 1916). And on August 28ᵗʰ, 1917, he was deployed with the Nelson Battalion to Calais in France. Shortly after arriving in France, he was hospitalised twice, the first time, in Rouen, in November, 1917, for "ICT [Inflammation of the Connective Tissue] Hand"; and the second time, in le Havre, between late December, 1917 and early January, 1918, for an undiagnosed condition. Following his final discharge from hospital, he spent some time at a Convalescent Depot in le Havre, and then at a Base Depot in Calais. Finally, the Nelson Battalion having been disbanded on February 23ʳᵈ, 1918, he joined the Anson Battalion of the 188ᵗʰ Brigade of the 63ʳᵈ (R.N.) Division on February 28ᵗʰ. And he was sent to the Flesquieres-Havrincourt Salient, on the front-line, the following day, St David's Day, March 1ˢᵗ. He wrote a letter to his parents on his way to the front on March 1ˢᵗ, which read in part as follows: "Dear Father + Mother, Just a few lines to let you know I have joined the Battalion at last and that my present address is Inf. R/3413, 3 Platoon, A Co., Anson Batt., B.E.F. [British Expeditionary Force]. We are at present in a village about 10 miles from the front, but we are going up farther tonight. .... I am feeling alright now .... I have not got much time to write today. I shall write again when we come back here which I hope will be Sunday. From Wynn". It would be the last that his parents would hear of him for many anxious weeks.

FWJ was reported as "missing" on the Flesquieres-Havrincourt Salient on March 23rd, 1918, during the Battle of St Quentin, the first of the First Battles of the Somme, 1918. Judging from the Anson Battalion's "*Battalion War Diary*", this must have been somewhere between Havrincourt and Bertincourt, very close to where his future brother-in-law, my maternal grandfather, Private Charles Rueben Clements of the 24th Battalion, the Royal Fusiliers, was in action at the same time (see Appendix 2). An unofficial letter to the effect that FWJ was "missing" was sent to his parents, from the Anson Battalion Chaplain, on April 13th; and an official one, from the Officer in Charge of Records in the Record Office of the 63rd Division, on April 20th. It was not until around April 25th that they eventually received the longed-for news that their son was safe, by way of a post-boy on a bicycle. Bless him, he rode to their farm excitedly shouting out to all within earshot on his way, "*Mae Wynn yn byw, mae Wynn yn byw*" (Welsh for "Wynn is alive"). It was an emotional moment.

FWJ had in fact been captured, and spent the last six months of the war initially in temporary Prisoner-of-War/Labour camps at Le Transloy and at St Amand in France, and subsequently in Belgium, while being registered as being in a permanent camp at Limburg in Germany (*Figures 50-51*). He was somewhere south of Tongres or Tongeren in Belgium at the time of the Armistice on November 11th, 1918. A week later, on November 18th he wrote a letter there to his parents, describing the conditions of his captivity. It read in its entirety as follows:

"My dear Father + Mother,

At last I am able to write to you once more, but under very different circumstances from the last time. The war is over at last, thank God, and we are free once more. Our sentries left us several days ago about 40 miles south of this place and told us to find our way the best we could to Holland, but the Dutch Government will not let us cross the border as we have got to stay here until our Army comes. The Germans are still here but do not interfere with us in any way + give us no food so we have to depend on the civilian population + they seem only too glad to do it. The Belgian Relief Fund supplies food for us all but many civilian families have adopted one, two or three soldiers + those that are lucky enough to have these billets are looked after like lords. One friend of mine has the best bed in a house while the German officers billeted on the same people have to sleep amongst the potatoes! I and another young fellow get our dinner with a private family + other meals from the Relief Fund + we cannot wish for better.

Well, I suppose I had better tell you some of my history for the last eight months. When I was captured I was taken with about 100 others to a camp at a place called Le Transloy near Bapaume. Of course I could not tell you before, but we were on very short rations and as for the dinners – well, you give better stuff every day to the pigs. When I come home don't expect to see me looking exactly fat. Although I am run down, I consider myself to look well compared with some of the other poor fellows. Many have died from exposure + want of food. – From Le Transloy we shifted to a town called St Amand in Northern France + there we stayed till we started on the march through Belgium in October. The food was a bit better there but there is no nourishment in any of the food they give us. Since the beginning of October we have been gradually marching back before the advance of our army doing a few days' work here + there + then marching back. – I need not give you any more particulars now, I can give you them when I come home.

I am in the best of health, the only trouble has been that the change from bad to good food upset my stomach a few days ago but I am alright now.

Trusting you are all alright + hoping to see you shortly. I look forward to Xmas at home as it will be the first since 1912. Kind regards to all,

Your loving son,

Wynn

P.S. You will see no more of the "60 mile an hour" word on the envelope! I don't know if this is censored, but it won't be by Germans".

Ten days later, on November 28th, FWJ wrote another letter in Amersfoort in Holland, letting his parents know he was on his way home. It read in part as follows:

"My Dear Father + Mother,

Just a few lines to let you know that I am slowly making my way back to the old country although I may be some time yet before I reach it. I am at present with about 3,000 others in a big camp in a place called Amersfoort waiting for arrangements to be made to send us on to England. We left Maastricht on the Belgian border last Friday ... . I understand the Dutch frontier is closed to prisoners again, as all the camps in Holland are full up, so I think I was lucky to cross when I did.

We are in very comfortable quarters here, but of course we are all anxious to see the boat that will take us back home again. When I do arrive in England, I am hoping to have at least a month's leave to make up for the flesh I have lost during the last eight months. I am sure it will not take long to do that on uwd [Welsh for porage] and shot instead of Germany's pig food. Although I am a bit run down like the rest of the boys here, I am feeling alright so you need not worry about me at all.

I have been wondering whether D.J. [his younger brother Dei] has had to go abroad but of course now the war is over he will be alright.

Well, I have no more news to tell you today, but I hope to be able to tell you all about it round the fire before very long.

King regards to all

Your loving son

Wynn".

FWJ's enamel mug stamped "*Wupperman* 18", the standard issue to German soldiers and Prisoners-of-War, has now come down to me, as has the hand-made wooden box - given to him by a fellow PoW - in which he brought all his meagre belongings home from the Great War.

Havrincourt

There is little in this peaceful farm-land now
to show that it is fertilised by blood.
But yet it is. By blood shed by Britain
and her distant Dominions, and by France
and hers, and by Germany. By a lost
generation, a hundred years ago.
Blood shed as the great war-machine ground on
under star-shells and clouds of poison gas
among the ceaseless clatter of small arms
to soak into the soil where gravestones grow.

My grandfathers became blood-brothers here
one cold March morning, fighting side-by-side.
One was captured. The other one escaped.
The front then to-ed and fro-ed a hundred miles,
and brought him back again to this same place.
This time he was very gravely wounded
(his life was saved by a comrade-in-arms).
If either one had died in Havrincourt,
then, I would not be here to muse on Fate.
I owe them everything - my grandfathers.

SOURCES

1) Ashworth, T., 1980. *Trench Warfare 1914-1918 – The Live and Let Live System.* MacMillan.

2) Babington, A., 1983. *For the Sake of Example.* Leo Cooper (republished in revised form by Penguin in 1993). An account by a judge, highlighting the injustice of many of the capital courts-martial that took place during the Great War and its immediate aftermath. See also: Moore, W., 1974. *The Thin Yellow Line.* Leo Cooper. Documents both judicial and extra-judicial executions for supposed cowardice.

3) Barton, P. (writer and presenter), 2016. *The Somme from both Sides of the Wire.* BBC. A DVD of a three-part television series. See also Barton, P., 2006. *The Somme – A New Panoramic Perspective.* Constable (in association with the Imperial War Museum).

4) Bilton, D., 2005. *Arras - Oppy Wood.* Pen & Sword (Battleground Series). See also: Cave, N., 1996. *Arras – Vimy Ridge.* Pen & Sword (Battleground Series).

5) Binding, R.G., 1929. *A Fatalist at War.* George Allen & Unwin. An English translation of Binding's war diaries and letters, originally written in German. Binding was born in Basel in Switzerland in 1867. Before the Great War, he studied Medicine and Law, before joining the Hussars. And during the war, he commanded a Squadron of Dragoons. Afterwards, incidentally, he won a silver medal – for Art – at the Olympic Games in Amsterdam in 1928. He died in 1938.

6) Blunden, E., 1928. *Undertones of War.* Richard Cobden Sanderson. Blunden's autobiographical account of his Great War experiences as an officer with the Royal Sussex Regiment, including in the Battles of the Somme in 1916, and the Battle of Ypres (Passchendaele) in 1917. Blunden survived the Great War without suffering any serious physical injury, which he attributed to his diminutive stature rendering him "an inconspicuous target". His psychological scars, though, were to remain with him throughout his long life.

7) Bowser, T., 1917. *Britain's Civilian Volunteers - The Story of British V.A.D. Work in the Great War.* A. Melrose

(republished by the Imperial War Museum in 2003; and again, as part of *The V.A.Ds. – Accounts of the Voluntary Aid Detachment During the First World War 1914-18*, by Leonaur in 2014). Sister Ida Thekla Bowser served as a V.A.D. or Voluntary Aid Detachment nurse on the Western Front during the Great War, and died, of injuries suffered there, in January, 1919. As well as nurses, the V.A.D. also provided ward-maids, laundresses, cooks, clerks and drivers (including ambulance drivers).

8) Brophy, J. & Partridge, E., 1930. *Songs and Slang of the British Soldier.* Republished - as *The Daily Telegraph Dictionary of Tommies' Songs and Slang, 1914-1918* - by Pen & Sword in 2008. See also the German equivalent: Graff, S. & Bormann, W., 1925. *Schwere Brocken* ... .

9) Brown, M., 1991. *The Imperial War Museum Book of the First World War* ... . Sidgwick & Johnson.

10) Brown, M., 1993. *The Imperial Museum Book of the Western Front.* Sidgwick & Jackson.

11) Brown, M., 1996. *The Imperial War Museum Book of the Somme.* Sidgwick & Jackson. Covers the 1918 as well as the 1916 battles. See also: Evans, M.M., 1986. *The Battles of the Somme.* Weidenfeld & Nicolson.

12) Bull, S., 2014. *The Old Front Line – The Centenary of the Western Front in Pictures.* Casemate. Features an abundance of old and new photographs. See also: Giles, J., 1986. *The Somme Then and Now.* An After the Battle Publication. And: Giles, J., 1992. *The Western Front Then and Now* ... . An After the Battle Publication.

13) Cave, N., 1994. *Somme – Beaumont Hamel* ... . Leo Cooper (an imprint of Pen & Sword).

14) Cave, N., 1999. *Somme - Delville Wood.* Leo Cooper, an imprint of Pen & Sword (Battleground Series).

15) Chambers, S.J., 2004. *Uniforms and Equipment of the British Army in World War I – A Study in Period Photographs.* A Schiffer Military History Book.

16) Chapman, G., 1933. *A Passionate Prodigality – Fragments of Autobiography.* Ivor Nicholson & Watson (republished by Ashford, Buchan & Enright in 1985).

17) Chasseaud, P., 1991. *Topography of Armageddon – A British Trench Map Atlas of the Western Front 1914-1918.* Mapbooks (republished by The Naval & Military Press in 1994). See also: Chasseaud, P., 2006. *Rats Alley – Trench Names of the Western Front, 1914-1918.* Spellmount.

18) Chasseaud, P., 2013. *Mapping the First World War.* Collins, in association with Imperial War Museums. The story of the Great War told through maps. See also: Gilbert, M., 1970. *The Atlas of the First World War.* Weidenfeld & Nicolson (revised and republished by Routledge in 1994, and again in 2008).

19) Cheyne, G.Y., 1988. *The Last Great Battle of the Somme – Beaumont-Hamel 1916.* John Donald Publishers Limited, Edinburgh. Emphasises the role of the 51st (Highland) Division.

20) Committee of Imperial Defence, 1923-49. *History of the Great War based on official documents ... .* 40 volumes. The *Official History.*

21) Connelly, M., 2002. *The Great War, Memory and Ritual – Commemoration in the City and East London, 1916-1939.* A Royal Historical Society publication, published by The Boydell Press.

22) Coombs, R.E.B., 1983. *Before Endeavours Fade – A Guide to the Battlefields of the First World War.* An After the Battle Publication.

23) Davis, W., 2012. *Into the Silence – The Great War, Mallory, and the Conquest of Everest.* The Bodley Head. Features biographical details and a photographic image of Private Herford of the 24th Battalion.

24) Downing, T., 2016. *Breakdown – The Crisis of Shell Shock on the Somme, 1916.* Little, Brown.

25) Doyle, P., 2017. *Disrupted Earth - Geology and Trench Warfare on the Western Front, 1914-18.* Uniform.

26) Doyle, P. & Schafer, R., 2015. *Fritz and Tommy – Across the Barbed Wire.* The History Press. Features accounts of events from soldiers from both sides.

27) Duffy, C., 2008. *Through German Eyes – The British & The Somme 1916.* Weidenfeld & Nicolson.

28) Dyer, G., 1994. *The Missing of the Somme.* Hamish Hamilton. The title is perhaps a little misleading. The book is principally about remembrance.

29) Ellis, J., 1976. *Eye-Deep in Hell – The Western Front 1914-18.* Croom Helm (republished by Book Club Associates in 1979).

30) Foley, M., 2007. *Hard as Nails - The Sportsmen's Battalion of World War One.* Spellmount. Contains some information on the 24th (2nd Sportsmen's) Battalion as well as the 23rd (1st Sportsmen's). See also Harris, C. & Whippy, J., 2008. *The Greater Game – Sporting Icons who fell in the Great War.* Pen & Sword. Contains a chapter on the two "Sportsmen's" Battalions.

31) Foss, M., 1967. *The Royal Fusiliers.* Hamish Hamilton (Famous Regiments Series).

32) Gibson, M., 1979. *Warneford VC – The First Naval Airman to be awarded the VC.* Friends of the Fleet Air Arm Museum. A biography of Reginald Warneford, sometime of the 24th Battalion, by his second cousin Mary Gibson.

33) Gilbert, M., 2006. *Somme – The Heroism and Horror of War.* John Murray. The same author also wrote: Gilbert, M., 1994. *The First World War – A Complete History.* Weidenfeld & Nicolson.

34) Griffith, P., 1994. *Battle Tactics of the Western Front – The British Army's Art of Attack 1916-18.* Yale University Press.

35) Griffith, W., 1931. *Up to Mametz.* Faber & Faber. Wyn Griffith's autobiographical account of his Great War experiences as an officer with the Royal Welch Fusiliers, including in the Battles of the Somme (his younger brother Watcyn was killed at Mametz Wood on July 10th, 1916). See also: Griffith, W. (Riley, J., ed.), 2021. *Up to Mametz ... and beyond.* Pen & Sword. A revised edition incorporating Griffith's previously unpublished diaries and letters, picking up his story at Mametz in 1916, and carrying it through to the end of the war in 1918 (and beyond).

36) Gudmundson, B.I., 1989. *Stormtroop Tactics – Innovation in the German Army, 1914-1918.* Praeger.

37) Hart, P., 2005. *The Somme.* Weidenfeld & Nicolson (republished by Cassell in 2006). Features extracts from interviews with surviving veterans (the author, Peter Hart, was an Oral Historian at the Imperial War Museum).

38) Holmes, R., 1995. *The Western Front.* BBC Books.

39) Holmes, R., 2004. *Tommy – the British Soldier on the Western Front.* HarperCollins Publishers.

40) Horsfall, J. & Cave, N., 2002. *Hindenburg Line - Cambrai – Bourlon Wood.* Leo Cooper, an imprint of Pen & Sword (Battleground Series). See also: Oldham, P., 1997. *The Hindenburg Line.* Pen & Sword (Battleground Series).

41) Hurst, S.C., 1929. *The Silent Cities – An Illustrated Guide to the War Cemeteries and Memorials to the "Missing" in France and Flanders: 1914-1918.* Methuen & Co. (republished by The Naval & Military Press in 1993). A comprehensive guide produced in association with the Imperial War Graves Commission (now the Commonwealth War Graves Commission). See also: Crane, D., 2013. *Empires of the Dead – How One Man's Vision Led to the Creation of World War One's War Graves.* William Collins. The story of Fabian Ware and the founding of the Imperial War Graves Commission.

42) Hutchison, G.S., 1933. *Pilgrimage.* Rich & Cowan. The author of this book, Lieutenant-Colonel Graham Seton Hutchison, D.S.O., M.C., who fought in the Great War with the Argyll and Sutherland Highlanders, and later with the Machine Gun Corps, was a controversial figure. According to his own account, on April 14th, 1918, three days after Haig's "Backs to the Wall" Order, he ordered the machine-gunning of a party of forty British troops attempting to surrender to the Germans, of whom only two survived. After the war, though, he began to take an active interest in the welfare of former soldiers, founding the Old Contemptibles Association, and playing a role in the founding of the British Legion. He went on to found the British Empire Fascist Party in 1933.

43) Hutchison, G.S., 1938. *Machine Guns: Their History and Tactical Employment.* MacMillan & Co. (republished by The Naval & Military Press in 2004).

44) Imperial War Museums, 2014. *The Battle of the Somme.* Imperial War Museums. A digitally remastered DVD of

Geoffrey Malins's film, originally released in 1916. The sequel, *The Battle of the Ancre and Advance of the Tanks*, originally released in early 1917, is also now available in digital format. At the time of writing, the third part of the trilogy, *The German Retreat and the Battle of Arras*, originally released in late 1917, is in the process of being digitised.

45) Junger, E., 2003. *Storm of Steel*. Allen Lane. An English translation of Junger's memoir, originally written in German. Junger was an author, philosopher, naturalist and entomologist, and evidently also possessed of something of an adventurous spirit. He ran away to join the French Foreign Legion in 1913, aged only eighteen. He then fought throughout the Great War, from 1914-18, and was wounded no fewer than seven times, and awarded the *Pour le Merite*, the German equivalent of the Victoria Cross, in 1918. And he later served as an intelligence officer in the Second World War, from 1939-44, when he was dismissed for suspected involvement in the von Stauffenberg plot to assassinate Hitler. At some not inconsiderable risk, he also passed on intelligence about upcoming transports to concentration camps, and thereby helped to save many Jewish lives. He died in 1998 - aged 102.

46) Kipling, R., 1915. *The New Army in Training*. MacMillan and Co. The author and poet Rudyard Kipling's only son, Lieutenant John Kipling of the Irish Guards, was killed at the Battle of Loos in 1915, aged only eighteen, and is buried in Haisnes in France (and also commemorated in the church of St Bartholomew in Burwash in Sussex, close to the family home of Batemans). After the Great War, Kipling Senior worked with the Imperial War Graves Commission on the selection of appropriate epitaphs for war graves and memorials. There is no epitaph or personal inscription on his son's grave.

47) Lewis-Stempel, J., 2014. *The War behind the Wire – The Life, Death and Glory of British Prisoners Of War, 1914-18*. Weidenfeld & Nicolson. See also: Wilkinson, O., 2017. *British Prisoners-of-War in First World War Germany*. Cambridge University Press.

48) Linge, P. & Linge, K., 2015. *Missing But Not Forgotten – Men of the Thiepval Memorial*. Pen & Sword. Features biographical details and a photographic image of Private

D'Abadie of the 24th Battalion. See also: Stamp, G., 2016. *The Memorial to the Missing of the Somme. Revised Edition.* Profile Books. And: Sackville-West, R., 2021. *The Searchers – The Quest for the Lost of the First World War.* Bloomsbury. Concerns the search for the "Missing" of the Great War, which continues to this day.

49) Lloyd, N., 2013. *Hundred Days – The End of the Great War.* Viking.

50) Lloyd, N., 2021. *The Western Front – A History of the First World War.* Penguin.

51) MacDonald, L., 1980. *The Roses of No Man's Land.* Michael Joseph. Features extracts from interviews with the nurses and doctors of the Western and Home Fronts, and their patients.

52) MacDonald, L., 1983. *Somme.* Michael Joseph.

53) MacDonald, L., 1993. *1915 – The Death of Innocence.* Headline Book Publishing.

54) MacDonald, L., 1998. *To the Last Man – Spring 1918.* Viking.

55) Masefield, J., 1919. *The Battle of the Somme.* William Heinemann (reprinted in 1968 by Cedric Chivers).

56) Mayhew, E., 2013. *Wounded.* The Bodley Head. The story of the Field Ambulances, Casualty Clearing Stations and Hospitals of the Western Front.

57) Middlebrook, M., 1971. *The First Day on the Somme.* Allen Lane (republished in revised form by Pen & Sword in 2016). Features extracts from interviews with surviving veterans.

58) Middlebrook, M., 1978. *The Kaiser's Battle.* Allen Lane.

59) Ministry of Pensions, The, 1923. *Location of Hospitals and Casualty Clearing Stations, British Expeditionary Force, 1914-1919.* (Re)published by The Naval & Military Press in 2014.

60) Montague, C.E., 1922. Disenchantment. Chatto & Windus.

61) Olusoga, D., 2015. *The World's War.* Head of Zeus. Emphasises the global nature of the Great War, and in particular the role of the millions of non-white soldiers and labourers who took part in it. See also: Van Galen Last, D. & Futselaar, D. (eds.), 2015. *Black Shame – African Soldiers in*

Europe, 1914-22. Bloomsbury (English translation). Morton-Jack, G., 2018. *The Indian Empire at War: From Jihad to Victory - The Untold Story of the Indian Army in the Great War.* Little, Brown. And: Wood, F. & Arnander, C., 2016. *Betrayed Ally – China in the Great War.* Pen & Sword.
62) O'Neill, H.C., 1922. *The Royal Fusiliers in the Great War.* William Heinemann. See also: Pinney, R., 1926. *The Royal Fusiliers in an Outline of Military History, 1685-1926.* Gale & Polden.
63) Pegler, M., 2012. *The Lee-Enfield Rifle.* Osprey Publishing (Weapon Series, No. 17).
64) Pegler, M., 2013. *The Vickers-Maxim Machine Gun.* Osprey Publishing (Weapon Series, No. 25).
65) Philpott, W., 2009. *Bloody Victory – The Sacrifice on the Somme ... .* Little, Brown. The same author also wrote: Philpott, W., 2014. *Attrition – Fighting the First World War.* Little, Brown.
66) Pitt, B., 1962. *1918 – The Last Act.* Cassell. See also: Thompson, J., 2018. *1918 – How the First World War was Won.* Welbeck (in association with the Imperial War Museums).
67) Prior, R. & Wilson, T., 1992. *Command on the Western Front – The Military Career of Sir Henry Rawlinson 1914-1918.* Blackwell (republished by Pen & Sword in 2004). Ostensibly a biography of Rawlinson, but also deals with Haig, Allenby, Byng, Gough, Monash and Currie. See also: Travers, T., 1992. *How the War was Won – Command and Technology in the British Army on the Western Front, 1917-1918.* Routledge (republished by Pen & Sword in 2005).
68) Rawson, A., 2014. *Somme Campaign.* Pen & Sword.
69) Rawson, A., 2017a. *The Arras Campaign, 2017.* Pen & Sword.
70) Rawson, A., 2017b. *The Cambrai Campaign, 2017.* Pen & Sword.
71) Rawson, A., 2018a. *Somme Offensive, March 1918.* Pen & Sword.
72) Rawson, A., 2018b. *Advance to Victory, July to September 1918.* Pen & Sword.

73) Rawson, A., 2018c. *The Final Advance, September to November 1918.* Pen & Sword.

74) Renshaw, M., 2004. *Somme - Redan Ridge.* Pen & Sword (Battleground Series).

75) Richards, F., 1933. *Old Soldiers Never Die.* Faber and Faber (reprinted by The Naval & Military Press). Richards's autobiographical account of his Great War experiences as a Private soldier with the Royal Welch Fusiliers, including in the Battles of Ypres in 1914, Loos in 1915, the Somme in 1916, and Arras and Ypres in 1917, and in the German "Spring" Offensive and Allied "Hundred Days" Offensive in 1918. Described by one critic as "arguably the greatest of all published memoirs of the Great War". Richards's was certainly an authentic voice, free of officer-class affectation.

76) Robertshaw, A. & Kenyon, D., 2008. *Digging the Trenches – The Archaeology of the Western Front.* Pen & Sword. See also: Saunders, N.J., 2007. *Killing Time – Archaeology and the First World War.* Sutton.

77) Rogerson, S., 1933. *Twelve Days on the Somme – A Memoir of the Trenches, 1916.* Republished by Greenhill Books in 2003.

78) Scotland, T.R. & Heys, S. (eds.), 2012. *War Surgery 1914-18.* Helion & Company. Includes chapters entitled "Evacuation Pathway for the Wounded" and "Developments in Orthopaedic Surgery". It was in the field of orthopaedics that perhaps the most significant medical advance of the war was made. The introduction of the Thomas Splint by Robert Jones and Henry Gray helped to reduce the mortality rate from a compound fracture of the femur from around 80% in 1914-15 to less than 20% in one study of over one thousand cases in 1917.

79) Sebag-Montefiore, H., 2016. *Somme – Into the Breach.* Viking.

80) Sheffield, G., 2003. *The Somme.* Cassell. The same author also wrote: Sheffield, G., 2001. *Forgotten Victory: The First World War - Myths and Reality.* Headline (republished by Sharpe Books in 2018).

81) Spencer, T. (ed.), 2008. *Stanley Spencer's Great War Diary 1915-1918.* Pen & Sword. A diary recounting the

author's war service with the 24th Battalion, the Royal Fusiliers from 1915-17, and with the West Yorkshire Regiment in 1918. Includes descriptions of his involvement with the 24th Battalion in the Battles of the Somme in 1916 and of Arras in 1917.

82) Stedman, M., 1998. *Somme – Guillemont.* Leo Cooper, an imprint of Pen & Sword (Battleground Series).

83) Sulzbach, H., 1973. *With the German Guns – Four Years on the Western Front.* Leo Cooper (republished by Frederick Warne in 1981). An English translation of Sulzbach's Great War diary, originally written, and subsequently published, in German. Sulzbach survived the Great War, and afterwards returned to Germany, only to have to flee to Britain in 1937 in order to escape the then escalating Nazi persecution of Jews. He spent the first few months of the Second World War in an internment camp on the Isle of Man, before, rather remarkably, joining the British Army in 1940, and receiving a commission in 1945. After the Second World War, he served as a cultural officer at the German Embassy in London, in which role his principal concern was the promotion of Anglo-German friendship.

84) Terraine, J., 1982. *White Heat – The New Warfare 1914-18.* Sidgwick & Jackson. For more on advanced weapons technology, see: Fletcher, D., 2004. *British Mk I Tank, 1916.* Osprey. And: Cooper, B., 2010. *The Ironclads of Cambrai,* Pen & Sword.

85) Terraine, J. & Barnett, C. (writers), 2009. *The Great War.* BBC (in collaboration with the Imperial War Museum). A series of DVDs of a twenty-six part television series produced by the BBC in 1963-64 (accompanied by an elegantly compressed book of the same name). See also Strachan, H. (writer), 2013. *The First World War.* A series of DVDs of a television series produced by Channel 4 in 2003 (accompanied by a book of the same name). And: Skelding, E. & Cave, N. (writers), 2013. *Walking the Western Front.* A series of DVDs of a television series produced by ITV in 2012-13 (accompanied by a series of books).

86) Treacher, K., 2000. *Siegfried Herford – An Edwardian Rock Climber.* Ernest Press.

87) Uys, I., 1983. *Delville Wood*. Uys Publishers. Emphasises the role of the South African Infantry Brigade.

88) Van Emden, R., 2016. *The Somme – The Epic Battle in Soldiers' Own Words and Photographs*. Pen & Sword. The same author also wrote: Van Emden, R., 2008. *The Soldiers' War – The Great War through Veterans' Eyes*. Bloomsbury.

89) Various Authors, 2015a. *2 Division, 5 Infantry Brigade, Royal Fusiliers (City of London Regiment), 24th Battalion, 8 November 1915-31 March 1919 (First World War, War Diary, WO95/1349)*. The Naval and Military Press. Published in association with The National Archives.

90) Various Authors, 2015b. *2 Division, 99 Infantry Brigade, Royal Fusiliers (City of London Regiment), 17th, 22nd and 23rd Battalions ... (First World War, War Diary, WO95/1372/1-2)*. The Naval and Military Press. Published in association with The National Archives.

91) War Office, The, 1914a. *Field Service Pocket Book - 1914*. His Majesty's Stationery Office (republished by David & Charles in 1971).

92) War Office, The, 1914b. *Infantry Training - 1914* . His Majesty's Stationery Office

93) War Office, The, 1916. *Notes for Officers on Trench Warfare*. His Majesty's Stationery Office (republished, as part of *"The Tommies' Manual – 1916*, by Amberley Publishing, in 2016).

94) War Office, The, 1919. *Officers Died in the Great War, 1914-19*. His Majesty's Stationery Office (republished by J.L.R. Sansom in 1975, and again by Samson Books in 1979). Contains approximately forty thousand names. See also: Clutterbuck, L.A., 1914-16. *A Biographical Record of British Officers who fell in the Great War*. Anglo-African Publishing (recently republished by The Naval & Military Press). And: De Ruvigny, Marquis, 1916-22. *The Roll of Honour – A Biographical Record of All Members of His Majesty's Naval and Military Forces who have fallen in the War*. The Standard Art Book Company (recently republished by The Naval & Military Press). Contains, in five volumes, approximately 25 000 biographies, and seven thousand photographs, principally of officers.

95) War Office, The, 1921. *Soldiers Died in the Great War, 1914-19, Part 12 – Royal Fusiliers (City of London Regiment).* His Majesty's Stationery Office (republished by J.B. Hayward & Sons in 1989). Contains approximately twenty thousand names. See also: Various Authors, 1920. *The National Roll of the Great War, 1914-1918.* National Publishing (recently republished by The Naval & Military Press). Contains, in fifteen volumes, approximately 150 000 biographies, principally of men who served and survived.

96) War Office, The, 1922a. *Report of the War Office Committee of Enquiry into "Shell-Shock".* His Majesty's Stationery Office (republished by The Naval & Military Press in 2014). See also: Babington, A., 1997. *Shell Shock – A History of the Changing Attitudes to War Neurosis.* Leo Cooper. And: Sassoon, S., 1937. *The Complete Memoirs of George Sherston.* Faber and Faber (republished in its constituent parts by the Folio Society in 1971-74). A fictionalised autobiography, including an account of the author's wartime treatment for "shell shock" in Craiglockhart War Hospital in Slateford, near Edinburgh, by the eminent neurologist Captain William Halse Rivers Rivers of the Royal Army Medical Corps.

97) War Office, The, 1922b. *Statistics of the Military Effort of the British Empire during the Great War, 1914-1920.* His Majesty's Stationery Office.

98) Ward, F., 1920. *The 23rd (Service) Battalion, Royal Fusiliers (First Sportsman's).* Sidgwick & Jackson (republished by Leonaur in 2010).

99) Westlake, R., 1994. *British Battalions on the Somme – 1916.* Leo Cooper, an imprint of Pen & Sword. See also: James, E.A., 1978. *British Regiments 1914-18 … .* Samson Books (republished by The Naval & Military Press in 2021).

100) White, J, 2014. *Zeppelin Nights – London in the First World War.* The Bodley Head.

101) Wynn, S., 2016. *Romford in the Great War.* Pen & Sword.

102) Yorke, T., 2014. *The Trench – Life and Death on the Western Front, 1914-1918.* Countryside Books. Features a selection of photographs and cut-away diagrams clearly

illustrating   trench design and construction (and aspects of trench life).

103) Zabecki, D., 1994. *Steel Wind – Colonel Georg Bruchmuller and the Birth of Modern Artillery.* Praeger. See also: Haber, L.F., 1986. *The Poisonous Cloud – Chemical Warfare in the First World War.* Oxford University Press.

ONLINE RESOURCES

www.armyservicenumbers.blogspot.com [website].

www.astreetnearyou.org [website]. Enables online access to searchable digital maps of places of origin of thousands of British and Empire service personnel who were killed in the Great War.

www.bedfordregiment.org.uk [website]. Includes biographical information on Private Medlock of the 24th Battalion, who is commemorated on the Great Gransden War Memorial.

www.britisharmyancestors.co.uk [website].

www.britishempire.co.uk [website]. Contains useful information on Army units.

www.cwgc.org [Commonwealth War Graves Commission website]. Contains invaluable information on Commonwealth War Graves and cemeteries. Search functions enable individual graves to be located.

www.derbyshireterritorials.com [website]. Features biographical details and a photographic image of Private Bond of the 24th Battalion.

www.europeana.eu [website]. Enables access to digitised primary and secondary sources on the Great War.

www.everyoneremembered.org [Royal British Legion website].

www.findagrave.com [website]. The world's largest gravesite collection.

www.firstworldwar.com [website]. Aims to provide "a multimedia history of World War One".

www.footballandthefirstworldwar.org [website]. Contains biographical information on Serjeant Evans and Private Purver of the 24th Battalion, who both played professional football before the war.

www.forces-war-records.co.uk [website]. Enables online access to, among other things, maps showing troop movements in the Great War.

www.fusiliermuseumlondon.org [website].

www.gatehouse-folk.org [Gatehouse of Fleet website]. Contains biographical information on Serjeant Armstrong, who was from near Gatehouse.

www.grandeguerre.icrc.org [website]. Features a searchable database of Great War Prisoners-of-War compiled from the archives of the International Committee of the Red Cross.

www.greatwar.co.uk [website]. Covers all aspects of the history of the war on the Western Front. Also contains numerous useful links, including one to Pam and Ken Linge's Thiepval Database Project.

www.great-war-casualties.com [website]. Enables online access to a searchable relational CD-ROM database of soldiers who died in the war (charge applies).

www.greatwardigital.com [website]. Enables online access to catalogue of "LinesMan" digitised Trench Maps, draped onto Digital Elevation Models, these being available to purchase (and downloadable onto portable devices for use in the field).

www.greatwarforum.org [website]. The premier site for discussing all aspects of the war. Among other things, contains biographical information on Lance-Corporal Beard, Private Clayton, Private Mahoney, Private Morrell, Lance-Corporal Edgar James Smith and Private Yorke Smith of the 24th Battalion, and on Hylton Cleaver, sometime of the Battalion.

www.greatwarhospitals.wordpress.com [website].

www.hadleighhistory.org.uk [website]. Contains biographical information on Private Peake of the 24th Battalion, who had lived in Hadleigh before the war.

www.heritage.keble.ox.ac.uk [website]. Contains biographical information on Private Limpus, who had been a student at Keble College, Oxford before the war.

www.hoxnehistory.org.uk [website]. Contains biographical information on Private Kirby of the 24th Battalion, who was born in Hoxne.

www.inmemories.com [website]. Pierre Vandervelden's website dedicated to Commonwealth soldiers' burial sites in Belgium and France.

www.isleworthww1.co.uk [website]. Features biographical details and a photographic image of Private Purver of the 24th Battalion, who was born in Isleworth. Also includes information on Private Degens, who was living there at the outbreak of the Great War.

www.iwm.org [Imperial War Museums website].

www.jeffreygreen.co.uk [website]. Features a blog on *African-Descent Soldiers in British Regiments in 1916-1918* (No. 122).
www.limpsfield.org.uk [website]. Contains biographical information on Private Dykes, who lived in Limpsfield before the Great War.
www.longlongtrail.co.uk [website]. Contains a wealth of information on the British Army in the Great War.
www.manchester.ac.uk [website]. Contains biographical information on Private Westphal of the 24th Battalion, who was a student at the University of Manchester before the Great War.
www.nationalarchives.gov.uk [website]. Enables online access to digitised copies of units' war diaries, individual soldiers' service records etc., these being available to download (charges apply).
www.nam.ac.uk [National Army Museum website].
www.newfoundlandonthesomme.com [website]. Features, among other things, an annotated aerial photograph of the Somme battlefield in the Newfoundland Memorial Park at Beaumont-Hamel.
www.nls.uk [National Library of Scotland website]. Enables online access to digitised Great War Trench Maps. The maps are viewable, and downloadable in electronic - .pdf – format, for free, and reproducible on condition of appropriate attribution (see "Copyright" terms and conditions). They are also downloadable in electronic - .jpg – format, or available in printed hard-copy format, for a fee.
www.nmarchive.com [Naval & Military Archive website].
www.newportpast.com [website]. Contains information on Harry Packer of the 24th Battalion.
www.nottinghamlocalnews.com [website]. Contains biographical information on Lance-Corporal Benn, who was born in Retford in Nottinghamshire.
www.nottinghamshire.gov.uk [website]. Contains biographical details and photographic images of Second Lieutenant Harry Daft and Private - John Henry – Hayes of the 24th Battalion (in the "Roll of Honour" section). Also contains biographical details of Corporal Moon and Private O'Kavanagh.

www.ocsociety.org [Old Cranleigians Society website]. Contains biographical information on Private Loibl and Second Lieutenant Mott of the 24th Battalion, who were both students at Cranleigh School before the Great War.

www.oldcestrefeldians.org.uk [website]. Contains biographical information on Private Bond of the 24th Battalion, who was a student at Chesterfield Grammar School before the war.

www.plattmemorialhall.org [website]. Includes biographical information on Private Parris, who was had been living in Platt at the outbreak of the war.

www.pudseycenotaph.co.uk [website]. Includes biographical information on lance-Corporal Hyland, who was born in Pudsey, and still living there at the outbreak of the war.

www.ramc-ww1.com [website]. Contains much useful information on the R.A.M.C or Royal Army Medical Corps in the war. Includes information on the "chain of evacuation".

www.rememberourdeadregimentallist.weebly.com [website]. Contains biographical information on Private Baron, Corporal Firstbrook, Second Lieutenant Gregory and Private Robinson of the 24th Battalion.

www.researchingww1.co.uk [website].

www.roll-of-honour.com [Stock Exchange website]. Includes biographical information on Private Courtney, sometime of the Stockbrokers' and 2nd Sportsmen's Battalions.

www.royalsignalsmuseum.co.uk [website].

www.saintsplayers.co.uk [Southampton FC website]. Contains information on Corporal Lewis Richard Lewis of the 24th Battalion.

www.sportsmansgazette.blogspot.com [website]. Contains a record of the Sportsmen's Battalions in the Great War.

www.stanfords.co.uk [website]. Enables online access to catalogue of reproduction hard-copy Trench Maps, these being available to purchase.

www.sudburysuffolk.co.uk [website]. Includes biographical information on Private Cross of the 24th Battalion, who was from Sudbury.

www.ukphotoarchive.org.uk [website]. Features images of Private Mitchell, Lieutenant Radcliffe, Herbert Raphael, Private

Simco, Lance-Serjeant Taylor, Private Urry and Private Warth of the 24th Battalion.

www.undyingmemory.net [website]. Includes biographical information on Private Wells of the 24th Battalion (in the "Elveden Remembers" section).

www.universitiesatwar.org.uk [website]. Includes biographical information on Private Paget of the 24th Battalion, who attended Hertford College, Oxford, and Durham University before the war.

www.wartimememoriesproject.com [website]. Includes biographical details of Warrant-Officer Second-Class Joseph Henry Hughes of the 24th Battalion, written by his grandson, Colin MacDonald. Also features biographical details and a photographic image of Serjeant Punchard, and a photographic image of Private Collins.

www.waymarking.com [website]. Includes biographical information on Lance-Corporal Dack (in the feature on the Repps-with-Bastwick Church war memorial).

www.westernfrontassociation.com [website].

www.wickhamskeith.suffolk.cloud [website]. Contains biographical information on Corporal Isaac, who was from Wickham Skeith.

www.wlv.ac.uk [University of Wolverhampton website – and host-site of the "Football and War Network"].

www.worldwar1luton.com [website]. Contains biographical details of Privates Dunham and Godfrey of the 24th Battalion, who were from Luton. Also contains a photographic image of Private Dunham.

www.worldwar1veterans.blogspot.com [website]. Features a transcript of the tape-recorded interview with Serjeant Quinnell of the 9th Battalion, the Royal Fusiliers, conducted at the Royal Hospital, Chelsea in 1982 (concerning the action at Ovillers on the Somme on July 7th, 1916). Quinnell was also interviewed at the Imperial War Museum in 1975. His was one of the voices used in Peter Jackson's film, "*They Shall Not Grow Old*", released in 2018.

www.ww1battlefields.co.uk [website].

www.ww1cemeteries.com [website]. Features images of Privates Bell and Loibl of the 24th Battalion.

www.ww1photos.com [website]. Enables online access to a searchable database of thousands of identified photos, obituaries and service records of service and ancillary personnel who served in the war. Features images of Private Anderson, Private Baron, Private Barrowman, Private Bond, Lance-Corporal Boote, Captain Edwards, Private Ralph, Private Ridding, Second Lieutenant Stafford and Second Lieutenant Ullman of the 24th Battalion.

www.ww1playingthegame.org.uk   [website].   Features an image of Reginald Warneford, sometime of the 24th Battalion.

INDEX

Blaauw, Henry Thomas Gillman, Second Lieutenant 7, 8, 205
Black, William John, Private 94, 205
Blount, H.D., Private 92
Bond, Frederick Noel, Private 51, 205-206
Boote, John Arthur, Lance-Corporal 116, 206
Bowen, John Allen, Lance-Corporal 42, 206
Bowes, Edward, Private 50, 206
Bracey, Frederick Stanley, Lieutenant 66, 206
Bradberry, Cyril Christopher David, Private 66, 68, 206
Brinklow, Charles Frederick, Private 67, 206-207
Brock, Lance-Serjeant 9
Brown, Harry, Private 120, 207
Browne, C.E., Captain 7
Burge, George Joseph, Private 120, 207
Burnham, Andrew William, Second Lieutenant 66, 207
Burston, Charles William Gammicott, Private 56, 208
Burston, George Ernest, Private 54, 208
Burton, Serjeant 8
Busby, Quatermaster Serjeant 8

Carpenter, Richard James, Private 55, 208
Catchpole, Corporal 70
Challenger, Orderly-Room Serjeant 9
Cheston, John Alford, Captain 208, 257
Child, Frederick, Private 119, 208
Clair, Serjeant 8
Clare, Alfred Frederick, Lance-Corporal 78, 208
Clarke, Sidney Bertram, Private 55, 208
Clayton, Francis Robert, Private 67, 208-209
Cleaver, Hylton Reginald, Corporal and later Second
Lieutenant 29, 57, 209
Clements, Charles Reuben, Private 3, 101, 119, 129, 253-261
Clifford, Gilbert Colin, Second Lieutenant 79, 84, 209
Cole, David Allen, Private 50, 210
Collier, Charles Richard, Serjeant 86, 201
Collins, Arthur Thomas, Private 78, 201
Coppack, Charles Richard Stewart, Second Lieutenant 104, 210
Coppard, William John, Second Lieutenant 104, 201
Cordwell, Thomas, Private 67, 210

Corrie, William, Private 57
Coulson, William John, Private 51, 210
Courtney, Laurence Edward, Private 119, 210
Cox, Serjeant 9
Cradock, H.U., Major 21
Cronin, Quatermaster Serjeant 9
Crookes, Ronald Orme, Second Lieutenant 29, 210
Cross, Ernest William, Private 66, 210-211
Cross, Frederick, Lance-Serjeant 55, 211
Crosse, Bertram Edward, Private, and later Temporary Quarter-Master and Honorary Lieutenant 7, 211
Cunliffe-Owen, Alexander Robert, Lieutenant 7, 8, 211-212
Cunliffe-Owen, Emma Pauline, Mrs. 1-2, 3, 8
Curtis, C.M., Second Lieutenant 258

D'Abadie, Louis Lawrent, Private 57, 212``
Dack, George Seth, Lance-Corporal 115, 116, 212
Daft, Harry, Second Lieutenant 78, 212-213
Day, George, Lance-Corporal 92
Day, Serjeant 9
Degens, Albartus, Private 79, 213
Dent, Serjeant 9
Denton, Serjeant 9
Dey, Frederick William, Private 27, 213
Dorman, Arthur Gilbert Decimus, Private 66, 213
Drew, Quartermaster Serjeant 9
Dunham, Horace George, Private 66, 213
Dunn, Albert Edward, Captain 2, 213-214
Dunn, C.L., Second Lieutenant 53
Durand, Ralph Anthony, Private and later Second Lieutenant 7, 8, 214-215
Dykes, Alfred Baverstock, Private 78, 215

Eathorne, Francis John, Second Lieutenant 55, 215-216
Ebdon, R.A., Private 56
Edwards, Frank, Private, and later Lance-Corporal, Corporal and Serjeant 5, 216
Edwards, Guy Threlkeld, Second Lieutenant, and later Captain 7, 8, 57, 216-217

Ekins, L.A., Captain 257
Ellis, Serjeant 9
Elwell, P., Major 7
Enderby, Arthur Aaron, Lieutenant 7, 8, 217
Enderby, Harold Henry, Major and Adjutant 7, 8, 217
Essex, Serjeant 9
Evans, Arthur Nicholas, Serjeant 4, 9, 55, 217-218
Evans, Thomas William, Private 116, 218

Fairburn, Serjeant 9
Ferrie, W.S., Private 6, 218
Finch, Serjeant-Major 8
Firstbrook, Ernest Albert, Corporal 66, 218-219
Fish, George Harrop, Private 51, 219
Fitton, William, Lance-Corporal 120, 219
Ford, Charles, Lance-Corporal 55, 219
Fortnam, William Henry, Private 55, 219
Foskett, Alfred Edward, Private 123, 219
Fowler, Francis Caleb, Private 66, 219
Franks, G.A., Captain 7
Furlong, Second Lieutenant 70

Garcia, Arnold Russell, Private 50, 219
Gauntlett, Leonard, Private 57
Geary, Frederick John, Private 55, 219
Gillard, Arthur Samuel, Private 123, 220
Godfrey, Ernest Arthur, Private 79, 220
Gore, S.H., Second Lieutenant 53
Green, Charles Layton, Second Lieutenant 8, 220
Green, W.C., Lieutenant and later Captain 7, 8, 54
Greenwood, Francis Idris, Private 55, 220
Gregory, Stanley Harris, Second Lieutenant 67, 220
Griffiths, H.W., Lieutenant 115
Griffiths, Leon David, Lieutenant 79, 220
Grugan, Felix, Corporal 115, 220-221
Grundy, Frederick, Private 56, 221

Hadaway, Serjeant 9
Haigh, Billy 24

290

Johnson, Percy, Private 55, 226

Kay, J.S.G., Lieutenant 7
Kilmister, Harold Howard Linsdell, Second Lieutenant 84
King, William, Lance-Corporal 92
Kirby, Sydney Herbert, Private 66, 226
Knight, Walter G., Private 42, 227
Knust, Cyril Alexander, Second Lieutenant, and later Captain and Major 22, 50, 227

Laidley, H., Second Lieutenant 53
Lewis, Lewis Richard, Corporal 178, 227
Limpus, Bernard Henry, Private 72, 227
Linsdell, Arthur, Private 42, 227
Little, Arthur Joseph, Serjeant 9, 68, 227-228
Lloyd, Willis Rees, Private 55, 228
Loibl, Randolph Spencer, Private 51, 228

Mackay, Angus, Second Lieutenant 108, 228
MacSwiney, J.C., Major 21
Mahoney, Bernard James, Private 56, 120, 228
Marchant, Thomas Robert, Private 72, 228
Marrable, Hubert Henry, Private 78, 228
Marshall, Herbert George, Private 42, 228
Martin, Ernest John, Private 86, 228
Mason, Lance-Serjeant 9
May, Edwin Wilfred Wrayford,   Private 42, 229
May, Oliver Bertram, Serjeant 9, 87, 229
Mayes, John Alfred, Private 119, 229
McCabe, D., Serjeant 92
McCready, William Austin, Lance-Corporal 57, 229-230
McGahey, Charles Percy 4, 230
McKechnie, David Bruce, Private 51, 230-231
McRedmond, P.J., Captain 7
Meares, Cecil Stanley, Captain 54, 231
Medlicott, Walter Barrington, Second Lieutenant 64, 231-232
Medlock, Reginald George, Private 120, 232
Millar, John Henry Bright, Lance-Corporal 57, 78, 79, 232
Miller, Ernest Minty, Private 67, 232

Spittels, William Arthur, Private 79-246
Stafford, Cyril Francis, Second Lieutenant 77, 244
Stephenson, William, Private 42, 246
Stokes, Arthur Alexander, Private 54, 246
Stone, Bertram Charles, Private 57, 246
Stratford, Horace Oliver, Company Serjeant-Major 86, 247
Stuart, Quartermaster Serjeant 9
Sutherland, Charles, Private 59, 247

Tarlton, E., Serjeant 92
Taylor, John Basil, Private 78, 247
Taylor, Walter Prince, Lance-Serjeant 78, 247
Templeman, F.J., Lieutenant 7
Thomson, James Benjamin, Private 26, 247
Tipton, Arthur, Lance-Corporal 55, 247
Tottie, Serjeant 9
Towler, Serjeant-Major 8
Turner, Albert Edward, Private 55, 247

Ullman, Douglas Maurice Jacques, Second Lieutenant 79, 247
Urry, Frank Allan, Private 79, 247

Vickery, George Charles, Private 55, 247
Vincent, Jack Harry, Private 27, 247

Wakefield, Serjeant 9
Walshe, Henry Ernest, Lieutenant-Colonel 21, 248
Ward, Albert Edward, Private 120
Warneford, Reginald Alexander John, Private, and later Flight
Sub-Lieutenant 5, 248-249
Warriner, John Robert, Private 119, 129, 249
Warth, Bernard, Private 59, 249
Watson, Pioneer Serjeant 9
Waymark, William, Private 93, 249
Webb, George Tudor, Second Lieutenant 28, 249-250
Wellicome, Edwyn Cyril, Private 55, 250
Wellington, Serjeant 9
Wells, Charles William Edward, Private 79, 250
Wells, James Francis, Private 108

Printed in Great Britain
by Amazon

18841613R00180